ORGANIZING EARLY EXPERIENCE

Imagination and Cognition in Childhood

Editor:

DELMONT C. MORRISON

Baywood Publishing Company
AMITYVILLE, NEW YORK

Library of Congress Catalog Card Number: 87-37482
ISBN: 0-89503-051-9

© 1988, Baywood Publishing Company, Inc.

Library of Congress Cataloging in Publication Data
Main entry under title:

Organizing early experience: imagination and cognition in childhood/editor, Delmont C. Morrison
     p. cm.
    Bibliography: p.
    ISBN 0-89503-051-9
    1. Imagination in children. 2. Cognition in children. 3. Child psychology.

I. Morrison, Delmont C., 1932–
BF723.I5074 1988
155.4'13--dc19   87-37482
                                        CIP

Table of Contents

Preface   v

PART I: OVERVIEW

1. The Child's First Ways of Knowing
    Delmont Morrison   3

PART II: DEVELOPMENTAL PATTERNS

2. Socialization and Moral Development
    Michael Siegal and Robin Francis   17
3. Learned Helplessness in Children: Perception of Control
    and Causal Attributions
    Steven Friedlander   33
4. Music in the Organization of Childhood Experience
    Peter Ostwald and Delmont Morrison   54

PART III: THE CONTRIBUTION OF EXPERIENCE

5. Imagination and Creativity in Childhood: The Influence
    of the Family
    Diana Shmukler   77
6. A Cognitive-Affective Theory of the Development of
    Imagination: Family Mediation and Television Influences
    Jerome L. Singer and Dorothy G. Singer   92
7. Social Cognition and Social Competence in Childhood
    through Adolescence
    Lawrence A. Kurdek   116

PART IV: THE USES OF IMAGINATION

8. Process and Change in Child Therapy and Development:
    The Concept of Metaphor
    Sebastiano Santostefano   139
9. The Paracosm: A Special Form of Fantasy
    Robert Silvey and Stephen MacKeith   173
10. The Realities of Play
    Brian Vandenberg   198
11. E. Nesbit's Forty-First Year: Her Life, Times, and
    Symbolizations of Personality Growth
    Ravenna Helson   210
12. The Development of Romantic Ideation and J. M. Barrie's
    Image of the Lost Boy
    Delmont Morrison and Shirley Linden Morrison   226

PREFACE

The chapters in this text reflect a significant change in the focus of developmental psychology over the last twenty years. The dominant explanatory models have emphasized lawful relationships between environmental events and observable behavioral change. An example of this model is Reinforcement Theory. The theoretical shift is to models that include environmental events in the analysis of behavior change but also focus on the contribution of the child's cognitive organization to the observed change in behavior. The explanation of a child's behavior cannot be complete if behavior is viewed simply as a reaction to an external stimulus event. An adequate explanatory model must include the child's active and changing perceptions, affects, wishes, fantasies and cognitive organization that determine his/her interpretation of events. The cognitive organization itself is the result of the interaction of stage-specific cognitive structures and significant environmental events. There are numerous reasons for this change in focus but certainly the theories of Jean Piaget and John Bowlby have contributed to this process. Both of these theories stress the interaction between a child's cognitive organization during particular developmental periods and environmental events occurring during that period. Of major importance is that both theories have been stated in clear enough terms to be evaluated by research. A major difference between them is that Piaget does not stress interpersonal events while Bowlby does. The reader will find that the authors in this text give major consideration to the contribution of early interpersonal events to the child's imaginative, cognitive and affective development.

Eight of the following chapters have been published earlier in *Imagination, Cognition and Personality*. However, only one, Chapter 11 by Ravenna Helson, appears as it was originally published. Chapters 2, 3, 7, 8, 9, 10 and 12 have been published earlier but in modified form. The current versions have been expanded significantly to include more research and theory than was possible in the earlier publications. The remaining chapters are original contributions written specifically for the purposes of this text.

I wish to thank Kenneth Pope and Jerome Singer who encouraged me in the early stages of the book. Jerome Singer not only co-authored a chapter but also made useful suggestions concerning the organization of different sections as the book finally began to take its final shape. As an editor and contributor to this effort, I have enjoyed the experience and expanded my understanding of the development of imagination and cognition in childhood. I trust that the reader will have a similar experience.

Delmont Morrison
San Francisco 1988

PART I
Overview

CHAPTER 1

The Child's First Ways of Knowing

DELMONT MORRISON

This chapter describes the developmental process resulting in the differentiation and integration of two major sources of information in human experience: subjective and objective. The major theme in this effort is the differentiation in the child of the subjective and objective perspective and the rich but constantly changing information and awareness that evolves from the interaction of these two different ways of knowing. The subjective perspective in its earliest form is similar to what has been described as primary process thinking by Freud and sensorimotor intelligence and preoperational thought as described by Piaget. The development and change occurring in the subjective interpretation of experience has been explained by Freud and Freudian theorists in terms of instincts and conflicts between id, ego, and superego [1]. The objective awareness of reality grows as the ego modifies instinctual expression and satisfaction. Pathological cognitive states seen in neurosis are due to anxiety and the influence of the unconscious process on conscious thought. Cognitive development occurs in an affective context. The differentiation of subjective and objective awareness is the basic issue in the study of intelligence according to Piaget. However, in contrast to Freudian theory, this awareness occurs through inborn mechanisms developing largely in the context of the process of maturation and adaptive orientation to the external world. Affect may contribute or interfere with this process to some degree but is not a major factor in the sequence of cognitive development [2].

Recent research and theory indicate that both Freudian and Piagetian theory are inadequate explanations of how children evolve an understanding of the contribution of their inner states in the interpretation of experience and subsequently acquire a more objective view of experience. In this chapter, the cognitive aspects of this process are examined in the context of the development of self-nonself differentiation [3] as the child experiences those early interpersonal relationships that contribute to attachment [4]. This approach differs

3

significantly from both Freudian and Piagetian theory in that the most important modifications in the subjective and objective perspective are seen as due to an inseparable interaction between the child's cognitive organization and his/her first emotional personal relationships.

COGNITIVE STATES

As a working definition, the subjective perspective contributes to a child's interpretation of events through information, unconscious or conscious, that has an internal source. The most important cognitive source of this information is the child's affects, memory, wishes, and fantasies that contribute to his/her interpretation of early experience. The objective perspective, in contrast, is influenced by information that is external to the child. Like the subjective perspective, the objective is influenced by the child's unconscious and conscious information. The differentiation of the subjective and objective state is the complex reasoning children evolve to understand themselves, other people, social relations, social groups and institutions [5]. The child structures early experience with a perpetual confusion between inner and outer sources of information and it is only when the child is able cognitively to recognize consciously the contribution of his/her own internal states to the interpretation of experience that objective thought is acquired [6]. This objectification of experience is gradual and is acquired in the process of an expanding awareness of self that is by its nature affectively charged. As the child's awareness of events is more complex, there is a gradual recognition of a world that operates independent of self. With reflective thought the child becomes aware of self as thinker and the center of a will. With experience the child becomes aware that this will must be modulated in terms of objects and people that are not always influenced by the child's will as the child wishes or anticipates. This process is hypothesized to begin at about age two with the development of preoperational thought [3], but there is evidence that major interpersonal events occur before age two that probably greatly influence the differentiation of self-nonself [7].

When thought occurs under conditions where subjective sources of information are dominant and a limited capacity for reflective thought exists, as is true during the first years of life, children live within their presently occurring experience and assume that their actions bring events into existence, and that when their attention moves elsewhere the event ceases to exist. This narcissistic state of sensorimotor intelligence is transformed by the growing cognitive capacity to discriminate between internal and external sources of information and the consequent discovery of self and will. Events do not change but the child's experience of the event is changed by the cognitive capacity for objectification. This new understanding of a familiar experience is reorganized by preoperational systems of thought that structure the child's interpretation of the event, as well as the memory of the event and the anticipation of future events.

Preoperational thought is egocentric and action oriented. Assimilative functions are dominant and a major modality of representation is the metaphor. Through the metaphor unfamiliar events are transformed into relatively familiar ones, thereby reducing the cognitive aspect of novelty and the affective reaction to the unknown and strange. These representational systems are dominant between the ages of two and eight and are gradually modified by the development of the various forms of operational thought [8].

INTERPERSONAL EVENTS

A major transition occurs in the infant-parent interaction during the second half of the first year of life. Prior to this the infant has been engaged in a variety of sensorimotor explorations, such as the circular reactions, that contribute to the objectification of experience. However, at about six months, major motor milestones occur and the child's exploration of environmental novelty becomes more elaborate. The child now will subordinate and order his/her motor responses to obtain a goal: one of the first cognitive signs of the child's recognition of external information and an indication of intention. Prior to six months of age the infant has been engaged in an interpersonal relationship characterized by the management of the infant's tension by the caregiver. After six months the infant is more cognitively aware of the caregiver and behavioral interactions with this person are characterized by separation protests, retreating to the caregiver when too distressed by novelty, and positive greetings when the caregiver appears after an absence [7]. These exchanges are indicative of a major modification in subjective states reflected in a growing sense of self and will fused with anxiety and reduction of anxiety in an interpersonal context. The initial anxiety is intense and generalized and is reduced if the caregiver is reliable and consistent in mitigating stressful situations. This exchange results in the reduction of gross anxiety into more manageable signal anxiety which serves to indicate that under stressful situations the child can anticipate that the stress will be mitigated and anxiety reduced [9]. This mutual exchange between child and caregiver results in the child experiencing his/her pleasurable and negative subjective states as generally ending satisfactorily with a result that there is a continuity to the experience of self and increased self-esteem. The growing self-awareness of will is closely associated with the child's increasing awareness and eventual understanding of both love and aggression. In these continuing interpersonal exchanges the child becomes conscious that components of self are accepted and encouraged in the interpersonal events with the parent. However, these exchanges are also concluded at times with the child experiencing the parent in the context of frustration and rage. These images and feelings of anger are initially experienced cognitively as independent of the feelings of love and pleasure that are also directed at the same parent [10]. The repeated experience of receiving love and reducing anger satisfactorily with the same person results in the integration of these two feelings into a synthesized rather than fragmented cognitive-affective system [9].

With the development of crawling and walking during the interval of six to sixteen months the child's capacity to explore the environment is greatly increased. Cognitively, children demonstrate an awareness that an object continues to exist even when the child is not acting on it or cannot see it. Major modifications in subjective information occurs at this time when the child is able to decenter, process, and conserve two or more sources of perceptual information regarding objects and events at the same time. These cognitive shifts in the objective-subjective perspective are dependent on interpersonal experience. Although the child is curious and has an increased capacity to assimilate and accommodate more sources of information in an event, there is considerable evidence that there are limits to how much novelty a child can process comfortably. Too abrupt a shift in complexity, such as a stranger and/or a strange situation, arouses anxiety [11]. In the context of change and novelty the child must experience the parent as a familiar and anxiety reducing figure or there is a major disruption in the exploration of novelty [7-12]. The parent must become a constant reliable source of security for the child to apply his/her increasing cognitive skills to transform complex events into cognitive systems that further differentiate the subjective-objective perspective. As symbolic thought and language develop, the child and caregiver can remain in psychological contact, even when at a physical distance.

INITIAL WAYS OF UNDERSTANDING: COGNITION AND AFFECT

Probably the most important aspect of these earliest attachments is that they occur when the child interprets events with sensorimotor schema and pre-operational thought. These cognitive systems are greatly influenced by the subjective perspective with its idiosyncratic-egocentric images. The integrating effect of secure attachment eventually enables the child to elaborate on the various dimensions of self explored through events by the less subjective systems of operational thought. As a consequence, the probability is increased that a balance between subjective and objective perspective will develop. However, the chronic exposure to the unfamiliar without adequate attachment increases the chance that the growing cognitive capacity to attend to self becomes evaluative and negative. This inner conclusion regarding self is demonstrated in preschoolers who were known to have histories of anxious or avoidant attachment. When rated by their teachers on a measure of self-esteem, these children were rated as having lower self-esteem than children with earlier histories of secure attachment [13]. The pleasure the two year old has in exploring novelty with the familiar parent, and the growing awareness and assertion of will, can tax the parent's capacity to assert control, use discipline and set limits. At times the child may wish to explore in a situation that the caregiver perceives as inappropriate. The new process of self-assertion occurs in the child who is emotionally narcissistic and cognitively omnipotent. This combination sets the stage for the negativistic behavior observed during this time and the child's use of temper trantrums to negotiate in situations where caregivers must assert their will [14]. By its nature, this process of self-assertion is charged with emotional overtones and the temper tantrum, which is the prototype for future aggressive reactions to ego denial, becomes a major event for definition and evaluation of self. In the normal course of events the unbridled urge for pleasure and immediate gratification of will becomes modified by the need for parental approval. If parental methods for controlling negativism involve the overuse of verbal or nonverbal negative evaluations of the child, then low self-esteem can develop in the context of a preoperational understanding of self-assertion and anger.

Two major affects, anxiety and anger, experienced in the interpersonal exchanges basic to attachment and later interpersonal events such as the Oedipal triangle, contribute significantly to the child's objectification of experience. Affects do not emerge fully formed but must undergo their own extensive period of development. Initially, affective states may involve elements that are highly differentiated, such as the eight month old infant's greeting of the mother in the strange situation, without these elements being integrated or organized into a hierarchical structure [15]. The object of the affect is not differentiated from the affective event and the representation of self and others is fused with the affect. Because the preoperational child centers on the predominant isolated experience in an event, the dominant affective component may capture the child's attention and determine his or her total conception of the interpersonal interaction. Preoperational thought is unstable, discontinuous and irreversible. The latter means that the child cannot carry out transformations in thought that are necessary to solve perceptual problems such as the conservation of volume and number. This irreversibility is observed in the preoperational child who in one affective state cannot conceptualize having other contrasting affective states or evaluations of the same person. As objectification of self and affect occurs, the object of the affect and the affect itself are differentiated from each other. A further cognitive advancement occurs when the child recognizes that he/she may have mixed or contradictory feelings toward the same person and that some feelings toward a person have more personal meaning than do other feelings.

In summary, affects are initially experienced in the psychological state of an undifferentiated self and only with experience do affects become articulate. Affects such as love and anger are initially experienced as fused and later become differentiated. The attribution of affects to self or others and the expression of an articulated affect to a person can only occur after the representations of self and others are each integrated and consequently differentiated from the affect itself [10-15].

REFLECTIVE THOUGHT AND
THE PROCESS OF OBJECTIFICATION

The child's growing capacity to employ preoperational and operational systems of thought contributes to the reduction of egocentrism. This is a gradual process with a major shift occurring at about age nine [16]. Prior to age nine the child's capacity to reason about self and other people along psychological dimensions, or conceptualize relationships between individuals and groups, is characterized by concrete situation-specific thought that is dominated by the subjective perspective. For example, the preoperational child's perception of an authority or person who is in a position of leadership is determined by the child's own wishes and needs, while the nine year old can include concepts regarding reciprocity and contractual agreement in his/her understanding of such a relationship. As suggested by Piagetian theory, the development of reflective thought is characterized by stage-related cognitive capacities. However, the individual cognitive differences in children of the same age who demonstrate similar levels of cognitive organization suggest the importance of experience. In contrast to children who have an anxious or avoidant attachment, preschool children with secure attachment are capable of making friendships and are liked by other children. In terms of relationships with adults, preschool children with histories of secure attachment are treated matter of factly by their teachers whereas the same teacher will interact with children with histories of anxious attachment with much more control and the expectation that the child will not comply [17]. The influence of subjective affective states in the child's perception of other children and the effect of this perception on interpersonal relationships is seen in latency-aged children who are socially rejected or neglected by their peers. When compared to more popular children, the social perceptions of these socially isolated children are less accurate and the errors they make are biased toward attributing hostile motives to others [16].

Reflective thought, or thought that thinks about its own thinking, will be modulated by interpersonal experience and affects such as anxiety. Undifferentiated anxiety experienced intensely and chronically probably results in the pathological cognitive organization observed in the borderline child [9]. As anxiety becomes differentiated in later development it can signal an anticipated situation of stress which is instrumental in the child's effort to modify images and wishes to accord with the anticipated experience. These events and the psychological reactions may be transitory. However, if the anxious state becomes chronic the anxiety ladened preoperational images may not be subject to the cognitive reorganization of operational thought because they cannot be manipulated by conscious effort. However, these subjective images will continue to determine the child's interpretation of experience. This is seen in latency aged children with an attributional style of ascribing negative events to internal, stable and global factors. There are indications that this particular cognitive style results in a negative self-concept and social withdrawal [18].

THE SOCIALIZATION OF THOUGHT

The reduction of egocentric thought is a continuing process. Although the child's assertiveness and expanding awareness of self will almost always result in conflict with major caregivers and peers, the compensating need for attachment, love, and human affiliation provides the impetus for conflict resolution. As has been noted, the child's first knowledge of experience will be greatly influenced by narcissism and preoperational thought. Between the ages of two and eight, knowledge of events is a somewhat unstable cognitive conglomeration of the earlier representations interacting with developing operational systems. A great socialization influence is the child's tendency to imitate and identify with peers and adults who have emotional meaning for him/her [19]. Although there are cognitive stages in the development of social and moral cognitions, the child's developing awareness of self in a social system that is influenced by broader moral issues is greatly influenced by affect experienced in an interpersonal context. In the day to day interaction with the parent, the child negotiates to maintain the subjective perspective and protect narcissistic needs while the parent negotiates to develop shared semantic systems that become implicit and explicit contracts for certain situations. As a result of the parent's style, and a history of shared discipline encounters, the child and parent mutually assign the same social and moral meaning to particular social acts [20]. Through identification, the movement out of the subjective perspective and the objectification of experience not only involves information regarding self and others but social systems linked to the child's broader cultural history.

The child's subjective experience is one of constant assimilation and accommodation: existing preoperational systems assimilating the new information by metaphors that in turn accommodate to operational schema that are more socialized and based on stable hierarchies. In a stable home the child will have periods of time when explorations of this novelty can be done leisurely in isolation or in a social environment that allows assimilation to dominate. If the parent values imagination and creativity and the child has the opportunity to engage in creative activity, the child will use these as mediums to understand and organize experience. If the parents' style of understanding themselves, social relationships and moral behavior involves exploration and reviewing experience in a flexible, communicative way, their children will demonstrate a similar cognitive style [20-22].

CREATIVE THOUGHT: THE CONTRIBUTION OF SUBJECTIVE EXPERIENCE

The earliest signs of objectification are seen when the child at about age two is able to decenter and simultaneously conserve major perceptual elements in the process of reasoning about an event. Eventually the child is able to conserve subjective and objective information to differentiate aspects of self and intention as interacting with causality and the event which is thought about. Interpersonal events are the most important and although this sequence begins at about age two, it is obvious that the process of objectification goes on for a lifetime. As children become more aware of self and self-evaluative, they enter major social experiences, such as school, which are geared to educate them in the development and application of operational systems. The use of operational systems and achievement in the application of these systems in Western society contributes significantly to a child's self-esteem. In fact, the traditional definition of intelligence has been the measurement of skills that are mostly acquired through classroom experience [23]. As thought becomes socialized, external sources of information play an increasingly dominant role in the child's use of reflective thought and evaluation of self. Freud referred to this cognitive level as secondary process and Piaget referred to it as concrete and formal operational thought. It is clear that both viewed this level of cognitive organization as superior in terms of human adaptation to earlier occurring forms of thought [3-24]. This chapter concludes with an examination of the positive contribution of the child's first subjective images, symbols, affects and representations of experience in the enrichment and objectification of later human experience.

The child's first way of structuring and representing experience is preverbal and prelogical. Although these representations are in a constant state of disequilibrium, all new information is first assimilated into these systems: these representations are the first reality of the child. These early representations are constructed through interpersonal exchanges that establish the child's inner working models for attachment-trust, detachment, separation-individuation, assertiveness-aggressiveness, initiating-reciprocating, and competitiveness. Early experience is structured, and reality is interpreted through idiosyncratic cognitive systems of realism, animism, and artificialism [25]. As the child develops representational thought and sense of self, the words, thoughts, affect, postures and physical actions that represent the past and ancitipate future experience are expressed metaphorically [26]. Major interpersonal events are experienced by the child as requiring constant shifts in the assimilation and accommodation of the representations of interpersonal experience and self. The stress and anxiety experienced can be mitigated by the adequate caretaking of the parent and by the child's exploration of the meaning of the experience without having to meet the demands of the experience.

Play serves a variety of developmental purposes [24], but the use of play by the child to reconstruct past experience and explore definitions of self contributes significantly to the development of reflective thought and objectification of experience [22-27]. Childhood is unique in that there is much more new information generated from experience than there is old information that has been acquired from experience. Assimilation and accommodation are much more complex processes during childhood than during adulthood. However, it is in the nature of human experience in general, and specifically during periods of stress and major change, that previous definitions of experience and self are challenged and alternative sources of knowledge must be explored. The events that challenge adults will often be the same interpersonal events experienced in childhood and will often be understood by metaphors which are similar to the ones that were first constructed. In the mature adult, the self is differentiated from the event and analytical thought can be consciously manipulated toward a goal. However, if current experience is perceived to be psychologically similar to previous experience in childhood and evokes similar affect the individual will react in a similar way as in the past. There are clearly variations in this process and the degree to which the earlier metaphors are conscious and the affect manageable, the more unlikely the individual will be compelled to repeat previous experience. Thoughts organized by earlier metaphors will be particularly amenable to the evocation and expression of affect. In those situations where the adult experiences frustration in the pursuit of goals, or a threat to previous definition of self, the exploration and understanding of experience can be enriched by analytic thought which incorporates previous evocative metaphors accompanied by the remembered affect [3]. The two cognitive modes contribute to this process: the preoperational, organized by affect and metaphor, and the operational, organized by logical analysis and semantic structure. There may be a third: musical representation. Music is a mode of thought which is similar to preoperational modes in that it is evocative of affect and organized by cognitive structures that appear to be relatively independent of semantics. Music contributes to the emotional experience of an event and can be shared socially. Music is unique in that it is a way of expressing the subjective perspective of commonly shared emotional experiences through non-verbal means. If expressed by an exceptional composer, the music becomes a partial definition of the experience [28].

The content and structure of play changes significantly when the child is capable of using concrete and formal operational systems. Play at this time takes on a more realistic quality in that more children are included, it is less idiosyncratic, and sustained role playing is common. Although the assimilative compensatory quality of play dominated by preoperational modes is less common, the child can still construct and explore a world that is less susceptible to the demands of reality. These enduring organized fantasies are dominated by rules and order expressed in a society in which the compensatory wishes of the child find expression. However, self-observation is adequate and the child clearly discriminates between what is imagined and what really exists. These paracosms, or imaginary private worlds, have played a significant role in the lives of individuals who later became unusually creative such as C. S. Lewis and W. H. Auden [29]. The process of creative thinking is not necessarily the generation of new facts but the exploration of new ways of thinking about what had previously been obscure. The obscure quality to an idea may be in an intellectual context but it may be in an interpersonal context as well. There is evidence that conflicts generated in early interpersonal experience can be a source of original and creative thinking [30]. Early representations of self and others that are associated with too much signal anxiety are overdetermined by the subjective perspective and not readily available to reflective thought. These metaphors of early experience have been subject to substantial preoperational learning but excluded from the reorganization that results from learning acquired with operational thought. The conflicts will express themselves in adulthood in various ways but when expressed creatively they tend to be reworkings of the old metaphors in an attempt to come to a more conscious awareness of various aspects of self [27-31]. This reworking of experience combining the preoperational and operational modes of thought can be both cathartic as well as a modality for expanding the boundaries of self-awareness with a consequent new perspective of reality.

Objectification of experience can be only partially established through the use of logic and reference to socially accepted systems of meaning. Reflective thought used to understand preoperational representations with their passionate aspects and wish for change can be used to define an individual's present reality as well as future possibilities [24]. Objectification of experience is a continuing process which is broadened when the individual is able to reflect upon past and current experience with the fullest range of thought enriched by emotions. Like play, this is probably best done at times when the immediate demands on the individual are reduced. The repeated use of this experience can result in a broader definition of current self but also offer an opportunity to explore possible selves [32]. Objectification for the mature adult includes the awareness of the self as it has been experienced in the past and is currently experienced, but also the possible selves defined by the individual's hopes, fears, goals and the wish for change. Conscious awareness of the various cognitive components and motivations for the anticipated experience contributes to the awareness of a possible self which in turn becomes an incentive for future behavior.

REFERENCES

1. H. Hartman, *Ego Psychology and the Problem of Adaptation*, International Universities Press, New York, 1958.
2. J. Piaget, *Intelligence and Affectivity: Their Relationship during Child Development*, T. A. Crown and C. E. Kaego (eds.), Annual Reviews, Palo Alto, California, 1981.
3. I. Fast, *Event Theory: A Piaget-Freud Integration*, Lawrence Erlbaum Associates, Hillsdale, New Jersey, 1985.
4. J. Bowlby, *Attachment*, (Vol. 1), Basic Books, New York, 1969.
5. W. Damon and D. Hart, The Development of Self-Understanding from Infancy through Adolescence, *Child Development*, *53*:4, pp. 841-864, 1982.
6. J. Piaget, *The Child's Conception of Physical Causality*, Kegan Paul, London, 1930.

7. A. Sroufe, The Coherence of Individual Development: Early Care, Attachment, and Subsequent Development Issues, *American Psychologist*, *34*:10, pp. 834-842, 1979.

8. J. H. Flavell, *The Developmental Psychology of Jean Piaget*, Van Nostrand Company, New York, 1963.

9. F. Pine, On the Development of the "Borderline-Child-To-Be," *American Journal of Orthopsychiatry*, *56*:3, pp. 450-457, 1986.

10. R. Melito, Cognitive Aspects of Splitting and Libidinal Object Constancy, *Bulletin of the American Psychoanalytic Association*, *39*:1, pp. 515-534, 1982.

11. M. D. S. Ainsworth, M. Blehar, E. Waters, and S. Wall, *Patterns of Attachment*, Lawrence Erlbaum Associates, Hillsdale, New Jersey, 1978.

12. D. Stern, The Goal and Function of Mother Infant Play, *Journal of the American Academy of Child Psychiatry*, *13*, pp. 402-421, 1974.

13. A. Sroufe, Infant-Caregiver Attachment and Patterns of Adaptation in the Preschool: *The Roots of Competence and Maladaptation*, M. Perlmutter (ed.), Minnesota Symposium in Child Psychology, (Vol. 16), Lawrence Erlbaum Associates, Hillsdale, New Jersey, 1983.

14. D. P. Ausubel, Negativism as a Phase of Ego Development, *The American Journal of Orthopsychiatry*, *20*:4, pp. 796-805, 1950.

15. A. E. Thompson, The Nature of Emotion and Its Development, in *Event Theory: A Piaget-Freud Integration*, I. Fast (ed.), Lawrence Erlbaum Associates, Hillsdale, New Jersey, 1985.

16. L. A. Kurdek, Social Cognition and Social Competence in Childhood through Adolescence, in *Organizing Early Experience: Imagination and Cognition in Childhood*, Baywood Publishing Company, Amityville, New York, pp. 116-135, 1988.

17. L. A. Sroufe, The Role of the Infant-Caregiver in Development, in *Clinical Implication of Attachment*, T. Belsky and T. Nezwoski (eds.), Lawrence Erlbaum Associates, Hillsdale, New Jersey (in press).

18. S. Friedlander, Learned Helplessness in Children: Perception of Control and Causal Attributions, in *Organizing Early Experience: Imagination and Cognition in Childhood*, Baywood Publishing Company, Amityville, New York, pp. 33-53, 1988.

19. A. L. Baldwin, *Theories of Child Development*, Wiley, New York, 1967.

20. M. Siegal and R. Francis, Socialization and Moral Development, in *Organizing Early Experience: Imagination and Cognition in Childhood*, Baywood Publishing Company, Amityville, New York, pp. 17-32, 1988.

21. D. Shmukler, Imagination and Creativity in Childhood: The Influence of the Family, in *Organizing Early Experience: Imagination and Cognition in Childhood*, Baywood Publishing Company, Amityville, New York, pp. 77-91, 1988.

22. J. L. Singer and D. G. Singer, A Cognitive-Affective Theory of the Development of Imagination: Family Mediation and Television Influences, in *Organizing Early Experience: Imagination and Cognition in Childhood*, Baywood Publishing Company, Amityville, New York, pp. 92-115, 1988.

23. J. McV. Hunt, *Intelligence and Experience*, Ronald Press, New York, 1961.

24. B. Vandenberg, The Realities of Play, in *Organizing Early Experience: Imagination and Cognition in Childhood*, Baywood Publishing Company, Amityville, New York, pp. 198-209, 1988.
25. J. Piaget, *The Child's Conception of the World*, Littlefield, Adams and Company, Totowa, New Jersey, 1979.
26. S. Santostefano, Process and Change in Child Therapy and Development: The Concept of Metaphor, in *Organizing Early Experience: Imagination and Cognition in Childhood*, Baywood Publishing Company, Amityville, New York, pp. 139-172, 1988.
27. D. Morrison and S. Morrison, The Development of Romantic Ideation and J. M. Barrie's Image of the Lost Boy, in *Organizing Early Experience: Imagination and Cognition in Childhood*, Baywood Publishing Company, Amityville, New York, pp. 226-241, 1988.
28. P. Ostwald and D. Morrison, Music in the Organization of Childhood Experience, in *Organizing Early Experience: Imagination and Cognition in Childhood*, Baywood Publishing Company, Amityville, New York, pp. 54-73, 1988.
29. R. Silvey and S. MacKeith, The Paracosm: A Special Form of Fantasy, in *Organizing Early Experience: Imagination and Cognition in Childhood*, Baywood Publishing Company, Amityville, New York, pp. 173-197, 1988.
30. P. Noy, Insight and Creativity, *Journal of the American Psychoanalytic Association, 26*, pp. 717-748, 1978.
31. R. Helson, E. Nesbit's Forty-First Year: Her Life, Times, and Symbolizations of Personality Growth, in *Organizing Early Experience: Imagination and Cognition in Childhood*, Baywood Publishing Company, Amityville, New York, pp. 210-225, 1988.
32. H. Markus and P. Nurius, Possible Selves, *American Psychologist, 41*:9, pp. 954-969, 1986.

PART II
Developmental Patterns

CHAPTER 2

Socialization and Moral Development

MICHAEL SIEGAL
AND ROBIN FRANCIS

Together with the contemporary interest in attributional and person perception approaches to social interaction, increasing attention has been devoted to the development of moral judgment and behavior in children. The cognitive developmental approaches of Piaget [1] and Kohlberg [2] continue to influence and dominate much of the research in the area. In this chapter we seek to explore types of cognitive antecedents to moral behavior in early childhood which may serve as a theoretical bridge between traditional measures of moral judgment and moral action, particularly in the absence of an external authority.

Both Piaget and Kohlberg hypothesize a stage sequence in which development proceeds from an egocentric moral orientation to a mature concern for the interests and intentions of others. Transition through these stages is claimed to be accomplished through cognitive-developmental changes in social understanding often brought about through peer group contact. Although the two accounts share many fundamental similarities, Kohlberg has modified and differentiated his model as one distinct from Piaget's, proposing a more detailed sequence of stages which extend to development in adolescence and adulthood.

The importance of cognitive factors in moral behavior has been evaluated in a comprehensive review by Blasi [3]. Moral behavior has often been hypothesized to be directly dependent on the subject's stage of moral reasoning, most commonly as defined by Kohlberg's Moral Judgment Scale. Behavioral control in the moral sphere has therefore been assumed to develop, at least, in parallel to moral judgment development. For example, behaviorally maladjusted children have been predicted to have lower stage scores than children who demonstrated more mature moral behavior. That is, they judge actions such as stealing in terms of the consequences of reward or punishment rather than orientations toward a consideration of the benefits of law and order or the rights of individuals within society. According to Blasi, the clearest indication of any judgment-behavior relationship involves the association between delinquency and moral judgment. The link between judgment on the one hand, and honesty and conformity on the other appears to be particularly weak with at least half the studies reporting ambiguous or non-significant results.

However, a closer inspection of the studies which pertain to the judgment-delinquency relationship shows that, even in this case a substantial number, eleven out of twenty-seven, reported no association. This lack of support is underscored by Jurkovic who describes equivocal findings with regard to the hypothesis that delinquents' moral reasoning is not as mature as that of non-offenders [4].

Despite a number of reported positive correlations between moral judgment and moral action, overall the empirical findings are not impressive. They do not clearly indicate the presence of a direct link between behavioral and cognitive-developmental measures.

In order to achieve a fuller account, it is necessary first to appraise the contribution of cognitive-developmental approaches. This will lead toward a perspective which incorporates both affective and volitional factors that has been influenced by the work of James Mark Baldwin.

COGNITIVE-DEVELOPMENTAL
APPROACHES TO MORAL REASONING

In his broad two stage model, Piaget claimed that increasing cognitive competence permits the child to regulate emotional impulses [1]. With age, rationality comes to moderate wholly affective responses. In conjunction with the development of abilities to reason about causality and motivation, the child begins a transition from an egocentric orientation to one in which there is a coordination of differing viewpoints. The social world comes to be seen in terms of a logic or reciprocity and cooperation. While Piaget allowed that moral development is naturally capable of being reinforced by the precepts and practical example of the adult, he claimed that in practice a mature morality "is largely independent of these influences, assigning a central role to peer group relations" [1, p. 66].

Kohlberg [2, 5] originally proposed a six-stage model which more recently [6] has been revised to five stages. The initial stages describe a preconventional morality where the rights of others are respected only insofar as they serve the needs of the individual. Development through these stages progresses to a conventional level where constraints of law and order are paramount. Finally it culminates in post-conventional or principled morality where universal principles of justice and respect for the rights of the individual prevail. Kohlberg has claimed that his model has greater validity than Piaget's two-stage model, that Piaget's stages fail to meet the criteria which define a stage and that Piaget ignored development beyond middle childhood.

Altough Piaget and Kohlberg are predominantly interested in the development of moral reasoning, both nevertheless suggest an effect of moral reasoning, on behavior. Piaget noted that "the peculiar function of cooperation is to lead the child to the practice of reciprocity, hence of moral universality and generosity in his relations with his playmates" [1, p. 66], and Kohlberg recently has maintained that the correspondence between moral judgment and action will be greatest at the highest moral judgment stages [7]. Kohlberg also acknowledged that moral judgment alone is not sufficient to effect moral action, and that volitional factors are also implicated in the decision process. At higher moral stages, he proposed tentatively that judgments of responsibility may mediate the decision to behave morally in suggesting that "moral action is determined not only by judgments of deontic justice (e.g., rights and contract) but by follow-through judgments of responsibility" [6, p. 555]. Moral stages are said to act as "conceptual filters" (in ways not precisely determined) which define adults' perception of the responsibility to act.

Yet Kohlberg does not apply this analysis to moral development in childhood. Explanations of the weak to modest relationship between moral judgment and moral behavior in young children have focused on:

1. The reliability and validity of the Moral Judgment Scale [8]. The difficulty of devising a "test" of moral reasoning, whether based on psychometric criteria or Piaget's clinical method, may still prove to be overcome through the use of a new scoring system [9]. Nevertheless, evidence suggests that, in support of Piaget and contrary to Kohlberg, young children judge an act as wrong regardless of whether it is rewarded or punished [10, 11]. A significant advance in this area is the work of Turiel [12], Nucci [13], and Smetana [14, 15] noted below.

2. The assumptions made by Kohlberg as to the relevance of his hypothetical moral dilemmas. For instance, discrepancies in the theoretical and practical reasoning of nondelinquent children have been reported [16-18]. Responses to the hypothetical dilemmas may be of questionable relevance to commonly-experienced reasoning about actual dilemmas.

3. A failure to consider the role of content-related cognitions. In citing evidence that tolerance of deviancy might be a factor in the antisocial behavior of delinquents [19], Jurkovic claims that cognitions which derive from subjectively held values and attitudes (i.e., content-related cognitions) might be more influential determinants of moral actions than cognitions which reflect one's moral stage [4]. Nisan proposes that moral choices are determined more by the context or norm attached to a moral issue rather than by the stage structure of moral reasoning [20].

4. The absence in stage models of reference to the role of affective factors which motivate moral behavior. In support of this proposition, Jurkovic contends that many moral choices may be made without recourse to rational moral reasoning or reasoning which reflects stage judgment abilities [4]. All in all, consideration of affective factors in moral development may lead to more powerful predictions of one's moral stage.

In contrast to this "cool" cognitive emphasis, it seems likely that in many commonly-experienced moral conflicts in childhood, close correspondence between thought and action may involve "hot" cognitions. These are cognitions which involve perceptions of persons and situations that have strong affective value and which ultimately contribute to effective socialization and the course and outcome of the moral decision process. In agreement with the importance of the role of affective factors, Gerson and Damon maintain that "moral emotions" are [21, p. 55]:

> ... often ... the lifeblood of moral behavior, that which makes moral objectives really seem to matter. Because of their intensity, either pleasant or unpleasant, they serve as important reasons for the child to follow moral objectives, particularly when these objectives conflict with non-moral ones.

While the significance of affective factors as influential determinants of children's moral action has been examined most often from social learning perspectives which stress the powerful socializing impact of rewards and punishment, such an approach assumes the primary of situational factors which reinforce certain responses. The active cognitive role of the individual in formulating moral courses of action is thus minimized or ignored.

In a similar way, the Kohlberg interview method can be said to underestimate grossly the active cognitive role in moral development of young children. Kohlberg insists that Piagetian stages of logical development as indicated by performance on conservation tasks is a necessary but not sufficient prerequisite for reasoning at a conventional moral level [6, p. 390]. By definition, young children cannot reason conventionally and do not discriminate between different sorts of rules, since they do not conserve. This reliance on orthodox Piagetian theory betrays the young child's ability to conserve as demonstrated in many recent experiments. For example, in line with the work of Gelman [22], McGarrigle and Donaldson [23], Moore and Frye [24], and Rose and Blank [25], Siegal, Waters and Dinwiddy [26] have found that preschoolers give external attributions for nonconservation responses. They indicate that such responses reflect a desire to please a grownup experimenter after he or she has repeated a request to compare quantities following a transformation. Consequently, the child's cognitive and moral development must be viewed with regard to the social context of shared meanings or symbols in interaction with others. A more comprehensive framework through which to conceptualize the reasoning/action process is to draw upon a symbolic interactionist process as articulated by Baldwin [27, 28] and Mead [29] and currently undergoing a revival [30-32].

SYMBOLIC-INTERACTIONISM AND A SOCIAL-COGNITIVE APPROACH TO MORAL DEVELOPMENT

Mead's contribution to moral development was to embed the foundation and ontogeny of symbolic thought within the notion of a "conservation of gestures" where actions of one individual toward other individuals depend upon the anticipated responses of the other [29]. Mead asserted that the social interaction informs individual cognition, a point of view shared by Vygotsky [33]. Knowledge of social phenomena then derives directly from the individual's experience in interpersonal relations.

Mead's work had an early precursor in Baldwin's rich account of social-cognitive development [27, 28]. Baldwin, like Freud, emphasized the importance of the development of the self and argued that such development took place within a system of interpersonal relations.

The self is considered to develop through interactions with others and experience of the self is dependent upon experiencing the world as containing other selves. According to Broughton and Riegel, perceptions of one's self and of other selves develop together [34]. As a result of social interactions, varying degrees of self-awareness are eventually achieved.

In Baldwin's model, children first have a projective sense of self in which they are stimulated by parents or those in authority to control their asocial impulses. They strive toward an ideal self which is exemplified in the behavior of others whom they perceive as good. The process is at first largely noncognitive in that children at this point do not reflect on the motivations underlying their behavior. In fact, the affective component which motivates moral behavior is largely untempered by "cool" cognitive considerations of morality.

However, as children begin to understand others they also begin to understand themselves. Development proceeds from the projective self to a subjective self when children consciously articulate the existence of an ideal self, sometimes exemplified in their personification of religious figures who embody the ultimate "good" toward which important others strive. The child perceives that to be like one's ideal self is to behave as one's parents or as individuals of enduring emotional attachments expect them to behave. To want to be like the parent may serve to satisfy the child's striving toward his or her ideal self. The child's disposition to "identify" with the parents' rules and standards for behavior now becomes more cognitive and reflective. The final differentiation of the self is toward an ejective state where the child reflects upon the discrepancies between the real and ideal self, and attempts to resolve the difference by evoking a dialectical process of argument and counter-argument. This point in development appears to correspond to Stage 5 of Kohlberg's model, one which assumes a formal-operational stage of development and which is characterized by reasoning founded on a belief in universal principles from which the rules and laws of society ideally derive.

While Baldwin's theory was devoid of concrete research proposals and has received little direct empirical attention, his contribution was to have recognized the importance of social and affective factors in moral cognition. In particular, it focused attention upon social interaction as the primary means to knowledge and understanding of others and, therefore, of the self.

The symbolic interactionist theory of Baldwin thus provides the basis for a social-cognitive approach to the study of moral development. Moral action in the absence of external authority may stem from the child's need for self-definition and feelings of competence in terms of their perceptions of attributes of other individuals whom they admire and respect. The definition of self and competence develops as a consequence of social interactions which have both cognitive and affective significance for children. It is in this sense that one can speak of, for instance, the child's "identification" with an important other (often the same-sex parent) and of its influence on moral development. It is likely that such "identification" would develop within the context of certain parenting styles, which promote the child's understanding of behavior governed by moral and social rules. Social interaction involves the attempts of the parent to foster shared semantic constructions of certain situations in discipline encounters between themselves and their children so that eventually both parent and child assign the same meanings to particular social acts as forbidden or permissible with regard to the context of behavior. Sometimes these attempts at socialization will proceed through straightforward didactic training. At other times the process may involve negotiation on the part of both parent and child (or indeed other significant individuals and child) until agreement is reached. One outcome is "internalization," the self-motivated following of rules of behavior in the absence of external surveillance, than mere compliance in the face of demands by others.

MORAL DEVELOPMENT AND SOCIALIZATION IN RELATION TO THE SHARED MEANING OF RULES AND SITUATIONS

Several studies are germane to the proposition that children develop moral cognitions through the development of shared meanings of social acts with important others. Research in school settings, on discipline within the home, and on children's social knowledge can be viewed from this perspective.

Evidence from School Settings

The first line of evidence comes from a recent study by Walton [35]. She compared three theoretically different cognitive approaches (cognitive-developmental, Heider's [36] attributional model and symbolic interactionist) to moral behavior within the context of negotiations of responsibility among kindergarteners and first and second graders. The children were observed in open classroom settings during school activities where they were encouraged to talk freely and to interact with one another while working. The findings supported a symbolic interactionist approach based on shared semantic constructions among peers. There was no evidence for an age-related shift in coordinating differing viewpoints and considering intentionality in assigning responsibility for acts as Piaget would have predicted [1]. There was also no increase in the frequency with age of appeals to reciprocity norms, contrary to Kohlberg's theory [2].

The data were more readily interpreted as "interchanges" which "did seem to involve a negotiation between the participants to determine how the situation was to be defined" [35, p. 734], "particularly in peer-peer interaction. For instance, in interactions with peers which involved rule violations, children were likely to respond with rejections of the validity of the rule they were accused of violating. When this response was rejected by their peers they were more likely, according to Walton, to offer another explanation or to repeat the first, or to "challenge the accuser."

Evidence from Parent-Child Relations and Discipline Encounters

The second type of evidence to support the role of shared meanings in moral cognitions comes from the controversy between social-learning and cognitive perspectives on socialization processes.

Baumrind examined the relation between particular parental child-rearing patterns and certain social behaviors in children involving self-control, viz. social responsibility, achievement, and independence [37-40]. Such behaviors can be considered to reflect certain levels of self-development and to be related to the extent of moral autonomy of the child [3].

It was found that "competent" children who scored high on the self-control dimension had parents who displayed "authoritative" parenting styles characterized by high maturity demands, firm control over their children's behavior and high levels of nurturance and clear communication. By contrast, children who scored low on self-control had parents who did not exercise consistent firm control and did not demand mature behaviors from their children.

Baumrind also identified two other parenting styles: harmonious and non-conforming. Each style is virtually identical to authoritative parenting except for the lack of salient firm control. Daughters of harmonious parents were equally as competent as daughters of authoritative parents and sons of non-conforming parents display similar levels of self-control as sons of authoritative parents.

Baumrind interpreted her results from a social-learning perspective arguing that "the use of reasoning accompanied by power-assertion should be more effective with young children than reasoning alone: with young children a display of power captures their attention and clarifies in their minds that compliance is required, whereas the use of reason without a display of power often signals to the child that the parent is indecisive about requiring compliance" [40, p. 14]. Baumrind does not consider that the young child's cognitive capacities and social understanding may determine the usefulness of firm control in the context of the child's perception of the parent and situation and shared meanings in parent-child relations. Socialization may thus be fostered at times by power assertive techniques involving threats, deprivation of privileges, and physical punishment. Firm control must be "moderately severe" in order to be effective.

Lewis in a reinterpretation of Baumrind's data claims that given the findings with respect to parental firm control for daughters of harmonious parents and sons of non-conforming parents, parental firm control may not necessarily be instrumental in promoting internalization of moral and social regulation in children [41]. From a cognitive perspective, she suggests that "measures of firm parental control may in many cases be interpreted as measures of the child's willingness to obey or of the abence of parent-child conflict. For some measures parents may be scored high in firm control because the child misbehaves infrequently (i.e., as a small percentage of all child-initiated behavior) rather than because the parent responds firmly to instances of misbehavior" [41, p. 560].

Lewis's proposal is based on research [e.g., 42] which demonstrated that internalization of a norm is more likely when the strength of an external control is just enough to secure compliance. Lepper found that greater external control than this minimally sufficient account actually inhibits later internalization of the norm in question [42]. Lewis argues that the use of firm parental control in authoritative parenting always accompanies other variables such as parental warmth and inductive reasoning and possibly the child's willingness to obey. These factors may in fact make a more powerful contribution to the development of self-control in children than the use of parental firm control. Thus Baumrind's data on firm control may be reinterpreted as showing that children who score highly on the self-control dimension also exercise a high degree of control over their behavior in compliance with the demands of their parents. In the harmonious household, for example, children are actively involved in the formulation and alteration of rules so that, "from the child's point of view, rules may not be imposed or enforced at all but distilled from the child's social interactions and amended by the child" [41, p. 562]. Lewis proposes that in fact, children's sense of control over rules may be far more central than parental firm control to the extent to which they internalize rules and norms.

In a rejoinder to Lewis, Baumrind rejects this argument claiming that Lewis misunderstood and misinterpreted the "configural" classification of parenting styles [40]. Baumrind resorts to the traditional social-learning model to explain internalization, a view which emphasizes the idea that self-control arises out of responses to unpleasant experiences, such as the consequences of non-compliance. Baumrind maintains that young children do not have the cognitive capacities to make inferences about the legitimacy of certain rules and norms, that in fact that compliance occurs and self-control develops in the absence of self-attributions on the part of children. But recent research on social-cognitive development suggests that Lewis's argument may have greater validity than Baumrind would accept.

Children's Social Knowledge: Morality and Convention

According to Turiel's analysis, children even at an early age can distinguish between social-conventional and moral rules [12]. Social-conventional rules (such as those regarding etiquette) are considered to be arbitrary, alterable and related to the social context whereas moral rules (such as those regarding fighting) are considered to generalize across contexts and are not tied to specific social settings. Smetana has found that children as young as three years evaluate moral transgressions as more serious than social-conventional transgressions and consider that they should be punished more severely [15].

Further, young children appear to be capable of making inferences about different types of transgressions that go beyond their personal experience of moral and social conventional rule violations. Smetana examined the responses of three- to six-year-old children to stories where transgressions were either moral or social-conventional and to stories where particular events were unspecified but which varied in terms of the consistency of the prohibitions regarding the events and the consequences of such events for others [16]. She found that children of all ages were able to use consistency of application and consequence information to distinguish moral and social-conventional transgressions and did not appear to rely on their knowledge of specific prohibitions in specific contexts. Adult prohibitions only appeared to be salient with respect to social-conventional transgressions and such events were judged to be permissible if the particular prohibition was removed. Children did not resort to adult prohibitions to judge the wrongness of moral acts even when they were not able to articulate why such an act was wrong. In this connection, young children prefer parents and authority figures to enforce moral rules rather than social-conventional ones [13, 43].

PARENTAL INVOLVEMENT AND
MORAL ATMOSPHERE AS A BASIS FOR
SOCIALIZATION AND MORAL DEVELOPMENT:
TOWARD AN INTEGRATIVE SYNTHESIS

Much research in the area of cognitive development has been stimulated by the work of Bryant [44], Gelman [22] and Donaldson [45] which has shown that young children have a pre-existing capacity to understand conservation and other Piagetian tasks. A cognitive-developmental stage analysis underestimates the abilities of preschoolers and children under seven years. By contrast, Piaget and Kohlberg have claimed that young children are primitive in their moral cognitions: that they either define moral rules in terms of a unilateral respect for the adult or in terms of the consequences of reward and punishment. A timely reappraisal is required since the cognitive-developmental approach to socialization is predicated on a particular stage analysis that now seems outdated [46].

The work of Walton, Lewis, Turiel and Smetana has shown that young children strive to share the meaning of rules with others and discriminate between the legitimate and illegitimate application of rules on the basis of social interaction. The implication is that young children's perceptions of parental socialization behavior is finely differentiated. Further, these perceptions or "hot" cognitions may mediate moral behavior.

In a series of studies over the past five years, we have sought to examine children's evaluations of parental discipline techniques. Siegal and Cowen [47] gave children from preschool to Grade 12 stories patterned after the categories of disobedience situations used by Grusec and Kuczynski [48]. The subjects were read each story and presented with the childrearing techniques of four mothers. They were asked to consider each mother in turn and told to indicate how right each of the mothers was to do as she did. The techniques fell into the broad categories defined by Hoffman [48]: 1) induction in which the mother was described to the subjects as reasoning with the culprit and pointing out the harmful consequences of the transgression for the self and others, 2) power assertion in which she was described as physically punishing the culprit, and 3) love withdrawal in which she was described as telling the culprit that she would not have anything more to do with the child for the time being. In addition, a four type of mother was described as choosing not to intervene, believing that the child would learn independently. The inclusion of permissiveness as a discipline technique allowed comparisons to be made between evaluations of nonintervention and different forms of intervention. At all ages, children generally expressed strong approval for induction backed by milder approval for physical punishment. Evaluations were highly influenced by the nature of the situation with children appreciating the mother's flexibility.

Yet in a followup study on evaluations of father's socialization behaviors using the same methodology and similar age groups [50], young children aged five to six years showed no clear preferences for the same techniques as used by fathers and their ratings were not strongly determined by the situation. Physical punishment often received approval comparable to induction. Moreover, in contrast to the study of perceptions of mothers, boys and girls differed in their ratings. Boys in general rated fathers more favorably than did girls, particularly in their use of physical punishment in situations of simple disobedience and physical harm to the self. Girls rated fathers' use of induction more highly than boys in the simple disobedience situation.

These results support the observation of Lynn [51] and Block [52] that, compared to the father, the mother is generally more visible in childrearing. Since mothers ordinarily have a greater day-to-day involvement in socialization encounters, they are likely to be seen by both boys and girls as more sensitive to individual situations which affect the child. The girl is provided with a model for sex-appropriate behavior which the boy lacks. Fathers, by contrast, are comparatively unavailable as sources of induction and sensitivity. The boy is left more on his own to search for the appropriate model and his rule conceptions may be less sensitive to social contexts and situations [14].

In the absence of the extensive day-to-day interaction that marks the mother-child relationship, father-child evaluations may be more likely to be influenced by mutual sex-typing. Boys' and girls' differential evaluations of the father's socialization behavior may be a function of the father's differential treatment strategies that are practiced early in children's socialization histories. In their review of the sex differences literature, Maccoby and Jacklin [53, p. 348] report that they were handicapped by a lack of information on the father. But in agreement with Johnson [54, 55], they speculated that "fathers may differentiate between the sexes to a much greater degree than mothers." Since then considerable research has indicated that fathers, more than mothers, do differentiate between boys and girls in their socialization behaviors [e.g., 56, 57]. While some studies have used multiple measures of parent-child interaction and often only a few of these have revealed differences attributable to the sex of the parent, results that are significant provide general support for a pattern of father-specific socialization behaviors [58]. In particular, the father gives more positive and negative reinforcement to boys than to girls, is more punitive, and uses more firm control techniques. While there are studies in which no differences at all have been found or ones related to the socialization behaviors of the same-sex or opposite-sex parent, differences restricted specifically to the mother have been virtually nonexistent.

All the same, moral and prosocial behavior may be affected by the quality of the father's involvement in the home. For example, although Siegal and Barclay [50] found that five- to six-year-old boys did not differentiate in their evaluations of fathers' socialization behavior, the boys' self-reports of empathic responsiveness on the scale devised by Bryant were related to their positive ratings of fathers' use of induction and were unrelated to the use of physical punishment [59].

Rutherford and Mussen found that four-year-old boys' generosity was related to perceptions of their fathers as warm, nurturant, and altruistic [60]. Francis and Siegal found that seven-year-old boys' perceptions of their fathers' fairness were related to resistance to temptation in the absence of external surveillance [61]. While similar results were reported by Bixenstine, De Corte and Bixenstine [62], additional research is necessary to determine the extent to which perceptions of socialization behavior is an antecedent rather than a consequence of children's compliance and internalization.

Perceptions of parental behavior and associated conceptions of moral rules and social conventions are influenced by the socialization atmosphere created by parents, teachers, peers, and children themselves. A harmonious home atmosphere may undermine the perceived legitimacy of power assertion and foster the parent's use of subtle inductive methods to encourage compliance. While young children have the capacity to discriminate between moral rules and social conventions, the content of their rule conceptions is culturally influenced. In Israel, Nisan has provided evidence that cultural or social norms affect children's notions of right and wrong [20]. He compared rule conceptions in Muslim children and religious, non-religious, and Kibbutz children. Cultural background determined whether a behavior was considered wrong irrespective of laws or prohibitions. For example, Muslim children regarded referring to adults by their first names as morally and universally wrong while the other three groups regarded this act as wrong within particular social settings.

Similarly, young children's rule conceptions can be seen in terms of the atmosphere of day care and peer group settings in which the shared meanings of rules is fostered through social interaction. For example, in two studies, Siegal and Storey compared conceptions of moral and social rules in preschoolers who were veterans at day care, having attended for at least eighteen months, with those who were newly enrolled [63]. In the first study, the newly enrolled judged transgressions against social rules as naughtier and more worthy of punishment than did the veterans. In the second study, compared to the veterans, the newly enrolled regarded social transgressions as naughtier and worse even if there was no punishment, and more worthy of adult intervention and anger. The newly enrolled did not clearly differentiate between rule violations in the two domains.

It is likely that the atmosphere of home and day care differentially affects the two groups' conceptions of rules. Compared to the newly enrolled, the veterans had more highly developed (or shared) expectations of the use of adult authority. They preferred that adult intervention be exercised in moral rather than social structures. Day care children have been reported to be more independent in their compliance with adult directives [64]. Contrary to the wishes of adults, they may find social transgressions acceptable and behave accordingly. Within the day care setting itself, aggressive, rejected children who are disliked by their peers appear least likely to discriminate between moral rules and social conventions, while popular and controversial children are most likely to make this discrimination [65].

To conclude, from a social-cognitive perspective, "hot" moral cognitions contribute to socialization and moral development and are associated with internalization and rule-guided behavior. These cognitions reflect collective norms, shared meaning and symbols in conceptions of rules and perceptions of significant others. The legitimacy of parental socialization behavior and rule conceptions is influenced by culture, home and school. Given recent work in cognitive development, an orthodox Piagetian stage analysis is not relevant and, contrary to Kohlberg [6, p. 269], the influence of moral atmosphere is persuasive, especially in childhood. In the context of parental involvement and atmosphere, hot moral cognitions relate to moral behavior. More evidence is required to determine the role of forms of cognition and social knowledge in the moral behavior of young children.

REFERENCES

1. J. Piaget, *The Moral Judgment of the Child*, Penguin, Harmondsworth, England, 1977. (Originally published by Routledge and Kegan Paul, London, 1932.)
2. L. Kohlberg, Stage and Sequence: The Cognitive-Developmental Approach to Socialization, in *Handbook of Socialization Theory and Research*, D. A. Goslin (ed.), Rand McNally, Chicago, 1969.
3. A. Blasi, Bridging Moral Cognition and Moral Action: A Critical Review of the Literature, *Psychological Bulletin, 88*, pp. 1-46, 1980.
4. G. Jurkovic, The Juvenile Delinquent as a Moral Philosopher: A Structural-Developmental Perspective, *Psychological Bulletin, 88*, pp. 709-727, 1980.
5. L. Kohlberg, "The Development of Modes of Moral Thinking and Choice in the Years Ten to Sixteen," unpublished doctoral dissertation, University of Chicago, 1958.
6. ____, *Essays on Moral Development, Volume II. The Psychology of Moral Development*, Harper and Row, Chicago, 1984.
7. L. Kohlberg and D. Candee, The Relationship of Moral Judgment to Moral Action, in *Morality, Moral Behavior, and Moral Development*, W. M. Kurtines and J. L. Gerwirtz (eds.), Wiley, New York, 1984.
8. W. Kurtines and E. Greif, The Development of Moral Thought: Review and Evaluation of Kohlberg's Approach, *Psychological Bulletin, 81*, pp. 453-470, 1974.
9. A. Colby, L. Kohlberg, J. Gibbs, and M. Lieberman, A Longitudinal Study of Moral Judgment, *Monographs of the Society for Research in Child Development, 47*:199, 1982.
10. L. C. Jensen and K. Hughston, The Relationship between Type of Sanction, Story Content, and Children's Judgments Which Are Independent of Sanction, *Journal of Genetic Psychology, 122*, pp. 49-54, 1973.

11. E. Ozols and J. B. Gilmore, Respecting Children: Moral Reasoning When Right Conduct Joins Punishing Outcomes, *Canadian Journal of Behavioral Science*, *10*, pp. 296-307, 1978.

12. E. Turiel, *The Development of Social Knowledge: Morality and Convention*, Cambridge University Press, New York, 1983.

13. L. Nucci and E. Turiel, Social Interactions and the Development of Social Concepts in Preschool Children, *Child Development*, *49*, pp. 400-407, 1978.

14. J. G. Smetana, Preschool Children's Conceptions of Moral and Social Rules, *Child Development*, *52*, pp. 1333-1336, 1981.

15. J. G. Smetana, Preschool Children's Conceptions of Transgressions: Effects of Varying Moral and Conventional Domain-Related Attributes, *Developmental Psychology*, *21*, pp. 18-29, 1985.

16. J. S. Leming, Intrapersonal Variations in Stage of Moral Reasoning among Adolescents as a Function of Situational Context, *Journal of Youth and Adolescence*, *4*, pp. 405-426, 1978.

17. S. Yussen, Characteristics of Moral Dilemmas Written by Adolescents, *Developmental Psychology*, *13*, pp. 162-163, 1977.

18. N. Haan, Hypothetical and Actual Moral Reasoning in a Situation of Civil Disobedience, *Journal of Personality and Social Psychology*, *32*, pp. 255-270, 1975.

19. R. A. Gordon, J. F. Short, D. S. Cartwright, and F. L. Strodtbeck, Values and Gang Delinquency: A Study of Street Corner Groups, *American Journal of Sociology*, *69*, pp. 109-128, 1963.

20. M. Nisan, Content and Structure and Moral Judgment: An Integrative View, in *Morality, Moral Behavior, and Moral Development*, W. M. Kurtines and J. L. Gerwirtz (eds.), Wiley, New York, 1984.

21. R. Gerson and W. Damon, Moral Understanding and Children's Conduct, in *Moral Development, New Directions in Child Development*, (Vol. I), W. Damon (ed.), Jossey-Bass, San Francsico, 1978.

22. R. Gelman, Accessing One-to-one Correspondence: Still Another Paper About Conservation, *British Journal of Psychology*, *73*, pp. 209-220, 1982.

23. J. McGarrigle and M. Donaldson, Conservation Accidents, *Cognition*, *3*, pp. 341-350, 1975.

24. C. Moore and D. Frye, The Effect of Experimenter's Intention on the Child's Understanding of Conservation, *Cognition*, *22*, pp. 283-298, 1986.

25. S. A. Rose and M. Blank, The Potency of Context in Children's Cognition: An Illustration through Conservation, *Child Development*, *45*, pp. 499-502, 1974.

26. M. Siegal, L. J. Waters, and L. S. Dinwiddy, Misleading Children: Causal Attributions for Inconsistency Under Repeated Questioning, *Journal of Experimental Child Psychology*, in press.

27. J. M. Baldwin, *Social and Ethical Interpretations in Mental Development*, Macmillan, London, 1896.

28. _____, *Mental Development in the Child and the Race*, Macmillan, London, 1906.

29. G. H. Mead, *Mind, Self and Society*, University of Chicago Press, Chicago, 1934.

30. J. M. Broughton, The Genetic Psychology of James Mark Baldwin, *American Psychologist*, *36*, pp. 396-407, 1981.
31. J. M. Broughton and D. J. Freeman-Moir, *The Developmental Psychology of James Mark Baldwin*, Ablex, Norwood, New Jersey, 1981.
32. J. Russell, *The Acquisition of Knowledge*, Macmillan, London, 1978.
33. L. S. Vygotsky, *Thought and Language*, MIT Press, Cambridge, Massachusetts, 1962.
34. J. M. Broughton and K. F. Riegel, Developmental Psychology and the Self, *Annals of the New York Academy of Sciences*, *2*, pp. 149-167, 1977.
35. M. D. Walton, Negotiation of Responsibility: Judgments of Blameworthiness in a Natural Setting, *Developmental Psychology*, *21*, pp. 725-736, 1985.
36. F. Heider, *The Psychology of Interpersonal Relations*, Wiley, New York, 1958.
37. D. Baumrind, Current Patterns of Parental Authority, *Developmental Psychology Monographs*, *4*, (1, Part 2), 1971.
38. _____, Harmonious Parents and Their Preschool Children, *Developmental Psychology*, *4*, pp. 99-102, 1971.
39. _____, The Development of Instrumental Competence through Socialization, *Minnesota Symposia on Child Psychology*, *7*, A. D. Pick (ed.), University of Minnesota Press, Minneapolis, 1973.
40. _____, Rejoinder to Lewis's Reinterpretation of Parental Firm Control Effects: Are Authoritative Parents Really Harmonious? *Psychological Bulletin*, *94*, pp. 132-142, 1983.
41. C. C. Lewis, The Effects of Parental Firm Control: A Reinterpretation of Findings, *Psychological Bulletin*, *90*, pp. 547-563, 1981.
42. M. R. Lepper, Social Control Processes and the Internalization of Social Values: An Attributional Perspective, in *Social Cognition and Social Development: A Sociocultural Perspective*, D. N. Ruble and W. W. Hartup (eds.), Cambridge University Press, New York, 1983.
43. D. Weston and E. Turial, Act-Rule Relations: Children's Concept of Social Rules, *Developmental Psychology*, *16*, pp. 417-424, 1980.
44. P. Bryant, *Perception and Understanding in Young Children*, Methuen, London, 1974.
45. M. Donaldson, *Children's Minds*, Fontana, Glasgow, 1978.
46. M. Siegal, *Children, Parenthood, and Social Welfare in the Context of Developmental Psychology*, Oxford University Press, Oxford, 1985.
47. M. Siegal and J. Cowen, Appraisals of Intervention: The Mother versus the Culprit's Behavior as Determinants of Children's Evaluations of Discipline Techniques, *Child Development*, *55*, pp. 1760-1766, 1984.
48. J. E. Grusec and L. Kuczynski, Direction of Effect in Socialization: A Comparison of the Parent's versus the Child's Behavior as Determinants of Disciplinary Techniques, *Developmental Psychology*, *16*, pp. 1-9, 1980.
49. M. L. Hoffman, Moral Development, in *Carmichael's Manual of Child Psychology*, (Vol. II) (3rd Edition), P. Mussen (ed.), Wiley, New York, 1970.
50. M. Siegal and M. S. Barclay, Children's Evaluations of Fathers' Socialization Behavior, *Developmental Psychology*, *21*, pp. 1090-1096, 1985.

51. D. B. Lynn, Sex Role and Parental Identification, *Child Development, 33*, pp. 555-564, 1962.
52. J. H. Block, Differential Premises Arising from Differential Socialization of the Sexes: Some Conjectures, *Child Development, 54*, pp. 1335-1354, 1983.
53. E. E. Maccoby and C. N. Jacklin, *The Psychology of Sex Differences*, Stanford University Press, Stanford, 1974.
54. M. M. Johnson, Sex Role Learning in the Nuclear Family, *Child Development, 34*, pp. 319-334, 1963.
55. ____, Fathers, Mothers and Sex Typing, *Sociological Inquiry, 45*, pp. 15-26, 1963.
56. P. Bronstein, Differences in Mothers' and Fathers' Behaviors toward Children: A Cross-Cultural Comparison, *Developmental Psychology, 20*, pp. 995-1003, 1984.
57. J. H. Langlois and A. C. Downs, Mothers, Fathers, and Peers as Socialization Agents of Sex-typed Play Behaviors in Young Children, *Child Development, 51*, pp. 1217-1247, 1980.
58. M. Siegal, Are Sons and Daughters Treated More Differently by Fathers than by Mothers? *Developmental Review, 7*, pp. 183-209, 1987.
59. B. K. Bryant, An Index of Empathy for Children and Adolescents, *Child Development, 53*, pp. 413-425, 1982.
60. E. Rutherford and P. Mussen, Generosity in Nursery School Boys, *Child Development, 39*, pp. 755-765, 1968.
61. R. Francis and M. Siegal, Rule-Following Behavior and Children's Perceptions of Significant Others, in *Issues and Research in Child Development*, T. G. Cross and L. M. Riach (eds.), Institute of Early Childhood Development, Melbourne, 1985.
62. V. E. Bixenstine, M. S. De Corte, and B. A. Bixenstine, Conformity to Peer-sponsored Misbehavior at Four Age Levels, *Developmental Psychology, 12*, pp. 226-244, 1976.
63. M. Siegal and R. M. Storey, Day Care and Children's Conceptions of Moral and Social Rules, *Child Development, 56*, pp. 1001-1008, 1985.
64. J. L. Rubenstein, C. Howes, and P. Boyle, A Two-year Follow-up of Infants in Community-Based Daycare, *Journal of Child Psychology and Psychiatry, 22*, pp. 209-218, 1981.
65. J. A. Sanderson and M. Siegal, Conceptions of Moral and Social Rules in Rejected and Nonrejected Preschoolers, *Journal of Clinical Child Psychology*, in press.

CHAPTER 3

Learned Helplessness in Children: Perception of Control and Causal Attributions

STEVEN FRIEDLANDER

Learned helplessness refers to the behavioral condition that develops when, faced with uncontrollable aversive events, the individual presumably learns that responding does not control outcomes [1, 2]. This learning affects motivation, cognition and emotion in ways that have serious implications for adaptive functioning. Motivationally, the incentive to initiate responses in an effort to control outcomes is reduced. Further, the learning of response-outcome independence interferes with cognitive functioning by making the learning of response-outcome contingency more difficult. Finally, the initial emotional reaction of fear quickly evolves into depression and a feeling of helplessness.

Originally based on research with animals [1], helplessness effects have been repeatedly demonstrated in humans [3-7]. Although the original helplessness hypothesis was cognitive in that it posited that the *expectation* that outcomes are uncontrollable formed the basis of the development of helplessness deficits, the plethora of studies investigating helplessness in humans identified inadequacies in the original hypothesis, prompting a reformulation along attributional lines [8]. This revision has brought the helplessness hypothesis clearly within the purview of cognitive theory. According to the refomulation, helplessness is mediated by the causal attributions that are activated by the effort to understand one's inbility to control outcomes. It is the nature of the causal attributions generated in response to failure to control outcomes that determines the consequences of the experience for adaptive functioning. The revised hypothesis proposes that these attributions vary along the three bi-polar dimensions of

[1] This chapter is a revision and expansion of a paper that originally appeared in *Imagination, Cognition and Personality*, 4:1, 1984–85.

stable-unstable, global-specific, and internal-external, each of which correspondingly determines the chronicity and generality of the resulting helplessness deficits, as well as the consequences of the experience for the individual's self-esteem.

Learned helplessness has been proposed as a model of reactive depression in humans [2, 8], and there are data that both support and question the adequacy of the helplessness model of depression.[2] Independent of its adequacy as a model of depression, helplessness describes a phenomenon in which primarily cognitive factors, in the form of causal attributions, are hypothesized to have a significant impact on adaptive behavior. Although the role of cognitions as ultimate causes of behavior has been recently questioned [10], there is little question but that one's beliefs or expectations about the relationship between behavior and outcome can influence behavior [11] and, via that influence, affect performance-based feedback which, in turn, may exert a more direct influence on subsequent behavior [12].

As a phenomenon mediated by causal attributions and related to perceived uncontrollability, learned helplessness is at the interface of research on attribution theory, the perception of control and causality, as well as studies of internal-external locus of control [13-16]. As already noted, helplessness theory was born in the animal laboratory, and in both its original and reformulated versions has been extensively investigated with adult humans. Although helplessness has not been as thoroughly or directly investigated in children, the application of helplessness theory to children is by no means new. As a cognitive theory, however, and given that children's cognitive functioning is both qualitatively and quantitatively different from that of adults, the application of helplessness theory to children will require systematic consideration of cognitive-developmental factors [17]. A brief review of selected studies will provide the background for that consideration.

HELPLESSNESS AND CHILDREN

In an early application of helplessness theory to humans, Dweck and Repucci inquired whether children experiencing uncontrollable failure in an achievement situation would suffer the performance decrements associated with helplessness, and further attempted to identify those factors which distinguish children who respond to failure by "giving up" from those who do not [18]. The investigators divided their fifth grade subject sample into helpless and persistent groups based on their response to failure, and then evaluated the generalized expectancies for control of reinforcements in each group. Based on helplessness theory it was predicted that helpless children would assume relatively less personal responsibility for their success and failure, and when responsibility for outcomes was accepted, as evidenced by an internal attribution, such outcomes would be seen as due to the presence or absence of the stable quality of ability rather than effort. On the other hand, it was predicted that persistent children would assume responsibility for their successes and failures, and would attribute outcomes to the modifiable quality of effort rather than ability, thus accounting for their sustained or enhanced effort in the face of failure. The results confirmed these predictions. In contrast to persistent children, helpless children were found to attribute failure to external factors and, when making an internal attribution, tended to see failure as a function of ability rather than motivation.

Dweck and Repucci's results clearly imply that by the age of about ten years, a consistent and systematic attributional pattern has developed that results in a circumstance in which a child may not try to solve a problem even though the problem is within the limits of the child's ability [18]. Thus, when confronted with failure, some children will respond as if the situation is potentially within their control and persist in their efforts, while others will respond as if they are helpless to alter their circumstances and cease trying. These contrasting responses are presumably mediated by the attributions the child makes for the failure. Clearly such a circumstance has the potential for profound impact in the child's subsequent adaptive behavior.

In an effort to determine whether altering a child's failure attributions would affect this maladaptive response to failure, Dweck identified twelve helpless children based on their expectation of failure and the deterioration of their performance in the face of failure [19]. These children were matched on measures of their response to failure, and randomly assigned either to a success only treatment in which failure was avoided, or an attribution retraining treatment in which periodic failure was programmed into the experience, and when it occurred, was attributed by the experimenter to insufficient effort as opposed to lack of ability, the latter of which presumably would have been the natural attribution of such helpless children. It was hypothesized that if the helpless child could be trained to attribute failure to effort, a variable factor under personal control, rather than to the stable factor of ability, then the response to failure might, in parallel fashion, change from passive helplessness to persistent effort. The results supported the hypothesis and demonstrated that helpless children could be taught to attribute failure to lack of effort and, by thus taking responsibility for it, place it under personal control. In addition to demonstrating the susceptibility of attributional patterns to modification by concurrent life experience, this study confirmed the notion that the manner in which a child understands his or her experience, that is, the causal attributions made by the youngster, can have a significant effect on the child's reaction to the event as well as on his or her subsequent behavior.

Since cognitions, specifically causal attributions, appeared to be the major determinant of youngsters' helpless response to failure, Diener and Dweck directly studied the achievement-related cognitions of both helpless and persistent children [20]. Building on the two studies just reviewed, they identified helpless and persistent subjects on the basis of their respective tendency to ignore or emphasize the role of effort in accounting for failure. Subjects who tended to attribute failure to effort were placed in the mastery-oriented group, and those who tended not to attribute failure to effort were designated helpless. Children's cognitions following failure were monitored, in one study by asking the child, "Why do you think you had trouble with these problems?" and in a second study by having the child "think out loud" while attempting to solve problems.

Results of both studies showed consistent differences between the two groups. In response to the inquiry as to the cause of their failure, over 50 percent of the helpless children spontaneously cited their lack of ability (e.g., "not smart enough"), while not a single mastery-oriented child offered such an ability attribution, tending rather toward effort attributions or attribution to external factors such as luck or task difficulty. Further, analysis of the childrens' spontaneously generated attributions indicated that in the face of failure experiences helpless children made ineffective task-strategy statements and attributions for their failure, while the mastery-oriented children made few attributions of any kind, tending instead to engage in self-monitoring and self-instruction regarding their ongoing efforts at problem solving. Interestingly, Diener and Dweck noted that mastery-oriented children did not seem to experience the feedback that their response was incorrect as evidence of failure or as predictive of future failure, but rather as information that could be used in further efforts to solve the problem [20].

While the work of Dweck and her associates provides substantial evidence that children differ in the way they understand or process failure, and that these attributional differences are associated with the cognitive and motivational deficits of helplessness, little light has been shed on the affective and self-esteem consequences proposed to be associated with uncontrollable events. In a study relevant to these dimensions of helplessness with children, Johnson proposed that chronic school failure could be conceptualized as a lack of control over important outcomes, thus constituting naturally occurring helplessness training [21]. Based on the reformulated helplessness hypothesis, she predicted that high self-esteem would be associated with success, with external attributions for failure, and with internal attributions for success. Average, failing, and learning disabled children in remedial classrooms were compared on measures of self-concept, internal-external control of reinforcement for academic outcomes, which provided a measure of attributions for success and failure, and a behavioral test of persistence in the face of failure. The prediction was confirmed—school achievement (failure/success), persistence in the face of failure, self-concept and the nature of causal attribution were significantly related to one another.

In summary, the data would seem to be consistent in support of the direct applicability of the learned helplessness hypothesis to children, particularly in regard to achievement oriented behavior. Uncontrollable events, operationalized primarily as failure on cognitive tasks, elicit cognitive activity in the form of attributions, the precise nature of which appear to determine whether or not the youngster will develop the motivational, cognitive and self-esteem deficits associated with helplessness. Children appear to develop systematized attributional patterns that lend a degree of stability and predictability to their response to failure. Further, these patterns differ in the extent to which they render the youngster either susceptible or resistant to helplessness effects. Indeed, these ideas have been so attractive that they have found their way into the educational literature, forming the conceptual basis for helping teachers to understand children's failure-related behavior, and even for providing guidelines for teachers on how to "remedy learned helplessness" [22]. There would seem therefore to be no need to consider the potentially complicating factor of developmental changes in children's cognitive competencies as mediating factors in the manifestation of helplessness-based behaviors.

These tentative conclusions are based on rather homogeneous subject samples, however, particularly in regard to age. Neither Dweck and Repucci [18] nor Diener and Dweck [20] reported exact ages of their fifth grade subjects, but it may be assumed that they were no younger than ten years old. Dweck's [19] subjects ranged from eight to thirteen years, but only one of the twelve subjects was eight years old, and Johnson's [21] sample of boys ranged from nine to twelve years of age. Data on younger children are conspicuously absent. Given the salient role of causal attributions in helplessness theory, and the changes in attribution and the understanding of causality that occur from preschool through the age of ten or twelve years [23], it might be expected that preschool age children would respond to helplessness inducing failure differently than do ten- or twelve-year-olds.

In a straightforward test of this hypothesis, Rholes, Blackwell, Jordan and Walters assessed the relative susceptibility of different aged children to learned helplessness [24]. Kindergarten (M age = 5.9 years), first (M age = 7.1 years), third (M age = 8.7 years), and fifth (M age = 10.9 years) graders were pretreated with success or failure on a hidden figures task, and decrements in task performance and persistence following these pretreatments were the measures of helplessness. Based on developmental studies which suggest that younger children do not view failure as related to ability [25, 26] or as having implications for future performance [27], Rholes et al. predicted that younger children would be less susceptible to helplessness than older ones [24]. The results supported this prediction, with post-failure persistence and performance indices of helplessness evident only among fifth graders. Similarly, success or failure had a significant impact on mood only among fifth graders. In a later developmental study of helplessness, Miller subjected both second graders, (M age = 8.3 years), and sixth graders (M age = 12.4 years) to helplessness inducing failure. The performance deficits indicative of helplessness appeared only in the sixth graders [28].

Interestingly, Rholes et al. also found that the attributions of their younger subjects differed from those of the fifth graders in systematic ways [24]. Whereas the correlation between fifth graders' attributions and the behavioral indices of helplessness was consistent with helplessness theory, there was less evidence of a relationship between attributions and behavior in kindergarteners and first graders. This led them to suggest that the attributional patterns associated with helplessness are not "characteristic of children whose mental age is substantially less than nine and a half years" [24, p. 623]. It would thus appear that the attributional basis of helplessness does not become firmly established until about nine or ten years of age. This, of course, does not suggest that helplessness deficits are not evident in younger children [cf., 24, 29]. It does, however, raise important questions regarding the mediating variables in the development of helplessness in young children, as well as the nature of the developmental variation in those aspects of the helplessness phenomenon other than causal attributions, such as the perception of failure or uncontrollability.

THE CAUSES OF HELPLESSNESS: A DEVELOPMENTAL VIEW

The process that presumably eventuates in a state of learned helplessness includes two necessary conditions—the perception of no control and the generation of specific kinds of causal attribution to explain that perception [8]. The child must first perceive that he or she is helpless, that is, that there is a lack of contingency between behavior and outcome. Put in terms of the most common experimental operationalization of uncontrollability, the child must first experience him or herself as having failed. If there is no perception of independence of effort and outcome, of a lack of contingency, of uncontrollability, in short, of failure, then the second condition, the generation of causal attributions to explain or account for the helplessness, lack of control, or failure will not follow.

The theory posits that helplessness will develop given the perception of uncontrollability and the attribution of that uncontrollability to internal, stable and global factors. It is argued that the adaptive consequences of the perception of uncontrollability are a logical function of the nature of the causal attribution. So, for example, an adult who attributes perceived uncontrollability of negative outcomes to ability would manifest the range of deficits associated with helplessness. However, whether such an outcome would result from a similar attribution in young children has not yet been determined. Although Seligman and Peterson argue that an internal attribution in children would affect helplessness and depression in the same way it does an adult [30], there is evidence to suggest that differences in the way children understand the concept of ability, an internal attribution, may result in very different adaptive consequences in spite of comparable perceptions of uncontrollability and causal attributions. Thus, developmentally based cognitive factors may influence the development of helplessness in children via the perception of uncontrollability or the nature of the causal attribution. It may also be that because of these developmental considerations both of the necessary conditions for the development of adult helplessness may be met and young children still may not manifest the same helplessness deficits as do adults and older children.

Perception of Control

According to Piaget and Inhelder, the perception of uncontrollability requires the appreciation of the independence of events, an understanding that comes later in development than that of dependent relations [31]. The concept of chance, so central to much of the experimental work on noncontingency, is thus thought by these theorists to be absent in young children. This would imply that young children would have difficulty perceiving a lack of contingency even under circumstances, such as chance determined outcomes, in which the events in question are independent.

Indeed, Langer has demonstrated that even among adults, perceived controllability of outcomes is not a simple function of objective contingencies [32]. Adults often manifest an *illusion of control*, acting as if uncontrollable events, specifically chance determined outcomes, were, in fact, under their control. Langer has even suggested that such an illusion of control might be the inverse of learned helplessness [32]. Further, Alloy and Abramson have demonstrated that such errors in judging contingency are not random, but are systematically related to the subjects' emotional state and the valence of the outcome [33]. Depressed adults accurately judge degree of contingency, whereas nondepressed subjects overestimate degree of contingency when the outcome is frequent and/or desirable, and underestimate contingency when the outcome is undesirable. Given these findings with adults, it would not be surprising to find children subject to the same phenomenon, tending to perceive contingency and control where none exists, a tendency that might counteract the development of helplnessness.

Weisz presented kindergarteners and fourth graders with a chance determined card task and, parallel to the demonstration of illusory contingency in adults, showed that while fourth graders manifested some evidence of an illusory belief in contingency, (e.g., prediction of greater winnings for children who tried hard on a chance task), the younger children more consistently and intensively manifested such an illusion of control [34].

It will be recalled that Rholes et al. found younger children to be less susceptible to helplessness than older children [24]. This finding was predicted on the basis of converging sets of data from the developmental literature.[3] One such set of data addressed the way in which children understand the relationship between effort, ability and outcome. As do adults, older children tend to perceive a compensatory relationship among effort, ability and outcome such that one factor compensates for the other. Thus, for example, a positive outcome in the context of high ability would be seen to be a function of low effort. Younger children, however, tend to view effort, ability and outcome as positively corre- lated. This "halo scheme" [25, 35] results in positive outcomes being viewed as a result of both high ability and high effort, whereas negative outcomes are seen to be a function of both low ability and low effort. Consistent with this, Rholes et al. found a positive correlation between effort and ability ratings of young children (halo scheme) and a negative correlation (compensatory scheme) between effort and ability in their fifth graders [24]. They note that this may reflect "attributional immaturity" on the part of younger children, but go on to suggest that the halo scheme may immunize the young child to helplessness by maintaining a positive relationship between effort and ability, factors that pre- sumably have opposite effects on helplessness.

Both the notion of illusory control and the potentially protective function of the halo scheme raise the possibility that developmentally determined cognitive capacities of young children tend to protect them from one or more of the deficits associated with helplessness and may thereby serve a defensive function. That adults may distort their experience of reality as a defensive maneuver is inherent in the illusion of control data [32, 33].[4] In fact, the self-serving and self-esteem enhancing nature of the attributional errors made by nondepressed subjects in judging degree of contingency clearly implies a defensive function and prompted Alloy and Abramson to suggest that depressed individuals were "sadder but wiser" [32]. Further, Rotter has acknowledged the possibility that for some, an external locus of control may represent a defense against or ration- alization for expected failure [15].

Evidence from the locus of control literature provides support for the notion of defensive distortion in children. A review of this literature suggested that normal children between ten and fourteen years of age may defensively disown responsibility for failure, and supported a general conclusion that children develop external views of the cause of failure as a defensive measure [16]. Recall that Dweck and Repucci found that not only were helpless children characterized by a lack of effort, but they tended to attribute failure to external factors [18]. It may be that these children, designated as helpless based on response to failure, do not try in order to avoid the pain of failure. If one does not try, then one cannot fail. That these children may be particularly sensitive to failure, suffering inordinate self-esteem deficits in response to it, and therefore seek to avoid it is

---

[3] See reference [23] Sedlak and Kurtz for a thorough review of children's causal inferences.
[4] Such attributional distortion has been fully discussed elsewhere [36-38].

consistent with this notion [19]. From this perspective, the external attribution of failure would be the *result* of an adaptive problem (sensitivity to failure) rather than, or in addition to the cause of one (helplessness).

The Processing of Failure

The discussion to this point has emphasized that failure, in one way or another, is at the heart of the helplessness experience with children. Response to failure or attributions regarding failure have been used to operationalize helplessness [18, 20], naturally occurring academic failure has been assumed to constitute helplessness training [21], and experimentally manipulated failure has been employed to induce helplessness in the laboratory [24]. However, the distinction between simply not solving a problem or not achieving a goal and experiencing that event as failure is a complex one that involves, among other things, recognition of the potential for a relationship between one's actions, one's ability, and outcomes [39], as well as a particular kind of attribution or cognitive processing of the event. Thus, for example, Bialer [39] has argued that only when an unfavorable outcome is ascribed to one's own shortcomings does it become failure [cf., 8].

The capacity to experience failure would appear to be a cognitively based developmental achievement intimately related to the child's understanding of causality. According to Piaget and Inhelder, the preoperational child does not recognize that logical laws must necessarily be true [31]. It may be for this reason that young children do not recognize the stable, unchanging nature of a causal relationship. Thus, although A may be recognized as causing B, the young child does not necessarily see this as a reliable relationship which can lead to the confident prediction that if A occurs then B will always follow [23]. It is apparently as a derivative of this fact that young children do not always respond to failure as do adults and older children, and may not even experience the specified event as failure.

Among adults, usually as a result of ability attributions, failure experiences affect expectancies for success, which, in turn, have a dramatic effect on one's persistence and quality of performance [40]. In contrast to adults and older children however, when a younger child makes an ability attribution for failure it does not necessarily lead to the formation of stable expectations for, or ability consistent predictions of future behavior [41]. Repeated success and failure has no systematic effect on preschoolers' expectancies of future success or failure, whereas older children show the expected increase and decrease in expectancies as a function of success and failure [27]. Thus, surmising that younger children do not view failure as having stable implications for their future performance, Rholes et al. demonstrated that failure had little effect on the child's persistence and quality of performance on a hidden figures task, or on the ability attributions of kindergarteners as compared to fifth graders, concluding that the younger children were thus relatively resistant to helplessness [24]. Finally, in two studies of children ranging in age from four to eleven, Ruble, Parsons and Ross demonstrated that failure led older children to much more negative ratings of their affect and ability than it did younger children [26]. In fact, whereas six-year-olds never reported negative affect after failure, ten-year-olds regularly showed negative affect following failure. In general, their results indicated that failure had relatively little influence on younger children, who may actually perceive failure as variable and thus as not relevant to the assessment of ability.

There appear to be two separate groups of children who respond to failure in behaviorally similar ways: Mastery-oriented or persistent children [18, 20], and young, probably preoperational children. Both groups do not respond to failure with performance decrements and are thus relatively less susceptible to helplessness. The persistent child would seem to be either insensitive to, or tending toward a higher threshold for experiencing the negative consequences of failure. In the case of the young child, however, the resistance to the negative consequences of failure is apparently rooted in cognitive immaturity which may lead to the inability to experience failure as adults do. Weisz and Stipek have related this immaturity to a failure to appreciate the stability of a psychological construct like ability, which, in turn, is related to the preoperational child's difficulties with conservation of physical qualities [17]. They suggest that the "conservation of competence" [17, p. 274] might be an important variable in understanding attributional implications across developmental periods. In light of the previous discussions of defensive patterns in children, and at the risk of tautological, adaptionist reasoning, it is intriguing to speculate about the inherently protective function of the young child's cognitive immaturity. Given the frequency with which young children encounter "failure," disappointment and frustration [cf., 26] as they increasingly engage and explore the environment and venture into the world of objects and people outside the family, it is noteworthy that there is a built-in mechanism whereby they are relatively protected from discouragement and the various other cognitive, motivational and emotional consequences attendant on failure and helplessness.

Causal Attributions

In the absence of the *perception* of uncontrollability helplessness will not develop [cf., 11]. Given the perception of no control, the ensuing causal attribution will be a primary determinant of the adaptive consequences. The discussion of the perception of no control, and particularly the processing of that special case of uncontrollability known as failure, has necessarily touched on the attribution process and the nature of causality. Just as the child's developing cognitive capacities required attention in understanding the perception of no control, so too the attribution process is shaped by the quality of the child's cognition.

Internal vs. External Causes. Whether the cause of the perceived lack of control is attributed to internal or external factors will significantly affect subsequent behavior [8]. Because of their different adaptive consequences, the question of whether there is a developmentally-based tendency toward internal or external attributions is of considerable interest. There is some debate as to whether children move developmentally from a generally external orientation to an increasingly internal one, or whether the process proceeds in the reverse direction. The former point of view is predicated on the observation that the young child is relatively helpless and unable to control reinforcements, and with the increasing development of competencies and abilities, there is a trend toward greater internality [42, 43]. The latter point of view is represented by the Piagetian cognitive-developmentalists who suggest that the young child's egocentricity and overestimation of personal control [44] is associated with a tendency toward internality which gives way with increasing maturity to the recognition of a lack of control over events and a general shift toward externality.

Weisz and Stipek have reviewed the empirical evidence for these conflicting propositions and found support for both [17]. In a cogent argument, they proposed that the conflicting data might be a function of conceptual confusion in regard to the notion of control. They suggested that control is a function of the presence of two necessary conditions: First, contingency, that is, there must be the possibility of a causal connection between behavior and outcome; and second, competence, that is, the individual must possess the abilities necessary to achieve the outcome or "capitalize on the contingency" [17, p. 262]. Only in the presence of both conditions can an outcome be controlled. They further suggested that changes in perceived contingency will result in a developmental decrease in perceived control, whereas there will be a developmental increase in perceived control based on changes in competence.

Although the data on general developmental trends toward internality or externality are equivocal, there is some indication of systematic developmental differences in the tendency toward internal or external attributions when the nature or valence of the event is considered. Hence, Newhouse found that young children tended to take credit for success but not for failure [45]. Further, as children get older, this tendency decreases and they tend increasingly to attribute negative outcomes to internal factors. Parallel differences are evident in other selected groups of children. Thus, Boersma and Chapman compared the locus of control orientations of learning disabled (LD) and normally achieving third through sixth graders and found that whereas both groups showed a tendency toward increasingly internal attributions for failure, LD children differed in their tendency to attribute school success to external factors [46]. Also, Pearl showed that third and fourth grade LD children tended to see their successes as a function of luck or other presumably external factors, and their failures as less a function of factors over which they have control [47].

Similarly, DuCette, Wolk and Soucar compared the locus of control patterns of adjusted and maladjusted children and found differences in terms of the assumption of responsibility for positive and negative events [48]. The patterns were complex ones such that the maladjusted child tended toward an unbalanced pattern in which attribution to internal factors for either positive or negative events was emphasized, whereas nonreferred children manifested an equal tendency toward internal attributions for both positive and negative events. The authors argued that it is an unbalanced pattern in the perception of control (i.e., attribution) of positive and negative events that is associated with maladjustment. This notion is conceptually similar to that of the depressive attributional style in which particular patterns of attributions for positive and negative events are thought to be responsible for depressive symptoms [8, 49-51]. Such systematic attributional patterns may play a salient role in the breadth and quality of a child's daily experience, contributing not only to persistence and motivation, but also to self-esteem.

Basic to the discussion thus far has been the notion of attribution to internal vs. external causes. Again, much of the data has been based on children eight years of age and older. The abstract concept of an external cause of behavior is typically operationalized, for the purpose of measurement, as luck, chance or fate. Piaget and Inhelder have suggested that the preoperational child is not able to distinguish chance from logical necessity, and the earlier discussion of the illusion of control under chance conditions supports this position [31]. Weisz and Stipek also point out that young children are inclined to see chance outcomes as controllable [17]. They suggest that the concept of luck, presumably a prime example of an external, uncontrollable attribution rooted in chance, is actually perceived by young children more like an internal attribute (e.g., "I'm a lucky person"), one that might even be acquired, as for example through hard work, "being good," or the securing of a rabbit's foot. Thus, for young children, the distinction between internal and external factors, and thereby that between attributions to such factors, is far less clear than it might be with older children and requires systematic study and further clarification before it is assumed to have comparable consequences to those demonstrated with older children and adults.

Effort vs. Ability. If the distinction between attribution to internal and external factors is less than clear for young children, then the even more subtle one between effort and ability is also likely to be more complex than it would seem on the surface. Heider regarded effort and ability as the major internal causes of success and failure, and proposed that they relate to outcome in a multiplicative fashion with ability and effort compensating for one another in producing outcome [52]. As already noted, however, Kun has shown that among six-year-olds this is not the case [35]. Rather, for young children ability and effort are correlated such that given a particular outcome, high ability is taken to mean great effort, and vice-versa. By the time a child is in third grade, inverse compensation for effort emerges, but ability is still judged according to the so-called "halo scheme." The inverse compensatory relationship between effort and ability that characterizes mature reasoning may not be fully understood even in adolescence. In a definitive study, Nicholls conceptualized four levels of reasoning about ability and effort and demonstrated an age progression in which children below seven did not distinguish among ability, effort and outcome [25]. At this first level, children tended to center on one or the other quality, usually effort. At about ten years, ability began to be used intermittently, and not until twelve or thirteen years of age were all three concepts distinguished and used appropriately. Although more recent studies [53] have suggested that younger children (4-6 years) can be far more sophisticated in their causal understanding of achievement outcomes than suggested by Kun [35] and Nicholls [25], methodological differences may account for the discrepancy.

Although the ages at which children achieve different levels of reasoning may vary from study to study, as do the methodologies and measures, it is clear that children differ systematically and developmentally in their ability to reason about effort and ability. It should come as no surprise then that attribution of an outcome to ability or effort might be expected to have different consequences and implications for young children than for older children. The consequences of an attribution of failure to ability are likely to be dramatically different depending upon whether ability is perceived as an enduring, unchangeable trait, as it is by most older children and adults, or whether it is seen as a variable factor that may change tomorrow or with the presentation of the next problem.

Additionally, it would not be inconsistent with the data if such attributions were not even made by young children. In this regard it is noted that many of the studies assessing attributions employ scales in which the child is given a choice between alternative attributions for a given event. That a child chooses one attribution over another in such a forced-choice situation does not imply that the choice accurately reflects what the child's spontaneous cognitive activity might have been.[5] In fact, the one study that assessed children's spontaneous cognitions demonstrated that some children do not engage in any kind of attributional activity following failure [20].

Social Comparison. Implicit in the processing of failure is the notion of social comparison [39], and, although not a necessary condition for the production of helplessness, to the extent that the perception of a lack of control exerts a negative influence on self-esteem, social comparison is implicated. In this regard, social comparison plays a subtle but very important role in the reformulated model of helplessness in regard to whether one perceives a particular uncontrollable negative outcome as being one over which relevant peers would be able to exert control [8]. If an outcome is judged uncontrollable by

---

[5] See reference [17], Weisz and Stipek, for a thoughtful critical review of children's locus of control measures.

the self but controllable by relevant peers, and the failure is attributed to an internal cause, then self-esteem deficits will follow. Such self-esteem deficits are, in part, definitive of the helplessness model of depression. The rate and adequacy with which children make use of social comparison is likely to vary developmentally, and thus so would the implications for self-esteem deficits, helplessness theory, and adaptive responding in general. Consideration of the range of adaptive consequences associated with the child's causal attributions thus requires brief attention to representative studies in the developmental literature on social comparison.

Ruble, Feldman and Boggiano showed that preschoolers were less likely to engage in social comparison than older children [54]. Further, Ruble, Parsons and Ross demonstrated that task ease information, based on social comparison, only influenced the ratings of children eight years or older, leading them to suggest that children younger than seven years use outcome rather than social comparison data for formulating self-evaluation [26]. They concluded that attribution processes involving social norms or task ease information increase in importance with age. Similarly, Nicholls demonstrated a developmental trend in the accuracy of children's self-rankings of ability, suggesting that young children are not adept at social comparison, an activity that becomes increasingly salient however for older children [25].

Attributions for failure clearly have an increasing impact on expectations and behavior as children get older [24], and there is also evidence that self-concept is increasingly affected by attributions for failure [21]. Parsons and Ruble have identified a developmental trend toward increasing responsibility for failure [27], and Nicholls has suggested that normative evaluation is likely to promote attributions of failure to ability, and thus result in helplessness [25]. Data suggesting the relative imperviousness of younger children to failure or helplessness have already been mentioned. Taken together, these data suggest that social comparison becomes increasingly salient as children get older, and that such a trend may be associated with a corresponding developmental increase in vulnerability to loss of self-esteem, personal helplessness [8], and perhaps even the adult-like manifestations of depression.

CONCLUDING COMMENTS

This chapter has attempted to evaluate the applicability of the learned helplessness hypothesis, a cognitive theory with profound implications for adaptive behavior, to children of varying ages. The isomorphic transposition of helplessness theory to children was seen to rest on the assumption that children process and respond to helplessness inducing failure or lack of control in the same way adults do. The data presented seem quite clearly to indicate that this is not the case. Application of helplessness theory to young children must take careful account of developmentally-based cognitive factors that significantly influence the perception of uncontrollability, the experience of failure, and the nature of causal attributions, each of which is central to the development of helplessness.

The developmental characteristics of young children, referring primarily to preoperational children, tend actually to work against the development of help-lessness. Thus, for example, both the perception of illusory control in chance situations and the halo scheme in regard to perceptions of how effort and ability relate to outcome tend to render young children less susceptible to the deficits associated with helplessness [25]. Although from the point of view of actual competencies, young children are objectively more helpless than are adults, in the realm of cognitive theory objective reality often takes a back seat to percep-tions, subjective experience, and what one *thinks* is the case [11]. The young child's relative resistance to helplessness may simply be a fortuitous artifact of immature cognitive and information processing skills. Artifactual or not, how-ever, it appears to serve an adaptive function in protecting the vulnerable young child from the debilitating effects of helplessness.

This cognitively mediated resistance to helplessness may actually combine with other facts of the young child's life such that the level of *perceived* control remains relatively constant. That is, rather than increasing, as suggested by the child's growing competencies, or decreasing, as implied by the developmental decrease in egocentrism and associated cognitive distortion, under optimal condi-tions the subjective sense of control would be constant and relatively high. Early on, although the infant is relatively helpless, the presence of an attentive and skilled caretaker would permit the experience of self as powerful and in control, with needs anticipated and gratified almost immediately and food available virtually on demand. It is presumably as a product of this experience that the infant begins to develop a sense of basic trust [55], confidence in the world and in the self, and a burgeoning sense of efficacy. Thus, the infant may feel in con-trol by virtue of the attentive and responsive caretaker, thereby enjoying a kind of secondary or vicarious control. With development, the basis of this sense of control may become increasingly a function of the individual child's growing competencies and independence and less a function of the adequacy of the infant-caretaker dyad. From this perspective, in which development is viewed as a reciprocal process, the basis of the subjective sense of control is variously a function of the infant-caretaker dyad; the actual and developing competencies of the child; existing environmental contingencies; chance events; so called distorted perceptions and immature cognitions; and the child's evolving cognitive capabilities. Develop-mental changes in competence and contingency, the basic components of con-trol [17], may have opposite effects on perceived control, with early lack of instrumental competence offset by cognitive distortion, and the developmental growth of competencies paralleled by cognitive maturation that permits more accurate assessment of contingency. These factors would converge so as to con-tribute to the maintenance of perceived control at a relatively constant level.

PERCEPTION OF NO CONTROL:
ACTION VERSUS COGNITION?

Individuals strive to maintain control over the environment. This is the motive for mastery, competence, or control that, in its various forms, has found its way into many theories of personality [13, 56-59]. In response to environmental challenge, and in striving for a sense of mastery, control, and self-efficacy, the individual attempts via instrumental behavior to control the environment. In the face of unexpected events, or under circumstances in which the individual's instrumental efforts are ineffective, cognitions emerge which may then influence subsequent behavior [60]. Although cognitions associated with successful efforts at control may also influence behavior, it is primarily the cognitions attendant upon failure to control the environment that appear to have the greatest potential for affecting adaptive behavior.

Helplessness theory proposes that in the face of uncontrollability, individuals give up in their efforts to control important events. Rothbaum, Weisz, and Snyder have proposed an alternative model of perceived control that delineates two general classes of behavior [61]. In the first, people try to control the environment in accordance to their wishes, thereby exerting *primary control*. In circumstances in which events are uncontrollable and primary control therefore not feasible, Rothbaum et al. argued that individuals do not relinquish control and thereby become helpless, but rather engage in cognitive activity designed to achieve *secondary control*. In this latter case, attributions enhance the perception of control by altering the individual's internal state so as to be consistent with environmental realities. This two process model echoes the distinction between competence and contingency proposed by Weisz and Stipek [17], as well as the concepts of assimilation and accommodation so central to Piaget's theory of cognitive development, and the notions of personal and universal helplessness set forth in the attributional reformulation of the helplessness model of depression [8].

One can be in control, or one can think one is in control, and the functional difference between the two has not yet been studied. Clearly, thinking one is in control when that is not the case can have both adaptive and maladaptive consequences. It may be that concepts like secondary control, including perhaps the cognitive-developmental basis for the perception of control in the absence of primary control, as well as the control achieved through an attentive caretaker, have special relevance to and serve an important protective function for young children who are realistically limited in their instrumental competencies and thus the extent to which they can exercise and experience primary control.

To the extent that young children experience helplessness, the factors underlying its development would seem to be different from those operative in adults. Research is needed to identify the mechanisms mediating the development of helplessness in preoperational children. To the extent that helplessness provides a model for adult depression, similar developmental considerations will be necessary if that model is to be meaningfully applied to depression in young children. This would seem to be particularly important regarding those aspects of depressive phenomena presumed to be mediated by cognitive mechanisms.

From this perspective, the younger child would be less likely to manifest the range of symptoms typical of the adult depressive syndrome, most specifically those cognitive symptoms related to self-esteem deficits. If, for example, five-year-olds tend not to engage in social comparison, then self-esteem deficits might be proportionately decreased among depressed five-year-old children. This notion is consistent with that of the many observers who have argued for the importance of developmental considerations in regard to the occurrence and/or manifestation of depressive symptoms in children [62-64]. Although investigators differ on the precise age at which children emerge as capable of the complex cognitive processes that underlie the development of certain adult-like depressive symptoms, there is growing agreement that such a developmental transition occurs. In a study of depressive symptoms among elementary school age children, Kaslow, Rehm, and Siegel suggest that their phenomenological data indicate that by the age of seven years "most, if not all, children possess the basic cognitive processes commonly associated with, and necessary to, depression (e.g., Attributions, Self-Evaluations, Expectations)" [65, p. 618].

The major thesis of this chapter has been that the weight of the evidence from the developmental literature strongly supports the oft-invoked notion that developmental factors play a significant role in the occurrence and manifestation of both helplessness and depressive phenomena in children. The data further point to the age of about nine years as the time at which the cognitive processes that underlie helplessness, and perhaps depression, are fully developed. Strikingly, most studies of these phenomena in children rarely employ subjects younger than eight years of age, although we see consistent differences between younger and older children on virtually all measures of cognitive phenomena related to both depression and helplessness, including attributions, the understanding of effort and ability, the understanding of the causes of behavior, and the capacity for social comparison, to mention but a few. The question of the nature of both depression and helplessness in the younger, and especially the pre-school child appears, in fact, to remain largely untested. Studies of children younger than nine years of age which focus on factors such as self-esteem, self-blame, feelings of inadequacy and other such cognitively mediated depressive phenomena would go a long way in clarification of these issues, and may also help clarify the basis of inconsistent results in the literatures of both helplessness and depression in children. The absence of systematic research in this younger age range may reflect the difficult measurement problems inherent in assessing such phenomena in young children. Indeed, the very fact of the measurement problem and the related paucity of data on children in this age range may be evidence in and of itself for the importance of this distinction. Not only are systematic studies of children younger than nine years of age essential, but we need further to understand specifically what it is that underlies the relevance of this distinction. This is especially important in meaningfully tracing the developmental course and expression of depression and depressive affect in children.

REFERENCES

1. S. F. Maier and M. E. P. Seligman, Learned Helplessness: Theory and Evidence, *Journal of Experimental Psychology: General, 105*, pp. 3-46, 1976.
2. M. E. P. Seligman, *Helplessness*, Freeman, San Francisco, 1975.
3. E. Fosco and J. H. Geer, Effects of Gaining Control over Aversive Stimuli after Differing Amount of No Control, *Psychological Reports, 29*, pp. 1153-1154, 1971.
4. S. Friedlander and G. M. Chartier, Self-Attributed Mastery and Other-Attributed Mastery in the Alleviation of Learned Helplessness, *Journal of General Psychology, 105*, pp. 293-310, 1981.
5. D. S. Hiroto, Locus of Control and Learned Helplessness, *Journal of Experimental Psychology, 102*, pp. 187-193, 1974.
6. D. S. Hiroto and M. E. P. Seligman, Generality of Learned Helplessness in Man, *Journal of Personality and Social Psychology, 31*, pp. 311-327, 1975.
7. D. C. Klein, E. Fencil-Morse, and M. E. P. Seligman, Learned Helplessness, Depression and the Attribution of Failure, *Journal of Personality and Social Psychology, 33*, pp. 508-516, 1976.
8. L. Y. Abramson, M. E. P. Seligman, and J. D. Teasdale, Learned Helplessness in Humans: Critique and Reformulation, *Journal of Abnormal Psychology, 87*, pp. 49-74, 1978.
9. C. Peterson and M. E. P. Seligman, Causal Explanations as a Risk Factor for Depression: Theory and Evidence, *Psychological Review, 91*:3, pp. 347-374, 1984.
10. J. C. Coyne, A Critique of Cognitions as Causal Entities with Particular Reference to Depression, *Cognitive Therapy and Research, 6*:1, pp. 3-13, 1982.
11. H. M. Lefcourt, The Function of the Illusions of Control and Freedom, *American Psychologist, 28*, pp. 417-425, 1973.
12. A. Bandura, Self Efficacy: Toward a Unifying Theory of Behavioral Change, *Psychological Review, 84*, pp. 191-215, 1977.
13. J. B. Rotter, *Social Learning and Clinical Psychology*, Prentice-Hall, Englewood Cliffs, New Jersey, 1954.
14. ___, Generalized Expectancies for Internal Versus External Control of Reinforcement, *Psychological Monographs: General and Applied, 80*, pp. 1-28, 1966.
15. ___, Some Problems and Misconceptions Related to the Construct of Internal Versus External Control of Reinforcement, *Journal of Consulting and Clinical Psychology, 43*, pp. 56-67, 1975.
16. J. D. Searcy and J. Hawkins-Searcy, Locus of Control Research and Its Implications for Child Personality, in *Clinical Treatment and Research in*

Child Psychopathology, A. J. Finch, Jr. and P. Kendall (eds.), Spectrum Publication, Inc., Jamaica, New York, 1979.

17. J. R. Weisz and D. J. Stipek, Competence, Contingency, and the Development of Perceived Control, *Human Development*, *25*, pp. 250-281, 1982.

18. C. S. Dweck and N. D. Repucci, Learned Helplessness and Reinforcement Responsibility in Children, *Journal of Personality and Social Psychology*, *25*, pp. 109-116, 1973.

19. C. S. Dweck, The Role of Expectations and Attributions in the Alleviation of Learned Helplessness, *Journal of Personality and Social Psychology*, *31*, pp. 674-685, 1975.

20. C. I. Diener and C. S. Dweck, An Analysis of Learned Helplessness: Continuous Changes in Performance, Strategy, and Achievement Cognitions Following Failure, *Journal of Personality and Social Psychology*, *36*, pp 451-462, 1978.

21. D. S. Johnson, Naturally Acquired Learned Helplessness: The Relationship of School Failure to Achievement Behavior, Attribution, and Self Concept, *Journal of Educational Psychology*, *73*:2, pp. 174-180, 1981.

22. D. Balk, Learned Helplessness: A Model to Understand and Overcome a Child's Extreme Reaction to Failure, *Journal of School Health*, *53*:6, pp. 365-370, 1983.

23. A. J. Sedlak and S. T. Kurtz, A Review of Children's Use of Causal Inference Principles, *Child Development*, *52*, pp. 759-784, 1981.

24. W. S. Rholes, J. Blackwell, C. Jordan, and C. Walters, A Developmental Study of Learned Helplessness, *Developmental Psychology*, *16*:6, pp. 616-624, 1980.

25. J. G. Nicholls, The Development of the Concepts of Effort and Ability, Perception of Academic Attainment, and the Understanding That Difficult Tasks Require More Ability, *Child Development*, *49*, pp. 800-814, 1978.

26. D. Ruble, J. E. Parsons, and J. Ross, Self Evaluative Responses of Children in an Achievement Setting, *Child Development*, *47*, pp. 990-997, 1976.

27. J. E. Parsons and D. Ruble, The Development of Achievement Related Expectancies, *Child Development*, *48*, pp. 1075-1079, 1977.

28. A. Miller, A Developmental Study of the Cognitive Basis of Performance Impairment After Failure, *Journal of Personality and Social Psychology*, *49*:2, pp. 529-538, 1985.

29. P. Danker-Brown and D. H. Baucom, Cognitive Influences on the Development of Learned Helplessness, *Journal of Personality and Social Psychology*, *43*:4, pp. 793-801, 1982.

30. M. E. P. Seligman and C. Peterson, A Learned Helplessness Perspective on Childhood Depression: Theory and Research, in *Depression in Young People*, M. Rutter, C. E. Izard, and P. B. Read (eds.), The Guilford Press, New York, 1986.

31. J. Piaget and B. Inhelder, *The Origin of the Idea of Chance in Children*, [L. Leake, Jr., P. Burrell, and H. D. Fishbein (trans.)], Norton, New York, 1975. (Originally published 1951.)

32. E. J. Langer, The Illusion of Control, *Journal of Personality and Social Psychology*, *32*:2, pp. 311-328, 1975.

33. L. B. Alloy and L. Y. Abramson, Judgment of Contingency in Depressed and Nondepressed Students: Sadder but Wiser? *Journal of Experimental Psychology: General, 108*:4, pp. 441-485, 1979.

34. J. R. Weisz, Developmental Change in Perceived Control: Recognizing Non-contingency in the Laboratory and Perceiving It in the World, *Developmental Psychology, 16*, pp. 385-390, 1980.

35. A. Kun, Development of the Magnitude-Covariation and Compensation Schemata in Ability and Effort Attributions of Performance, *Child Development, 48*, pp. 862-873, 1977.

36. H. H. Kelley and J. L. Michela, Attribution Theory and Research, in *Annual Review of Psychology*, M. R. Rosenzweig and L. W. Porter (eds.), Annual Reviews, Palo Alto, 1980.

37. R. Rizley, Depression and Distortions in the Attribution of Causality, *Journal of Abnormal Psychology, 87*, pp. 32-48, 1978.

38. C. B. Wortman, R. P. Costanzo, and J. R. Witt, Effects of Anticipated Performance on the Attributions of Causality to Self and Others, *Journal of Personality and Social Psychology, 27*, pp. 372-381, 1973.

39. I. Bialer, Conceptualization of Success and Failure in Mentally Retarded and Normal Children, *Journal of Personality, 29*, pp. 303-320, 1961.

40. J. E. R. Luginbuhl, D. H. Crowe, and J. P. Kahan, Causal Attributions for Success and Failure, *Journal of Personality and Social Psychology, 31*:1, pp. 86-93, 1975.

41. W. Rholes and D. Ruble, Developmental Study of the Use of Personality Traits and Abilities to Predict Behavior, Princeton University, Princeton, unpublished, 1978, (Reported in Weisz and Stipek [17]).

42. V. C. Crandall, W. Katkovsky, and V. J. Crandall, Children's Beliefs in Their Own Control of Reinforcement in Intellectual-Academic Achievement Situations, *Child Development, 36*, pp. 91-109, 1965.

43. J. Lefcourt, *Locus of Control: Current Trends in Theory and Research*, Erlbaum, Hillsdale, New Jersey, 1976.

44. J. Piaget, *The Construction of Reality in the Child*, Basic Books, Inc., New York, 1954.

45. R. Newhouse, Reinforcement-Responsibility Differences in Birth-Order, Grade Level, and Sex of Children in Grades 4, 5, and 6, *Psychological Reports, 34*, pp. 699-705, 1974.

46. F. J. Boersma and J. W. Chapman, Academic Self-Concept, Achievement Expectations, and Locus of Control in Elementary Learning Disabled Children, *Canadian Journal of Behavioral Science, 13*:4, pp. 349-358, 1981.

47. R. Pearl, LD Children's Attributions for Success and Failure: A Replication with a Labeled LD Sample, *Learning Disability Quarterly, 5*, pp. 173-176, 1982.

48. J. DuCette, S. Wolk, and E. Soucar, Atypical Patterns in Locus of Control and Nonadaptive Behavior, *Journal of Personality, 40*, pp. 287-297, 1972.

49. S. Friedlander, J. A. Traylor, and D. S. Weiss, Depressive Symptoms and Attributional Style in Children, *Personality and Social Psychology Bulletin, 12*:4, pp. 442-453, 1987.

50. M. E. P. Seligman, L. Y. Abramson, A. Semmel, and C. Von Baeyer, Depressive Attributional Style, *Journal of Abnormal Psychology*, *88*, pp. 242-247, 1979.
51. M. E. P. Seligman, C. Peterson, N. J. Kaslow, R. L. Tannenbaum, L. B. Alloy, and L. Y. Abramson, Attributional Style and Depressive Symptoms Among Children, *Journal of Abnormal Psychology*, *93*, pp. 235-238, 1984.
52. F. Heider, *The Psychology of Interpersonal Relations*, Wiley, New York, 1958.
53. H. Wimmer, J. Wachter, and J. Perner, Cognitive Autonomy of the Development of Moral Evaluations of Achievement, *Child Development*, *53*, pp. 668-676, 1982.
54. D. Ruble, N. Feldman, and A. Boggiano, Social Comparison Between Young Children in Achievement Situations, *Developmental Psychology*, *12*, pp. 192-197, 1976.
55. E. H. Erikson, *Childhood and Society*, (2nd Edition), W. W. Norton and Company, Inc., New York, 1950.
56. A. Adler, *The Neurotic Constellation*, Dodd, Mead and Company, New York, 1926.
57. E. Fromm, *The Sane Society*, Rinehart and Company, New York, 1955.
58. G. A. Kelly, *The Psychology of Personal Constructs* (2 vols.), W. W. Norton and Company, Inc., New York, 1955.
59. R. W. White, Motivation Reconsidered: The Concept of Competence, *Psychological Review*, *66*, pp. 297-333, 1959.
60. B. Weiner, "Spontaneous" Causal Thinking, *Psychological Bulletin*, *97*:1, pp. 74-84, 1985.
61. F. Rothbaum, J. R. Weisz, and S. S. Snyder, Changing the World and Changing the Self: A Two Process Model of Perceived Control, *Journal of Personality and Social Psychology*, *42*:1, pp. 5-37, 1982.
62. J. Bemporad, Psychodynamics of Depression and Suicide in Children and Adolescents, in *Severe and Mild Depression*, S. Arieti and J. Bemporad (eds.), Basic Books, New York, 1978.
63. C. Malmquist, Depression in Childhood and Adolescence, I., *New England Journal of Medicine*, *284*, pp. 887-893, 1971.
64. I. Philips and S. Friedlander, Conceptual Problems in the Study of Childhood Depression, in *Psychiatry 1982: Annual Review*, L. Grinspoon (ed.), American Psychiatric Press, Washington, D.C., 1982.
65. N. J. Kaslow, L. P. Rehm, and A. W. Siegel, Social-Cognitive and Cognitive Correlates of Depression in Children, *Journal of Abnormal Child Psychology*, *12*:4, pp. 605-620, 1984.

CHAPTER 4

Music in the Organization of Childhood Experience

PETER OSTWALD
AND DELMONT MORRISON

From the beginning music, as the expression of emotional life not reducible to logical language, has been a medium for communicating ideals or urges as contrasted with ideas. It has been the language of mysticism, going far beyond the idealizations as expressed in poetry. It has expressed an attitude toward the gods and the spiritual world as a whole. As in the behavior of birds, it has expressed the sexual urge in all its rationalized and idealistic forms. As music for music's sake, it is a sort of dream language which carries the performer and the listener far beyond the routine of daily life [1].

Carl E. Seashore

Music has long been recognized to be of importance in the lives of children, especially in terms of the contact children have with the world of adults. Infants respond to the musical qualities of their mother's voices. Toddlers play with musical toys, and enjoy musical games. Teen-agers indulge in numerous musical activities—singing, dancing, playing instruments, collecting tapes and records, and attending concerts. Music also is used widely, and often expertly, in many programs of education. And yet, there seems to be little in the way of an organized body of knowledge about music in childhood. Research done in this field is relatively sparse, and there is as yet no adequate theory about the musical mind of the child [2].

The purpose of this chapter is to try to explain what we think happens when children are exposed to music. We begin with a brief definition of music, followed by a review of the three fields of inquiry with which we are most familiar: 1) biology, with its exploration of relations between music and the brain; 2) psychology with its emphasis on the development of musical skills and knowledge; and 3) psychoanalytic, psychotherapeutic, and psychobiographical studies of music and musicians. Our aim is to arrive at a better understanding of the role of music in organizing childhood experience.

First, a working definition: Music is the combination of sounds and silences into rhythms, melodies, harmonies, and contrapuntal patterns. It provides emotional satisfaction as well as motor excitement, relief of tension, intellectual stimulation, and social gratification. Operating essentially in the acoustic-auditory realm of human experience and closely related to language, music is a specialized form of communication, important for several of the performing arts (dance, theater, and entertainment).

THE BIOLOGY OF MUSIC MAKING

Investigation of the anatomical and physiological underpinnings of musical behavior has been very difficult [3]. There are many methodological and technical problems, not to mention the ethical limitations placed on research with human subjects, (infants and children in particular). Most studies, even the most modern and sophisticated ones using newer techniques such as positron emission tomography, deal primarily with diseased or abnormal children. Nevertheless, there is strong evidence indicating that while the sensori-motor cortex and cerebellum of the infant are quite active at birth, the visual areas are not [4]. These and other findings lend support to a theory, proposed in 1973 by Ostwald [5], that musical behavior may have its origins in certain intrauterine developmental events preceding the development of vision.

> Rhythmicity is of biological origin, beginning prenatally when the fetus produces rhythmic heartbeats, chest movements, and limb and body movements. By the third trimester the fetus usually responds to acoustical stimulation. Pregnant singers often report a change in fetal activity — usually the baby seems quieter — when they are singing. Pianists and other instrument-playing expectant mothers notice the fetus becoming more active while they are playing music or shortly afterwards.

Observations of intrauterine responsiveness to music are consistent with anatomical findings, since it is known that the middle-ear and inner-ear structures of the human fetus attain adult size by the fifth month of gestation. Furthermore, Armitage and co-workers have demonstrated that sounds produced at levels similar to normal conversation from outside the mother can reach the amniotic sac with relatively little attenuation, as do the sounds of the mother herself, including her eating, swallowing, breathing and intestinal noises [6]. Pulsations of the aorta and other large arteries in the pelvis close to the uterus would provide additional rhythmical and other sonic information about the mother. That the neonatal brain accepts acoustical input and processes it according to rules of pattern recognition is suggested by the fact that infants definitely prefer the sound of their mother's voice to other environmental sounds [7].

While there seems to be general agreement that mechanisms for categorical perception of speech as well as music are present from an early age, knowledge about those parts of the brain which participate in musical development is as yet limited. Some neurologists regard with skepticism the notion of preformed cortical areas subserving higher mental functions such as symbolization, language, or music [8]. They emphasize the importance of musical experience (i.e., listening and playing) as an organizing factor leading to the proliferation of neuronal networks in nonspecialized, multi-potential regions of the brain. Others have dissected the brains of prominent musicians and report astonishing physical configurations that would seem to confirm the notion of brain areas developing specialized capacities for music.

> Auerbach was the pioneer and at the same time the most important contributor [to brain localization of music]. His material included the brains of the conductors Felix Mottl and Hans von Bülow . . . in all cases the middle and posterior thirds of the superior temporal gyrus were strongly developed and showed great width; they were intimately connected with the equally well-developed gyrus supramarginalis. Auerbach was particularly impressed by the characteristic curved course of the middle portion of the superior temporal gyrus which was caused by blood vessels pushing in from above and below. . . . In the singer Stockhausen, Auerbach observed a striking development of the left second frontal convolution . . . the same striking size, but in this case on the right side [was] described in the second frontal gyrus [of a virtuoso cellist] who as a child, had possessed a fine voice [9].

The question of cerebral dominance has attracted considerable attention in musical circles. Before attempting to answer it, one must take note of the heated debates about proper relationships between music and language (a predominately left-sided brain function) that were so fashionable in the 19th Century [10] and have not been fully resolved in the 20th. Should music be regarded as a form of language, with phonological, syntactical, and pragmatic components that follow rules akin to those governing verbal behavior (but lacking a strong semantic component), or are we dealing here with entirely unique and distinctive modes of thinking, feeling, and behaving that would require neuroanatomical programs altogether separate from those subserving linguistic communication? A useful answer, insofar as communication theory and musicology are concerned, was provided by Leonard Meyer's thoughtful treatise about meaning and emotion in music [11]. And, from a neurological perspective, Antonio and Hanna Demasio suggest the following solution:

> Music does not act as significant to any signified external object, nor, consequently, does it signal the internal nervous representation

of any such effort. The way musical words combine into phrases, and phrases are organized into larger structures, depends upon the rules of musical grammar current at the time of writing, and to which the composer normally feels obliged to conform. This syntax does not lend itself to translation in terms of the more frequent cognitive calculus operations. The symbolizing power of music, by virtue of its lexical and syntactical nature, is thus restricted to the broad aspects of emotional states or general attitudes of problem-solving strategy. It does not translate things or relations between things in a transparent, linguistically effective manner. As a means of communication it does not serve the purpose of immediate conduction of behavior, met by the languages of words and gestures: it is a language of emotion [12].

Thus it would be reasonable to assume that for the general population, "dominance" by certain regions of the brain is not as well fixed for music as it is for language. Furthermore, cerebral dominance patterns undoubtedly reflect the degree of musical ability and training displayed by individual subjects.

The suggestion that the right hemisphere may be crucially involved in musical information processing stems from Milner's study of patients who had temporal lobectomies. Using the Seashore Test, she found a reduction of timbre discrimination and musical memory in those cases where the right temporal lobe had been removed [13]. (The importance of right temporal lobe control mechanisms for musical abilities has been confirmed by Zatorre, who also studied post-lobectomy patients [14].) Experiments with dichotic listening have lent additional support to the right-hemisphere hypothesis. However, as Bever and Chiarello have shown, training in music will influence the results of listening experiments [15]. Subjects who are musically experienced recognize simple melodies better in the right than the left ear, whereas the reverse is true for naive listeners. When the test performance of choirboys (9 to13 years old) was compared with that of untrained boys of the same age, the relative superiority of the right ear increased progressively with experience in the choir [15].

One of the most succinct statements about biological aspects of music applicable to childhood is by Wertheim:

> Musical perception and performance is an inborn capacity of the human brain. This ability is common among human beings and is independent of education or culture which can refine but not produce it. There are wide variations in the degree and development of the musical faculty but the anatomo-functional substratum is probably the same in a professional musician and a person lacking all musical training [16].

STUDIES IN PSYCHOLOGY AND EDUCATION

What constitutes musical genius? In ancient times, genius was thought to be a God-given quality. Later it was attributed to noble birth. In the 19th century a number of medical scientists, including Morel, Lombroso, and Moebius, proposed that genius is a product of genetic and mental "degeneracy" and thus linked to pathological conditions such as epilepsy, neurosis and psychosis [17]. More recently, it has been felt that genius is, among other things, a social attribute; while exceptional talents may be present, no one is called a genius until society declares him or her to be such a person [18]. For example, Johann Sebastian Bach, almost forgotten 175 years ago, is regarded today as a musical genius.

One of the most interesting and comprehensive studies of prodigious musical behavior in childhood was published in 1925 by Geza Revesz, Director of the Psychological Laboratory in Amsterdam. It concerns Erwin Nyiregyhazi, whose personality as a child bore a "marked resemblance to the infant Mozart" [19].

> Born in Budapest, Erwin's family had been connected with music for at least two generations. Both parents were musically talented, and their chief interest was centered on the boy "in whom they saw a future maestro." (The father's early death constituted a profound stress in later childhood.)
>
> Song imitation began before Erwin was a year old. In the second year, although speech development was "still very poor and defective," he could correctly reproduce melodies sung to him. Absolute pitch was discovered in his third year, and at the beginning of his fourth year he began to play at the piano "everything that he had heard." He also began to compose original melodies. Music lessons were started in his fifth year, and at age six he was enrolled in the Academy of Music, where professor Revesz personally observed his development until age twelve.
>
> Tests of mental development (the first set of Binet-Simon, 1908) were given when the boy was seven years old. These included: vocabulary, counting, digit memory, drawing of a rhombus, object and pattern recognition. He "did more than was to be expected from the average eight-year-old child," and also answered correctly all tests in a series for nine year children and many in a series for older children.

Revesz concluded that Erwin's "general mental development [was] at least three years in advance of his age ... according to Terman's system of intellectual measurements." Moreover, in testing the boy's musical abilities, he found him to have absolute pitch. His capacity for recognizing tone qualities, intervals, and chord-structure, was exceptional. Musical memory, sight reading, and the ability to transpose and transcribe were very highly developed.

However, the child prodigy Revesz analyzed did not become successful or world-famous. After reaching adulthood, his career went steadily downhill. For many years Erwin Nyiregyhazi did not perform at all, and none of his compositions are played today. Only in his dotage, as a slum-dwelling alcoholic, was this gifted musician rediscovered and invited to make a few recordings, which display his astonishing virtuosity. The story of his life lends support to Lange-Eichbaum's thesis that public acceptance and fame are needed before someone can be called a genius. Today we are more inclined to speak about musical intelligence rather than genius when talking about exceptional children [20].

The measurement of musical intelligence in children has developed more as an evaluation of acoustical perception or aesthetic judgment rather than an evaluation of the organizing cognitive structures required for creating, performing, or appreciating music. The earliest example of a test of perception is the battery developed by Seashore [21]. This test is comprised of six different measures: pitch, loudness, rhythm, time, timbre and time relationships. The pitch test consists of the presentation of fifty pairs of tones that are free of harmonics while intensity, timbre and time relationships are held constant. The subject is requested to judge whether the second of two successive tones is lower or higher than the first one. Scores on the different measures can be expressed as ranks and percentiles. The Test of Musical Intelligence was developed to select students of high musical aptitude for the study of instrumental music [22]. The four subtests of this battery include: 1) chord analysis: estimating the number of notes played in a single chord; 2) pitch change: detecting a change of a single note in a repeated chord; 3) rhythmic accent: choosing the better rhythmic accent in two performances of the same piece; and 4) harmony: judging the more appropriate phrasing in two performances of the same piece. These subtests appear to measure both auditory perception and musical aesthetics.

It is constructive to consider measures of musical intelligence in the context of the development of general measures of intelligence. These measures of musical intelligence were developed within the same theoretical framework as measures of general intelligence and share similar strengths as well as weaknesses. The Stanford-Binet was originally developed as a quantified system to determine which children should be assigned to special classes because they were intellectually incapable of benefiting from regular instruction [23]. Considerable effort was made to construct a measure with acceptable reliability and validity which defined normal intelligence by what normal children could do at different ages. The test was constructed to evaluate thinking in action on many different tasks so that the results would not be influenced by a specific skill. The level of intellectual development was indicated by a mental age score (MA). No particular theoretical view of intelligence influenced the development of the test. As the Stanford-Binet has been updated, the mental age and intelligence quotient have been complimented by standard scores [24]. The format of measuring various components of intelligence and establishing their relationship to age norms to provide an overall estimate of intelligence has been followed by more recent test developers [25, 26].

This approach to the measurement and definition of intelligence has received considerable criticism from a variety of sources [27] but only a few criticisms, relevant to the measurement of musical intelligence, will be addressed here. The use of a mental age, IQ, or any measure referring to a mean and standard deviation, is a kind of average in which success on each test item in a battery can substitute for success on any one of the others. These metrics imply a constant level of intellectual development across ages and obscure what we know about the structural and hierarchical nature of the developing abilities of an individual child [28]. In addition, such scores do not adequately reflect the importance of the integration of various abilities that truly reflect intelligence. Subscales such as vocabulary and arithmetic on the WISC-R can be viewed as gross measures of aptitude and achievement rather than intelligence.

A number of investigators have turned to Piaget's theory of the development of intelligence to construct measures for children. These efforts reflect the sequential order of intellectual development as well as the hierarchical nature of various information processing skills which contribute to cognitive integration and adaptation [29]. A brief review of Piaget's theory is necessary in order to demonstrate how this view of intellectual development differs from the statistical approach used to construct traditional measures of both general and musical intelligence [30].

In terms of musical intelligence it is important to note that in Piaget's theory the basis of all intellectual development is the sensorimotor period. The period lasts from birth until approximately twenty-four months and is characterized by the beginning differentiation and integration of sensory-motor activities. The child's active exploration of the environment through what Piaget terms the circular reactions results in consistent information being produced and the consequent development of coordinated abilities such as visual-motor and auditory-visual integration. Intelligence is intimately related to sensory integration and perception: factors that bear directly to the child's perception and sensitivity to music and performance of basic music skills. A major shift in information processing occurs when the child is less bound to sensory-motor methods of problem solving with the development of memory and representational thought. This cognitive development at about age two marks the beginning of pre-operational thought which is dominant until ages seven or eight. Perception is a major source of information during this period and the unique quality of the child's perception and thinking is important to the understanding of the development of musical abilities and intelligence.

During the initial stage of this period the child's perception is centered on only one biasing property of the stimulus field at a time and she/he cannot simultaneously attend to all the available information. Consequently, one perceptual property influences thought and the child is unable to perceive the invariant relationships that hold between properties such as mass and shape, or distance, time and velocity. For example, the preoperational child can observe two objects (A and B) moving in a straight line over the same interval with one of the objects (A) moving a longer distance than the other (B). When asked if both took the same amount of time, the child will insist that A took longer time. When asked for the reasons for this conclusion the child will say that A took longer because it ended up ahead of B or that B took a shorter time because it didn't have as far to go. This tendency to focus on a dominant perceptual cue, in this case space and end states, is termed centering. The other information available such as velocity and time are not taken into account. It is the integration of the information from these perceptual cues, requiring stable cognitive concepts representing the invariance in the relationships, that will enable the child to provide a valid answer to the problem. This differentiation and integration at a cognitive level discriminate the reasoning of a child with concrete operations from the child who is using preoperational thought.

Centration which is a dominant characteristic of preoperational thought is gradually replaced by conservation, a major characteristic of operational thought. Although based on perception, conservation is the cognition that certain properties, such as distance, velocity, time, etc., remain invariant (conserved) in the face of distorting perceptual cues, such as one object moving further than another in the same amount of time. Gradually the preoperational child through systematic variation in attention moves away from fixation on dominant cues to perceptual comparison and transformations. By simultaneously perceiving both time and distance these become differentiated and integrated into the concept of velocity. Using operational thought the child actively employs concepts, initially at a concrete level, but eventually at a more abstract level, to manipulate information and solve problems. Stability of operational thought is dependent on five laws of conservation: 1) combinativity of classes, 2) reversibility, in which any mathematical or logical operation can be cancelled by its inverse operation, 3) associativity, which allows for the combination of several operations without regard to sequence and combinations, 4) identity wherein any operation can be nullified by combining it with its opposite operation, and 5) tautology for logical classes and numbers.

Piaget's theory has stimulated a great deal of research on cognitive development that has generally been supportive of the theory [31]. Piaget's own work on the importance of the laws of conservation in the child's conceptual development of properties such as time, quantity, and seriation has served to encourage the application of his theory to define and measure musical intelligence in children. Musical ability would appear to be related to the capacity to perceive properties in tonal patterns and temporal structure that result in stable concepts of melody, rhythm, harmony and form. Initially one would expect the preoperational child to center on one of these properties at a time and then eventually perceive two or more simultaneously. Musical intelligence evolves as the child conceptually differentiates and integrates these properties by forming laws of conservation regarding musical elements. According to Pflederer there are five conservation laws that are essential for the stability of operational concepts of music [32]:

1. Identity refers to maintaining the essential characteristic of thematic material. For example, the identity of a musical theme when it is played on different instruments or when it is treated sequentially.

2. Metrical grouping is based on the perception of an accented element that influences the nonaccented members of the rhythmic stimulus series. As a result the child perceives relationships within the rhythmic grouping and eventually the child conceives the meter and it becomes a temporal unit capable of assimilating other rhythmic concepts. Conservation of meter enables the child to discriminate between meters and to maintain a meter even though the distribution of note values within measures varies.

3. Augmentation and diminution require the application of reversible thought to the temporal quality of notes. Augmentation refers to the presentation of a musical subject in doubled (augmented) and in halved (diminution) values. The discrimination that a melody has been played twice as fast or slow than when first presented is a time judgment requiring a relational framework among notes based on reversible operations.

4. Transposition results in a melody being perceived as an invariant when it is transported into a new key with intervallic relationships being maintained.

5. Inversion refers to the substitution of higher tones for lower tones and the converse of this operation. For example, in harmonic inversion a note can be shifted to the upper or lower octave. Reversible thought and the conservation of harmony is applied when the child realizes that the concept of a triad is invariant whether it is arranged 1-3-5, 5-1-3 or 3-5-1.

One test of the usefulness of a theory is if it produces innovative and productive ways of approaching problems and providing new information. The establishment of laws of conservation relevant to auditory perception certainly would move the study of musical intelligence away from the traditional one of having the child make qualitative judgments regarding the difference between tones, to the ability of the child to apply laws of conservation to acquire musical skills and create or appreciate music. This moves the measurement and definition of musical intelligence from perception to cognition. In addition, the assumption that there is a sequence in development and a hierarchical order in cognitive organization has implication for teaching music. A number of investigators have employed Piagetian tasks of seriation and conservation to demonstrate that the perception of meter [32] melody [33] and rhythm [34] are improved at age levels corresponding to the emergence of operational thought. However, more detailed research is needed to establish the laws of conservation in auditory perception and between different perceptual modalities of particular importance to music such as the auditory and visual modalities. There is also a need to investigate the relationship of musical conservation to more general measures of intelligence and to establish whether the conservation laws for melody, rhythm and such follow a similar sequence as the conservation laws for space, time, volume and mass. A number of studies have addressed these issues.

In a study of the relationship between visual and auditory conservation, thirty-four children with an average age of 6.1 years were tested on a series of Piagetian tasks [35]. Visual conservation of mass, liquid, and number were evaluated by tests developed by Elkind [36]. Auditory conservation was evaluated by a series of tonal and rhythm tasks which were administered by the experimenter demonstrating the music concept by singing, clapping and playing on bells. Two group-administered tonal and rhythm pattern tests were given to orient the children to the tasks and these were followed by individually administered tonal and rhythm conservation tasks. For the tonal conservation test, the child was asked if a tune being played was the same or different from one she/he had just heard played on bells. In some cases, the rhythm pattern was altered while the tune remained intact while in other cases the tune was different. The rhythm conservation task was administered the same way. In the tune conservation task the child had to discriminate the original tune in the context of potentially distorting perceptual cues of rhythm. In the rhythm conservation task the problem was reversed. The children were also assessed on a music ability test which evaluated abilities such as melodic direction (up or down), tonal patterns (same or different) and tempo (faster, slower, same). A test of receptive language vocabulary, the Peabody Picture Vocabulary Test, was administered to obtain a more general measure of verbal intelligence. The results indicated that there was no relationship between visual and auditory conservation. Only two subjects from this kindergarten population were both auditory and visual conservers. Auditory conservation did not relate to receptive language and visual conservation had a low but significant relationship with receptive language vocabulary ($r = .23$, $p < .01$). The correlation between visual conservation and music ability was nonsignificant ($r = .06$). Auditory conservers performed better on the music ability test ($r = .44$, $p < .01$) and a multiple regression analysis demonstrated that music ability alone was the best predictor of auditory conservation.

Although previous research had indicated a significant relationship between visual and auditory conservation [37], additional research has established that measures of auditory and visual conservation do not share sufficient common variance to form a single scale. The psychometric issues involved in developing a musical measure employing Piagetian tasks has been addressed by Rider [38]. The Musical-Perception Assessment of Cognitive Development (M-PACD) is appropriate for children from ages one to fifteen years. The M-PACD approaches the measurement of musical intelligence with more traditional techniques such as loudness discrimination, imitation of simple rhythms and matching of sounds, as well as techniques developed directly from Piagetian theory. Seriation, the ability to arrange objects in order according to some dimension such as length, is developed in the preoperational child of ages three to six. Seriation is measured on the M-PACD for both tempo and duration. For example, for seriation of tempo, the child is shown a toy animal that strikes a line of bells while moving at a certain speed. The child is asked how the bells might be struck faster while the animal moves at the same speed. The correct answer is to move the bells closer together. Conservation for rhythmic pulse, auditory number, tempo, and duration are evaluated by standard procedures. For example, in being evaluated for conservation of tempo the child first has to discriminate that a drum beat and resonator bell played in unison behind a screen are being played at the same tempo of sixty beats per minute. The instruments are then syncopated so that one is played on the first and third beats and the other on the second and fourth beats. The child has to discriminate that they are still playing at the same tempo.

One of the first requisites of a psychometric test is that the content measured be scalable. If the measurement is to be used with children, then performance of the content should improve systematically with age. To address these issues the M-PACD was administered to 109 children who were attending two day care centers and classes ranging from kindergarten to the first grade. The fifteen items on the M-PACD range in difficulty from the ability to repeat a two beat cadence to the ability to conserve duration. These items were arranged in order from most to least passed and entered into a Guttman scalogram analysis to determine the reliability of the scale. Both the coefficient of reproductibility (.98) and scalability (.90) indicate that the M-PACD has acceptable reliability as a developmental scale. Further analysis demonstrated a high correlation ($r = 80$) between the child's age and performance on the test. The value of this approach to the measurement of musical intelligence can only be established when it is shown that performance on such tasks is predictive of more complex musical acquisition and performance.

PSYCHOANALYTIC APPROACHES TO MUSIC

Although Sigmund Freud, the founder of psychoanalysis, complained at times that he was "almost incapable of obtaining any pleasure" from music [39], there can be little doubt about his sensitivity to the musical experiences of others. Two well-known Viennese musicians, Gustav Mahler and Bruno Walter, sought him out for treatment, and 40 references to musical topics appear in the Concordance to Freud's complete writings [40]. Among the subjects debated by Freud's disciples during their regular meetings in his apartment were the mental illness of composer Robert Schumann, the masturbatory significance of playing musical instruments, and the libidinal pleasure of listening to music [41].

One of the first psychoanalysts to attempt a "scientific" definition of the function of music in mental life was Heinz Kohut [42]. Using a structural approach, he focused attention on the excitation and relief of libidinal and aggressive tensions (an id function) provided by music, on the opportunities for displaying special skills in the performance of music (an ego function), and on the cultural and aesthetic values of music (a super-ego function). Another Freudian analyst, Richard Sterba, did a major survey of the psychoanalytic literature on music from 1917 to 1957. While most of these studies were found to be "highly speculative, [and] based on analogies and extrapolation," the following observations pertinent to childhood development were made.

> The gratification which music provides is based on a deep regression to the earliest states of extra-uterine mental development. It seems to be the consensus of opinion that music reaches back to a period of development previous to the establishment of ego boundaries and the separation of inside and outside world. This regressive pleasure, narcissistic, primary and basic as the one that underlies magical thinking and acting, is at the same organized in music *by the highest synthetic* functions of the ego. This is a safeguard against a regression of a massive and holistic kind which would be disturbing and dangerous. The combination of and interaction between deepest regression and highly developed organization makes music a unique experience. It creates the inner illusion of ego world identity, of an extension of the psychic organization which brings the cosmos under the domination of the self [43].

Pinchas Noy, a psychoanalyst who in 1967 critically evaluated all of the available literature about psychodynamic meaning in music, concluded that the psychoanalytic approach had focused too exclusively on patients who sought treatment "for reasons completely unconnected with music. . . . None of the writers bothered to investigate the average man who is interested in music; moreover, none suggests an experimental way of verifying his theoretical conceptions" [44].

Applying newer models, specifically those of communication theory, Noy then proceeded to make a fundamental distinction between:

1. Creative artists (composers) who have the capacity to create structures, and find "original forms of expression in this (musical) language,"

2. Performing artists who know how to articulate this language by "making its signs audible and intelligible," and

3. Listeners who are "sensitive enough to hear and understand" music [45].

Noy believes that musical communication is rooted in the very earliest (i.e., the preverbal) period of psychological organization, when boundaries between self and reality are not yet distinct, a developmental phase between birth and six months, when the infant is sensitive to "extreme variations" of emotional expression, especially the mother's, and "aware of slight changes in mood as these are expressed in the mother's voice." Unable as yet to relate to the semantic components of language, an infant responds strongly to the paralinguistic properties of speech, i.e., the changes of loudness, rhythm, tone, duration, and timbre of the voice. These, of course, are also the fundamental properties of music. Accordingly, Noy attributes not only the universality of music, but also its untranslatability, to the preverbal origins of musical experience. He invokes the hypothesis of a deficient "protective barrier" against acoustical stimuli to explain early hypersensitivities to music [46]. An infant who cannot ward off disturbing sounds "will have to build up specific defenses to protect itself against its musical sensitivity in order to reject, neutralize, or master the redundant stimuli." Gradual mastery of the auditory perceptual field involves a certain focusing on desirable stimuli, while other sounds are screened out and ignored. Again, the behavior of the mother, in particular her singing, is seen as an important ingredient for the infant's development of control and mastery over sounds, and the promotion of special musical aptitudes.

Sounds, both linguistic and musical ones, may in fact play an essential role in the mental life of the child as he/she begins to separate from the mother. In the form of words, the sounds repeated by a child resemble what psychoanalysts have called "transitional objects," [47] i.e., the pillows, toys, or other physical objects that many toddlers cling to as a way of maintaining their security away from the mother. Similarly, tunes, fragments of songs, and rhythms are taken along by a child in his/her quest for independence, to be repeated during moments of solitude, when playing, or while falling asleep. To the extent that a child may also elaborate on these familiar musical (and/or linguistic) structures, rearrange them, and compose or decompose new pieces, one could even assume that a creative ability emerges during the separation-individuation phase of development. As McDonald points out:

> ... some children who have experienced music from birth onward as an integral part of the loving motherly and fatherly caretaking environment, might ... find in music their own special "transitional phenomenon." Some may even select from a musical repertory a special "transitional tune" ... [or create] his own special music, a transitional tune by transferring onto this 'creation' the musical properties of both himself and of his mother (or parents) [48].

From this perspective, many of the problems of musicians reported in the psychoanalytic literature seem more understandable. For example, incomplete separation from the mother and fear of disapproval from the father is a recurring theme in psychoanalysis.

> A thirty-five-year-old conductor, while on stage, was excessively preoccupied with thoughts about admiring, attractive women. He had been very attached to his mother, herself a musician, who had taught him to play the piano and strongly encouraged him to seek advanced musical training. Conflicts around oedipal issues were prominent throughout his analysis [49].

The effects of sibling rivalry in undermining a musical child's feeling of security and self-esteem have also been observed.

A violinist who was hampered in his playing and generally inhibited in work and social relationships, reported undue submissiveness and self-effacement during childhood. Habitually he had played "second fiddle" to a younger brother. As the analysis progressed, the patient became more outspoken, started to write music, and made a career as a professional composer [50].

The loss of family continuity may have a disruptive effect on musical development that is only partially reversible, as demonstrated by the child of holocaust survivors who experienced very disturbing feelings of "timelessness, a religious, mystical sensibility" whenever she played in a concert [51].

Finally, there have been several reports in the psychoanalytic literature of musical instruments used symbolically to represent valued parts or extensions of the body.

A seven-year-old boy had acquired a trombone which, when he was an adolescent and undergoing analysis, symbolized his penis. As the treatment progressed and his castration anxieties, mourning depressions, and other psychopathological processes receded, he became musically creative, began inventing original tunes and participating in jazz performances [52].

This case study method of exploring musical development in childhood has recently been augmented by psychobiographical approaches which take account of much larger segments of life experience than can usually be observed clinically. For example, a study of Gustav Mahler showed recurring reactions to loss, grief and mourning to be influential in stimulating compositions such as the *Kindertotenlieder* [53]. The childhood of composer Gioacchino Rossini was marked by a severe disturbance in his relationship to his father who was imprisoned, leaving the boy's upbringing to his grandmother [54]. Ludwig van Beethoven's childhood too was marred by family problems, including the alcoholism of his father. As a young child he developed a persistent delusional belief that the Archduke Rudolf of Austria was his actual father [55]. Robert Schumann underwent a traumatic separation from his mother in infancy and a pathological reattachment to her after several years with a foster mother. This, plus the suicide of his sister and death of his father during adolescence led to decompensation, splitting, and a "vulnerable personality" subject to panic attacks, hypomania, and suicidal depressions. Music often briefly served to bring the personality into better balance [56].

Daniel Stern's recent major contribution to developmental theory may also be applicable to the subject of musical behavior. It emphasizes states of interpersonal relatedness rather than developmental phases geared to physiological zones. By synthesizing the available data about infancy from observational, experimental, and clinical research, Stern has come up with the concept of four senses of the self. "Each new sense of self defines the formation of a new domain of relatedness. While these domains of relatedness result in qualitative shifts in social experience, they are not phases; rather, they are forms of social experience that remain intact throughout life. Nonetheless, their initial phase of formation constitutes a sensitive period of development" [57].

The *emergent self* (0 to 3 months) establishes the basic organization of perceptual and motor patterns in the context of the infant's interdependence with essential caretakers. Perception is "amodal"—i.e., information received by one sensory modality, say audition, is translated with ease into another modality, say vision. Thus musical stimuli are felt throughout all the many dimensions of an infant's physical and mental being. Affective experience too is global, a "vitality" affect, to use Stern's terminology. He describes the "rushing" of emotions, the "unmeasurable waves" of feeling evoked by music. What Noy and others have called the "coenesthetic" phase of musical development would seem to correspond with this process of emergent-self experience.

The *core self* (3 to 8 months) integrates the experience of being a separate physical entity, an agent with a will apart from other people. Thus the infant would begin to appreciate himself or herself as an independent source of sound — cooing, crying, etc.—as contrasted with other soundmakers—their speech, movements, singing, etc. The first opportunities for aesthetic pleasure may arise, in the knowledge (obviously unconscious) that music can be "out there" as compared to "within" the baby. The sonic emanations of mother, toys, radios, etc. now have substance and can become meaningful.

The *subjective self* (8 to 15 months) is responsible for sensing how others may feel and think about the infant and how the infant feels and thinks about them. Thus a capacity for reciprocity, empathy, and of intersubjectivity arises. Music now begins to be a pleasure that can be shared. Stern uses the musical term "attunement" to characterize a process whereby the infant and his caretakers achieve mutuality in their attention and interest. Stern's formulation of the internal dynamics of an "evoked companion," which is a memory event filled with playful affect and traces of togetherness, could also explain the content of practicing, which musicians do for many hours alone with their instruments. Practice stimulates and also satisfies. It constitutes not only a conscious "rehearsal" for future performances, but also recalls unconsciously as well as consciously the musician's past experience of playing with parents, teachers, and others who have echoed the music being practiced along with the affects conveyed by the music.

The *symbolic self* (15 months to 3 years) acquires linguistic and other code-structured systems of communication with the social present, past, and future. The child now has mental tools for transcending reality, as well as distorting it. These are "double edged swords" capable of producing genius as well as madness. Symbolic behavior is the instrumental source of creativity. Written texts and notes can be interpreted and reinterpreted. New compositions can be notated. Music now leaves the arena of personally meaningful interactive behavior and enters the sphere of culturally relevant artistic behavior.

SUMMARY, CONCLUSIONS AND SOME THOUGHTS ABOUT FUTURE RESEARCH

We have defined music as a special form of human cognition and communication that provides emotional stimulation as well as intellectual, and social gratification. In focusing on the development of musical interests and abilities in the child, we have emphasized their very early, prenatal origins. Sounds and rhythms within the mother's body impinge on the fetus before it is exposed to light and visual stimuli. Perception remains amodal for several months following birth, and it is during this period of the "emergent self" that social attachment to the mother seems to take place as well as the psychological ramifications of that attachment. Her voice, which is audible in the dark, around corners and with eyes closed, becomes especially important for maintaining the bond between an infant and its mother or other care-taking persons. Information contained in the musical properties of her voice probably is processed by those parts of the brain sensitive to, or specialized for, the acquisition of musical and linguistic aptitudes. With the maturation of a "symbolic self" (between 15 months and 3 years), the child can begin to assimilate cultural rules and environmental practices in regard to music as well as other symbolic systems pertaining to the use of sounds for communication.

Exceptional musical abilities are usually discovered by the parents, a teacher, or the child him/herself. This may lead to early training or thwarting of such abilities. Tests of formal intelligence, of general musical intelligence, as well as specific musical skills have been devised. However, neither the emergence of prodigious musical behavior, nor the results of psychological tests in childhood, seem to predict a successful career in the performing arts. Considerable research is needed to clarify what factors may be essential and what may be detrimental for the furtherance of musical talents. One of the most critical issues seems to be the emotional climate of the home. Prolonged or complicated attachments, loss of a parent, intense sibling rivalry, conflicted relationships with teachers and other role models, patterns of social support for artistic behavior, special educational opportunities, and other influences, as well as the interaction of these factors, have been described in the psychological, psychoanalytic, and psychobiographical literature. Of critical importance seems to be the "transitional" nature of musical experience which, much like the transitional objects providing some security for a toddler, allows comfortable, relaxing, pleasurable emotions to be felt during a musical experience.

Further topics of importance for research in this field would be the question of the development, simultaneously or sequentially, of several artistic-symbolic-bodily forms of behavior, for example dancing, sports, and music. In terms of sensory-motor coordinations, these behaviors, ubiquitous in many observations or memories of childhood, probably involve closely-related parts of the brain.

Like the early play of children, the early musical expression of children offers an unusual opportunity to study the cognitive functions of children before they experience the homogenizing effect of formal education. The study of the musical perception and expression of the preoperational child as they are first organized and then modified by reflective and operational thought might offer new insights into early imagination, cognition, and the development of creativity. The study of the development of early musical behavior might also add important data as to how perceptual information is differentiated, integrated and synthesized by a cognitive system that may be relatively independent of language and the signs and symbols related to that cognitive organization. Neurobiological studies of highly gifted children (as well as children who are clearly not gifted) are needed to answer some of the fundamental questions about where special talents reside, and what the different kinds of special intelligence may be. Surely the musically gifted child is a desirable focus for further psychological and psychopathological investigation. The cultural value of music seems undeniable, and one can observe the high priority given to the fostering of musical prodigies throughout the world.

REFERENCES

1. C. E. Seashore, *In Search of Beauty in Music*, The Ronald Press, New York, p. 305, 1947.
2. J. A. Sloboda, *The Musical Mind – The Cognitive Psychology of Music*, Clarendon Press, Oxford, 1985.
3. F. Wilson (ed.), *The Biology of Music Making, Conference Proceedings 1984*, Colorado University Press (in preparation).
4. H. T. Chugani and M. E. Phelps, Maturational Changes in Cerebral Function in Infants Determined by [18]FDG Positron Emission Tomography, *Science*, *231*, pp. 840-843, 1986.
5. P. F. Ostwald, Musical Behavior in Early Childhood, *Developmental Medicine and Child Neurology*, *15*, pp. 367-375, 1973.
6. S. Armitage, B. Baldwin, and M. Vince, The Fetal Sound Environment of Sheep, *Science*, *208*, pp. 1173-1174, 1980.
7. A. DeCasper and W. Fifer, Of Human Bonding: Newborns Prefer Their Mother's Voices, *Science*, *208*, pp. 1174-1176, 1980.
8. M. Critchley, *Aphasiology and Other Aspects of Language*, Arnold, London, 1970.
9. A. Meyer, The Search for a Morphological Substrate in the Brains of Eminent Persons Including Musicians: A Historical Overview, in *Music and the Brain – Studies in the Neurology of Music*, M. Critchley and R. A. Henson (eds.), Heinemann, London, pp. 255-281, 1971.
10. R. W. Gutman, *Richard Wagner: The Man, His Mind, and His Music*, Harcourt, Brace and World, New York, 1968.

11. L. B. Meyer, *Emotion and Meaning in Music*, University of Chicago Press, Chicago, 1956.

12. A. R. Damasio and H. Damasio, Musical Faculty and Cerebral Dominance, in *Music and the Brain – Studies in the Neurology of Music*, M. Critchley and R. A. Henson (eds.), Heinemann, London, pp. 141-155, 1977.

13. B. Milner, Laterality Effects in Audition, in *Interhemispheric Relations and Cerebral Dominance*, V. B. Mountcastle (ed.), Johns Hopkins Press, Baltimore, p. 177, 1962.

14. R. J. Zatorre, Musical Perception and Cerebral Function, paper given at the Fourth Annual Symposium on Medical Problems of Musicians and Dancers, Aspen, Colorado, July 31-August 3, 1986.

15. T. G. Bever and R. J. Chiarello, Cerebral Dominance in Musicians and Non-Musicians, *Science, 185*, pp. 537-539, 1974.

16. N. Wertheim, Is There an Anatomical Localization for Musical Faculties? in *Music and the Brain – Studies in the Neurology of Music*, M. Critchley and R. A. Henson (eds.), Heinemann, London, pp. 282-297, 1977.

17. F. Schiller, *A Möbius Strip – Fin-de-Siecle Neuropsychiatry and Paul Möbius*, University of California, Berkeley, 1982.

18. W. Lange-Eichbaum, *Genie, Irrsinn und Ruhm: Eine Pathographie des Genies*, W. Kurth (ed.), Reinhardt, Munich, 1961.

19. G. Revesz, *The Psychology of a Musical Prodigy*, Harcourt, Brace and Company, New York, 1925.

20. H. Gardner, *Frames of Mind – The Theory of Multiple Intelligences*, Basic Books, New York, pp. 99-127, 1983.

21. C. E. Seashore, *Psychology of Music*, Dover Publication, New York, 1967.

22. H. D. Wing, A Factorial Study of Musical Tests, *British Journal of Psychology, 31*, pp. 341-355, 1941.

23. A. Binet and T. Simon, *The Development of Intelligence in Children*, Williams and Wilkins, Baltimore, 1916.

24. L. M. Terman and M. A. Merrill, *Stanford-Binet Intelligence Scale*, Houghton Mifflin, Boston, 1973.

25. A. S. Kaufman and N. L. Kaufman, *Kaufman Assessment Battery for Children*, American Guidance Service, Circle Pines, Minnesota, 1983.

26. D. Wechsler, *Manual for the Wechsler Intelligence Scale for Children*, Revised (WISC-R), The Psychological Corporation, New York, 1974.

27. B. R. McCandless, *Children, Behavior and Development* (2nd Edition), Holt, Rinehart and Winston, New York, Chapter 7, 1967.

28. J. McV. Hunt, The Utility of Ordinal Scales Inspired by Piaget's Observations, *Merill-Palmer Quarterly, 22*:1, pp. 31-47, 1976.

29. I. C. Uzgiris and J. McV. Hunt, *Assessment in Infancy: Ordinal Scale of Psychological Development*, University of Illinois Press, Urbana, Illinois, 1975.

30. J. Piaget, *The Origins of Intelligence in Children*, International Universities Press, New York, 1952.

31. F. B. Murray, *The Impact of Piagetian Theory*, University Park Press, Baltimore, 1979.

32. M. Pflederer, The Response of Children to Musical Tasks Embodying Piaget's Principles of Conservation, *Journal of Research in Music Education, 12*, pp. 251-267, 1964.
33. R. L. Larsen, Levels of Conceptual Development in Melodic Permutation Concepts Based on Piaget's Theory, *Journal of Research in Music Education, 21*, pp. 256-263, 1973.
34. R. L. Jones, Development of the Child's Conception of Meter, *Journal of Research in Music Education, 24*, pp. 142-154, 1976.
35. J. L. Norton, The Relationship of Music Ability and Intelligence to Auditory and Visual Conservation in Kindergarten Children, *Journal of Research in Music Education, 1*, pp. 3-13, 1979.
36. D. Elkind, Children's Discovery of the Conservation of Mass, Weight and Volume: Piaget Replication, Study II, *The Journal of Genetic Psychology, 98*, pp. 219-227, 1961.
37. M. S. Rider, The Relationship Between Auditory and Visual Perception on Tasks Employing Piaget's Concept of Conservation, *Journal of Music Therapy, 14*, pp. 126-138, 1977.
38. _____, The Assessment of Cognitive Functioning Level Through Musical Perception, *Journal of Music Therapy, 3*, pp. 110-119, 1981.
39. S. Freud, *Collected Papers*, Hogarth Press, London, *4*, p. 257, 1948.
40. S. Guttman, R. L. Jones, and S. M. Parrish, *The Concordance to the Standard Edition of the Complete Psychological Works of Sigmund Freud*, Hall, Boston, *4*, pp. 306-307, 1980.
41. *Minutes of the Vienna Psychoanalytic Society*, H. Nunberg and E. Federn (eds.), International Universities Press, New York, 1975.
42. H. Kohut, The Psychological Significance of Musical Activity, *Music Therapy*, 1951.
43. R. Sterba, Psychoanalysis and Music, *American Imago, 22*, pp. 96-111, 1965.
44. P. Noy, The Psychodynamic Meaning of Music, *Journal of Music Therapy, 3*, pp. 126-134, 1966; *4*, pp. 7-23, 45-51, 81-94, 117-125, 1967.
45. _____, The Development of Musical Ability, *Psychoanalytic Study of the Child, 23*, pp. 332-347, 1968.
46. P. Bergman and S. K. Escalona, Unusual Sensitivities in Very Young Children, *Psychoanalytic Study of the Child, 3/4*, pp. 33-352, 1949.
47. D. W. Winnicott, Transitional Objects and Transitional Phenomena, *International Journal of Psychoanalysis, 34*, pp. 89-97, 1953.
48. M. McDonald, Transitional Tunes and Musical Development, *Psychoanalytic Study of the Child, 25*, pp. 503-520, 1970.
49. P. Weissman, Early Development and Endowment of the Artistic Director, *Journal of the American Psychoanalytic Association, 12*, pp. 59-79, 1964.
50. R. Wittenberg, Aspects of the Creative Process in Music: A Case Report, *Journal of the American Psychoanalytic Association, 28*, pp. 439-459, 1980.
51. J. A. Arlow, Disturbances of the Sense of Time, with Special References to the Experience of Timelessness, *Psychoanalytic Quarterly, 53*, pp. 13-37, 1984.
52. J. Oremland, An Unexpected Result of the Analysis of a Talented Musician, *Psychoanalytic Study of the Child, 30*, pp. 375-408, 1975.

53. G. Pollock, Psychoanalysis of the Creative Artist: Gustav Mahler, *Fifth Regional Conference Report, Chicago Psychoanalytic Society*, pp. 82-156, 1976.
54. D. W. Schwartz, Rossini: A Psychoanalytic Approach to "the Great Renunciation," *Journal of the American Psychoanalytic Association*, *13*, pp. 551-569, 1965.
55. M. Solomon, *Beethoven*, Schirmers, New York, 1978.
56. P. F. Ostwald, *Schumann – The Inner Voices of a Musical Genius*, Northeastern, Boston, 1985.
57. D. S. Stern, *The Interpersonal World of the Infant*, Basic Books, New York, p. 34, 1985.

PART III

The Contribution of Experience

CHAPTER 5

Imagination and Creativity in Childhood: The Influence of the Family

DIANA SHMUKLER

Creativity is a much desired and valued talent in our society. One that we see as crucial in addressing some of the pressing problems that face us in the closing stages of this century. On an individual level it is a resource available to people, patients and children to enliven and enrich their lives, alleviate their psychic pain and conflict and provide some respite from the harshness of the reality principle. The problem of the identification and utilization of creative talent is no mean task. Consequently the focus of this chapter will be on those studies which attempt to delineate the environments, the social milieus, the psychological structures and physical resources that facilitate the development of imaginative play.

A basic assumption underlying the present approach is that an individual's childhood environment can strongly influence the development or retardation of his or her creative potential. The first play environment is the home and thus it seems to be the relevant place in which to seek the origins of imagination, imaginative play, and creativity. Long intrigued by the relationship of early home environment to the fostering and development of creative achievement and expression, I initially studied the development of imaginative play in the context of the mother-child relationship. In struggling for a synthesis of my background in development psychology, observational research and clinical training and experience, I have expanded the base of my perspective from an empirical one to include psychodynamic object relations theory. In a wonderful book written from exactly this perspective, Fred Pine makes this link as follows [1, p. 25]:

> The truly amazing thing about psychoanalysis, both its practise
> and its general theory, is how much has been learned or inferred
> about development from clinical work itself—from the analysis of

77

transference, acting out, and other repetitions, from attention to memories, and from reconstruction.

In the 1960s on the wave of optimism and enthusiasm generated by the subject of creativity, a few interesting but sporadic studies were conducted on the personality characteristics and some of the postulated home background features of creative adults, adolescents, and children. However, the home background variables relating to creative expression have not been well understood or as easily researched as other aspects of creativity.

By the mid-1970s, a whole new trend in psychological research had developed in the fields of imagination, mental imagery, and imaginative play. Play became a topic of practical and academic interest to researchers since it was related to broad questions and areas of development, having implications for education, intervention with the culturally disadvantaged and therapy with children. As a leading activity in early childhood it is clearly related to healthy development and good functioning. The features that foster its development depend on the same characteristics in the psychological environment that are related to the development of emotional health. Early experiences powerfully influence the child's approach to the unknown, his or her desire to initiate and discover, which gives rise to a feeling of competence and power, in turn leading to new desires for further explorations and encounters. However, early experience may also set up barriers to innovative thinking.

PSYCHOANALYTIC PERSPECTIVE OF THE ORIGIN OF PLAY

The capacity to play arises early in life. Imaginative play can be regarded as a skill developed in a child as a result of certain constitutional factors interacting with a particular set of early environmental circumstances. Of primary importance in this process is regular contact with a benign adult who serves both as a model and provides sufficient trust for building up a child's ego resources. As in the case of the child's other developing capacities, this grows in the matrix of the mother-child relationship. One of the clearest descriptions of the origins of play, its developmental importance and its centrality to health is given by the British psychoanalyst Donald Winnicott [2]. In fact the development of the capacity to play is central to his more general theory of the development of psychological well-being. He especially emphasizes the importance of the environment, particularly the child's early relationships with caretakers in this regard. Implicit in Winnicott's work is the stress on the environment or context as well as the intrapsychic and endowed capacities. Broadly speaking then, two features of the family environment appear to be important inducements to the development of creativity in the child. Conditions should be such, that the child is inclined to develop and utilize fantasy; and a particular set of interpersonal dynamics and relationships in the family should exist. These will be described more fully below and, as will be seen, these requisites are interdependent.

The infant needs a "holding" environment in which to flourish and grow. This statement reflects an axiomatic understanding about healthy development. Winnicott, in describing the process has clearly and accurately detailed what this means. A "holding" environment involves literal physical support for the infant, rocking, soothing and handling as well as support for the infant's frail capacity to deal with the external world. It also implies protection from sudden or unexpected impingement of the outside world. However, Winnicott stresses that an "ordinary good enough" mother intuitively provides adequately for her baby's needs. There will be times when she does not or is not able to meet the needs perfectly. Overall though, the baby is not unduly stressed or discomforted, particularly in the early months when it lacks the ego resources to deal well with extreme or sudden distress, since a young child is only capable of reacting to frustration or impingement rather than adaptation or adjustment.

The holding process creates an illusion in the child. An illusion of omnipotence in that the child experiences the external world as meeting its needs magically and as they arise. Although Winnicott speaks about the baby's experiences and these concepts mystically, yet his work is informed by the observation of hundreds of infants and their mothers, and the reconstructive evidence from his analytic work with patients.

DISILLUSIONMENT

A central task confronting the infant early in development is the necessity to start making a distinction between inner and outer reality and learning to cope with both. We imagine that the young infant has little knowledge of the external shared reality. With increasing cognitive/affective development, the "ordinary good enough" mother senses that the baby has the ability to hold on and wait for a while. She usually intuitively and unconsciously starts to make her adaptation to the baby's needs less perfect. The well-managed process of disillusionment being as important a part of the environmental provision as is the creation of the illusion in the beginning. The process of disillusionment promotes growth and is vital in shaping the child's ability to start adjusting to the external shared reality.

At this point in normal development, the baby takes a concrete object from the external world and invests it with psychological meaning. The object can be a toy, dummy, edge of a blanket or a bit of fluff. The object stands for mother and the mothering principle. In investing something external with inner meaning, the baby commits its first act of creation.

Winnicott called the object a transitional object. Transitional in the sense that it bridges the gap between inner and outer reality and occurs in an area that overlaps them, the transitional area. The object is both part of the self (me) and part of the external world (not me) at the same time. Paradoxically, transitional phenomena are both "me" and "not me" and we are not to ask the baby: "Is this you or not you?" but rather accept that it is both.

The freedom to develop transitional phenomena is connected to the development of a sense of a real self. It is dependent on a supportive environment in which the demands for adaptation are balanced by sufficient space and security. In these circumstances, free from pressing inner drives or undue concern with external demands, the child is able to attend to inner experience, experiment with and express it, in short play. Where this development is inhibited, the child experiences a strong need to adapt for fear of rejection. The fear of expressing the self and one's inner experience leads to a strengthening of an adapted or false self.

The ability to play in a safe way depends on the child's freedom to express him or herself and create something unique in the outside world. It is vital for the baby's emotional development in that it enables the child to come to grips with external reality without neglect of the inner psychic world. Play experiences develop throughout life and are linked to the cultural expressions of literature, art, music, and intimacy. They are "where we are" when we are involved in cultural and artistic activities, i.e., in the transitional space, neither completely in our own inner psychic world nor exclusively in the external shared reality but in some zone combining both. These experiences encompass spontaneity, autonomy and a capacity for close relationships: the features of healthy functioning, and provide us with the opportunity to relax our boundaries and momentarily blend with the other. In this way transitional phenomena form the pivot of autonomous and creative living. And as the young child abandons the original illusion of omnipotence, it forms an important compensation, as well as an inner resource, a buffer against external stress. Winnicott's own clinical work became increasingly linked with the idea of communication in the potential space: "Psychotherapy is done in the overlap of the two play areas, that of the patient and that of the therapist" [2, p. 63].

The mother role remains a crucial one in providing the holding environment which while enabling the young child the freedom to give over to internal experience at the same time protects the child for a while from external pressure. This process is similar to that described by Hartmann as "regression in the service of the ego" with the same concomitant links to creative expression [3]. Severe pathology is likely to be the consequence of failure at this early stage as the development of transitional phenomena is the key not only to play and creativity but more generally to future mental health.

SEPARATION-INDIVIDUATION

The child is not born with an inner sense of self clearly separate from others. The process of separation and individuation is a slow one and continues through the early years. Although as Erikson says, the child's first social achievement occurs when he can let mother out of sight, since she has become an inner certainty as well as an external reality, the process of separation-individuation is still a long way from complete [4]. Separation-individuation or acquiring a sense of inner separateness presents the young child with his or her next developmental hurdle. Few people attain a complete sense of autonomy with the concomitant ability to fully exercise their initiative. On the other hand, most psychologically healthy people attain a reasonable degree of inner separateness and individuality. Those who do not, present with disorders of this process such as borderline and narcissistic personality problems [5, 6].

According to Margaret Mahler, the separation-individuation process takes place in phases spanning the first three years. The early phases correspond to the creation of transitional space and her ideas regarding these phases are consistent with Winnicott's. The mother-child relationship remains the context in which this process occurs and is central to its healthy negotiation. As the healthy young child discovers his or her physical separateness and ability to move independently, he or she goes through a stage of being in "love with the world," i.e., showing curiosity fueled by excitement and a grasping of life with gay abandon and little anxiety. Mahler calls this stage one of differentiation and practicing, coming after the earlier one of emotional hatching [4]. This stage is marked by the beginning of symbolic development. As the symbolizing capacities of language, images and so on rapidly develop, play too becomes symbolic. The earliest forms of imaginative or pretend play involve schemata that are central to the child as well as familiar well-practiced behavior detached from their customary context such as pretending to eat or sleep, in the absence of the desire to eat or sleep. These sequences are observed at about twelve months.

Then, by about eighteen months, two characteristic shifts occur. Play now involves the self/other boundary and the child adopts the role of the nurturer, pretending to feed the mother or, a little later on making a further symbolic shift to a doll [7].

We see clearly here how playing reflects the psychological processes that the child is engaged in and how this highlights an important function of playing, namely the mastery of inner and outer reality.

The mother's role remains that of providing the holding, security and sensitivity to the child's needs. Although in supporting growing independence and separateness she can more and more expect the child to adapt and comply to the demands of the external world. Undue harshness with extreme consequences for the child's noncompliance however, can still lead to severe pathology as the child's ego resources are still fragile.

As the child reaches what Mahler terms the rapproachment phase, a new crisis in development arises. The increased cognitive-affective capacities of the child bring in their wake a renewed need for attachment, with an increasing awareness of separateness and the reality of the child's helplessness and dependency. This realization leads to a clearer sense of dependence and vulnerability. The child has a polar wish for autonomy on the one hand, and closeness to the mother on the other, and this process remains in childhood to be dramatically replayed in adolescence. As Piaget shows, however, a young child cannot hold conflicting views simultaneously, making the swings emotionally turbulent for mother and child. Succcessful negotiation of this crisis enables the child to move backwards and forwards between dependence and independence without fear of rejection, punishment, abandonment or engulfment. Ideally, the child in a stable context can explore and test out his or her own limits of curiosity and exploration. The increasing imaginative quality of the play allows the child to continue in the crucial exploration of reality and fantasy. This process depends on the mother maintaining the secure framework and boundary, while at the same time allowing the child the space and freedom to develop internal sequences and experiences in the external world. We will return to this theme of boundaries and space as it remains the major dynamic and overall organizing explanation at the later stages of development.

ON THE ROAD TO OBJECT PERMANENCE

By three, the child should have reached what Mahler terms "on the road to object constancy." The major developmental task of defining and separating out inner and outer reality, as well as attaining a psychological sense of separateness should now be complete. The significance of the first three years of life for healthy personality development is highlighted by Pine as follows:

> ... the core of boundary formation and self-feeling, the basic attitude toward one's own impulses and affects as well as their direction and degree of specification, basic attitudes toward, relationship with, and inner representations of others are all laid down in that early period [1, p. 164].

In healthy development the foundations of an integrated personality have now been laid.

Pine continued:

> Indeed I would turn to the issue of oedipal pathology around and ask: If someone gets stuck at that level, can things have been adequately developed before? Or, if things are adequately developed before, will someone get stuck on the issues of the oedipal level? Barring specific focused acting out of the parents during the child's oedipal age or specific trauma at that time, the answer I would give to both questions is: I doubt it very much [1, p. 165].

In this sense then, the oedipal stage comes by the time the major early developmental tasks are complete. Its impact on subsequent psychological health is less significant than Freud's earlier formulations. Modern developmental understanding of psychopathology emphasizes "first year of life" problems (Winnicott) and separation-individuation (Mahler) issues. Modern psychoanalysts agree that severe psychopathology, psychosis, borderline, narcissistic and other character disorders are all preoedipal. It seems that only specific trauma at the oedipal stage cause severe psychological problems and classic oedipal problems are now understood to reflect earlier mother-child relationships.

On the other hand, this stage is the beginning of fully blown imaginative play. Play sequences have by now become much longer, more complicated and unique and are no longer tied to representative objects. The preschool years see a rich flowering of imaginative play in the healthy child. Play presents the forum and the outlet for the emotional and intellectual dilemmas, puzzles, confusion and conflicts. The content of imaginative play in healthy children varies from sequences of everyday events like shopping, mommies and daddies, going to work and school, to T.V. characters and situations (television has become a major influence on imagination in our society, see e.g., Singer and Singer [8]); to, in the case of the creative imaginative child, stories of fantasy characters like fairies and giants and, in the case of the disturbed child, situations of conflict, anger, and pain.

The first play environment nonetheless is still the home and it is to here that we now turn and examine some of the empirical evidence from the studies of the impact of the family on both imagination and creativity. We are now on firmer ground dealing with older children and also with data that are less speculative, being based on empirical rather than theoretical and clinical evidence, although Winnicott, Mahler, and Pine's clinical theories are all informed by observational data.

RESEARCH ON PLAY

In Singer's seminal and extensive investigations in the field of imaginative play in children, he provides empirical evidence for some of the family variables of importance in fostering imaginative play [9]. Evidence is also drawn from the research on the home background variables which seem to affect children's creative potential. It seems safe to assume that the conditions facilitating the development of creativity, imagination, and imaginative play are similar (e.g., Sutton-Smith [10] and Lieberman [11]).

First we will examine the broad environmental factors and then the more subtle psychological ones.

Socioeconomic factors undeniably play a part. It has been repeatedly shown that creative potential in children is related to parental educational and occupational level and to the socioeconomic level of the home [12-15]. Creative subjects have consistently been found to have better educated parents, many of whom are professionals with intellectual interests. Such parents would be able to provide a varied and stimulating environment for their children. Singer concurs by stressing the importance of making available to the child the material for imagination in the form of stories, picture books, films, and play-props [9] and Feitelson and Ross point out that affluent societies can afford to mass-produce cheap suitable implements as toys for children [16]. The importance of providing children with toys which have make believe properties has also been shown by Pulaski [17].

Literary accounts and stories often describe make-believe play occurring in secluded gardens, attics, and barns and it would seem that free access to and availability of sufficient space is an important facilitating factor [10, 11, 18]. Privacy seems to be another relevant variable. The few studies investigating the phenomenon of the imaginary companion have shown the relationship between the need for privacy and imaginative behavior. The child who has imaginary friends tends to be lonely, an only child or one with a large age gap between himself and siblings [9]. Both Singer and Freyberg stress the importance of privacy in enabling the child to develop his/her imaginative capacities [9, 15].

Apart from the broad environmental factors there are also a number of specific factors involved in the development and facilitation of imaginative behavior in children. Of these parental attitudes, child-rearing practices and personalities would seem to be away the most crucial.

Singer suggested that a particular set of early environmental circumstances that provide for stimulation and encouragement is crucial for the development of imaginative behavior in children [9]. An optimal balance between benign parental contact and the opportunity to be left alone seems to be one of the circumstances conducive to the development of a rich fantasy life. That a certain set of circumstances occurring early in life may not only sustain creativity, but actually "create" it, is a view which was also put forward by Weisberg and Springer [19]. Their findings indicate that a family which is not overly close but, where nonetheless there is open expression of emotion, no pressure to conform and in which the child is able to regress easily at times encourages the development and expression of creativity.

Dewing and Taft sum up the main characteristics of parents of creative subjects as follows: 1) an unpossessive (but not unaffectionate) parent-child relationship [20], encouraging self-reliance and independence [19-21]; and 2) parents who have diverse intellectual interests and who are permissive as opposed to authoritarian and restrictive in their approach to child-rearing [12, 22-24].

Stein discusses the complexity in parent-child relationships which would permit the child to detach himself and become self-reliant [25]. Endorsing this, MacKinnon talks about respect for the child's competence and ability to cope [21]. Further the characteristics of adaptability and openmindedness and the important ability to avoid imposing restrictions and stereotyped beliefs on what is considered appropriate for children would be crucial attitudes in parents in facilitating the child's expressive behavior.

Parents' ability to entertain multiple views, "to take the role of the other" or to act "as if" might be seen to be helpful in assisting the child to employ fantasy during play. A picture of what Bishop and Chase call the "playful engendering" parent thus emerges [26]. Open-minded, adaptable, low on authoritarianism, unorthodox, flexible, and able to grant the child autonomy seem to be among the most salient features of this picture.

Such features do not occur in isolation, however, and as Harvey et al. show, they are likely to be part of a stable conceptual system found in parents [27]. These characteristics are likely to occur in someone who is more inclined to be abstract rather than concrete on an abstract-concrete continuum. Near the opposite pole is someone whose cognitive functioning can be characterized by concreteness, simplicity of beliefs, rigidity, conventional, authoritarian, and unadaptable. Bishop and Chase showed that mothers of more "creative" three- and four-year-olds were more abstract in their thinking than mothers of less creative children [26]. Further, the mothers of the abstract continuum provided a play environment at home more likely to enhance the playfulness of their children's play experience. They concluded that creative potential in children is related both to parents' cognitive style and the nature of the play environment they provide.

A study directly addressed to determining some of the family factors which may encourage or discourage imaginative play in children is Dennis' unpublished doctoral dissertation [28]. Strongly influenced by Singer [9] and Bishop and Chase [26], she selected a group of high and low fantasy children. Parents and siblings were tested for fantasy predisposition and conceptual style following Bishop and Chase. A home play environment questionnaire was administered and mother and child were rated in a play activity together. The main findings show that mothers' scores on fantasy predisposition and length of education were significantly correlated with the children's scores. Whereas the number of restrictive responses with regard to play in the home was negatively correlated with the child's fantasy predisposition. She failed to conform that the abstract or concrete conceptual style of parents distinguishes between high and low fantasy children. Neither were significant differences found in terms of sex, ordinal position, outside employment of mother, number of rooms in the house or people in the family, education or fantasy predisposition of father. The major parental influences are probably more subtle. Since Dennis' sample was restricted to middle class, "room for privacy" may be more important as a factor for imaginative play under circumstances of overcrowding and does not emerge when there is ample space in the homes. In the early years it also seems as though the mother's influence is more marked although one parent to serve as a model and endorse imaginative behavior consistently emerges as a feature [9].

PLAY AND THE CHILD'S MOTHER

Dewing and Taft found that the educational level of mothers as opposed to fathers was more important for subject's creative performance [20]. Furthermore, more potentially creative girls had working mothers and, although this variable was not related to boys' creative potential, it was related to the creative performance of both sexes. Generally it appears that the role models for girls of working mothers are more competent, "masculine" and creative, and so are likely to enhance the development of independence and creativity in their daughters. The work of Getzels and Jackson showed that the mothers of highly creative adolescents worked largely outside the home, thus spending less time with their children [18]. Such mothers were more likely to permit children greater freedom in exploring and manipulating the environment. Other trends that have emerged are that the mother's personality and her child-rearing attitudes appear to influence the child's potential for being creative. Dewey and Taft found mothers of creative children to be more egalitarian, permitting their children more contact with influences outside the home [20]. In similar vein, the parents of MacKinnon's subjects had given their youngsters rather unusual freedom in exploring their universe and making decisions for themselves [21].

This was the point at which I began my study into the family variables and specifically the mother-child relationship as it affected the child's developing imagination. I was struck by the lack of empirical evidence and the need to directly investigate the mother-child dimension in relation to the child's imaginative capacities and decided that an investigation of some of the psychological and interactive dimensions would be fruitful. My own research is, of course, limited by the fact that it, too, was done on a small specific sample and the results have not to date been replicated.

The study was based on hypotheses derived from the previous research of Singer and leaned heavily on his approach and understanding of imaginative play as a skill developed early in a child which is dependent on the combination of support and boundaries, space and freedom available to develop his or her own ability to express the self. This understanding, of course, is consistent with Winnicott's description of the importance of boundaries and space from the earliest months for authentic expression and experience. Boundaries and space although somewhat abstract notions are intimately related to the idea of transitional phenomena, play space and experiences and objects.

Hypotheses were formulated regarding the ability of mothers of creative children to create and provide imaginative interaction with their child; that they would be sensitive to the child and able to tolerate regression and ambiguity; that mother's ability to be sensitive to the child and accept him or her would be related to her own ability to accept herself. Finally that she would give the child the psychological space needed for creative expression.

The study was designed as an observational one and the central aspect was the observation of an unstructured play situation between mother and child. A great deal of other information, however, was also collected through interviews, Thematic Apperception Test stories and semantic differentials with mothers' observations and nursery school teacher ratings of the children's play. A sample of 111 mothers and their five-year-old children was selected from middle-class English-speaking nursery schools. All children were normal without any psychological problems and there was a more or less equal number of fifty-eight boys and fifty-three girls.

Children were identified as creative on the basis of their responses to the Singer Imaginative Play Predisposition Inventory, the Holtzman Inkblot test and ratings of their spontaneous play. It became clear that these mothers supported their children's imaginative play by creating structure and support in the unstructured play situation, at the same time giving the child psychological room to develop his/her own ideas. They would make suggestions about game possibilities, but having eased their children into the situation, they would withdraw and allow the child to develop the sequence or game in tune with his or her own needs. In contrast to this picture, the mothers of the uncreative children would have a need for the child to produce the "right" answers. It was easy to see the training for convergent thinking in "You can't bring a truck into the living room," "What do you call a baby cow," and the like. Among these mothers there was a lot of teaching, directing, and surveillance. These children were given the boundaries but not the space. Another pattern was observed in which mothers showed disinterest in their child and the play situation. They provided little structure, input or energy but seemed bored while waiting for the investigator to return. They provided the space but no boundary, support, or input for creative activity. These children emerged neither creative nor competent on the teachers' or the investigators' ratings [29].

Clearly then by five, discernible patterns of mother-child relationship and interaction can be observed, rated and related to the child's level of imaginative play, creative ability, and, in fact, to the broader dimensions of competence and effective functioning. Mothers support their children's capacities by their ability both to be with the child and also allow the child the freedom to explore, experiment, and use the play environment in a way that suits their needs. They feed the inner fantasy life through their own imaginative ability and capacities as well as their sensitivity to imagination and appreciation of imaginative products. Mothers of imaginative children accept their children for who and what they are without undue demands that they change and become more like the mother's image of what her child should be. The mothers are also imaginative themselves, in that they tell stories, make up games, and endorse the creative aspects of childhood. They seem to have the ability to tolerate "regression in the service of ego" as well as support the child's independence and often adult interests. The creative child has been characterized by both playing with childish things as well as having scientific or adult interest beyond their years [30].

The study then supported the notion of an optimal balance between benign support and concern, and space. Singer stresses the importance of a close relationship with one parent who, of course, could be the father. My study was limited by examining only the mother-child relationship and clearly in a family context other influences may support the child's creative capacities. The parent provides positive reinforcement for the child in the form of love and security, which results in a strong motive to please this adult. In the subsequent absence of the adult, the child has available a repertory of movement, words or postures that relieve his loneliness and provide new sources of pleasure. Moreover, while almost all children show a natural growth of imaginative skills, they need the encouragement and leadership of parents and other adults to sustain and broaden the scope of their play.

In line with the findings outlined above, the work of Smilansky in Israel and Singer already discussed, stresses the learned aspect of imaginative play as a central factor for its emergence [9, 31]. According to this view, some form of modeling is an essential precondition for the development of make believe, for unless a child sees another person engaged in symbolic play and activity, the "as if" stance usually associated with this kind of behavior will not occur on its own [16].

A study which examined environmental and cross-cultural correlates of children's fantasy play in South Africa and Israel was done by Udwin and Shmukler [32]. They showed that the interaction of children with their parents showed statistical significance with imagination for both Israeli and South African children. A number of other home background features considered prerequisites of fantasy development are in fact culture-based, and not universally applicable to all preschoolers. Specifically, it was found that the availability of "room for privacy" measured in terms of the number of children per family, number of rooms in the home, and the presence or absence of a private bedroom for the child, was significantly related to imagination in the South African sample, but not in the Israeli. If nothing else, this study again points to the urgent need for additional cross-cultural investigations into the environmental conditions which might facilitate fantasy development in early childhood.

Imaginative play and other forms of creative expression in children have an essential developmental function, by helping a child achieve a balance between inner and outer experience, and developing a reservoir of resourcefulness, liveliness, and self-esteem, encouraging both curiosity and the capacity for exploration. By its very nature, play demands that children use their potential to combine experiences into organized, yet flexible schemes. It is thus a powerful adjunct to early educational preventive and therapeutic procedures and, as such, should be central in any preschool activity.

The studies reviewed above suggest that imaginative play behavior is a dimension of experience and exploration available to most children, but one whose richness and frequency of employment grows from a set of optimal conditions. These seem to include the following.

An opportunity for the practice of fantasy in a relatively protected setting where the external environment is reasonably unobtrusive so that greater attention can be focused on internal activity. Singer spoke in this regard of the opportunity for the practice of fantasy in private and argued that children need time and space to themselves to think over and replay their experiences [9]. However, as noted above, Udwin and Shmukler found this requirement not universally applicable to children cross-culturally [32] and therefore the concept of "psychological space" seems preferable [29]. Shmukler showed that mothers should not crowd children psychologically but allow room for his or her inner resources to develop [29].

Not only do children need time and opportunity, but they also need wealth of content for their fantasy play. As such, a second requirement is the availability of a variety of materials in the form of stories told, books and playthings which increase the likelihood that the material presented to the child will be sufficiently interesting and novel to engage and hold their interest and attention with pleasure. Children also need an environment that is not too structured or well-ordered so they can develop greater flexibility in using the material at hand.

A further requirement is the availability of warm caring adults or older siblings or peers who encourage imagination and make believe activity and provide examples of how it is done, at the same time leaving the child space to develop nis or her own resources. Regular contact with an involved caring adult, genuinely interested in the child, is essential. Finally there needs to be a cultural acceptance of privacy and make believe as worthwhile.

A major problem with the work reviewed is that thus far play, imaginative play and creativity are almost always defined differently. In the absence of a single accepted definition of play, imaginative play and creativity, it is difficult to generalize across research. I have not attempted to address this issue in the present chapter but have tried to work with the broad general dimensions described and my own understanding of the issues involved. Another warning that must be sounded is that none of the studies above make any claim for representativeness; they are restricted in terms of relative homogeneity of intelligence, cultural background, numbers, socioeconomic status, and parental education, thereby seriously limiting the generalizability of their findings. While theories of play abound, systematic large scale studies necessary for testing hypotheses are unfortunately scarce.

In summing up then, the family background characteristics which support and sustain imaginative and creative capacities still remain somewhat ill-defined and clearly complex. The research and clinical evidence that we have points to certain features however. Nonetheless, on a practical note, suggestions for mothers, teachers, and other concerned adults lie in the finding which stresses the importance of providing the balance between the necessary stimulation and input and the psychological space and freedom from intrusion. Special stress is laid on the realization of creative potential, particularly in individuals who are endowed with talent and capability, as it seems that environmental support is necessary to sustain their creativity. However imagination and creative expression needs to be seen as a resource available to all.

Finally, the findings are consistent with the theory developed. The development of transitional areas and objects seems central to the capacity for imaginative play. Further, that the ability to be imaginative provides the child with a rich resource of inner material and proves to be a buffer against external stress. So that although the interest in the present discussion has revolved around creativity and imagination the points made refer also to the more general well-being of the child.

REFERENCES

1. F. Pine, *Developmental Theory and Clinical Process*, Yale University Press, New Haven and London, 1985.
2. D. W. Winnicott, *Playing and Reality*, Penguin Books Ltd., Harmondsworth, England, 1971.
3. H. Hartmann, *Ego Psychology and the Problem of Adaptation*, International Universities Press, New York, 1939.
4. E. H. Erikson, *Childhood and Society*, Penguin Books, London, England, 1950.
5. M. S. Mahler, F. Pine, and A. Bergman, *The Psychological Birth of the Human Infant*, Basic Books, Inc., Publishers, New York, 1975.
6. J. F. Masterson, *The Narcissistic and Borderline Disorders: An Integrated Developmental Approach*, Brunner/Mazel, Publishers, New York, 1981.
7. G. G. Fein, A Transformational Analysis of Pretending, *Developmental Psychology*, *11*:3, pp. 291-296, 1975.
8. J. L. Singer and D. Singer, A Cognitive-Affective Theory of the Development of Imagination: Family Mediation and Television Influences, in *Organizing Early Experience: Imagination and Cognition in Childhood*, D. C. Morrison (ed.), Baywood Publishing Company, Inc., Amityville, New York, pp. 92-115, 1988.
9. J. L. Singer, *The Child's World of Make Believe*, Academic Press, New York, 1973.
10. B. Sutton-Smith, A Syntax for Play and Games, in *Child's Play*, R. E. Herron and B. Sutton-Smith (eds.), Wiley, New York, 1971.
11. J. N. Lieberman, *Playfulness: Its Relationship to Imagination and Creativity*, Academic Press, New York, 1977.
12. C. E. Schaefer and A. Anastasi, A Biographical Inventory for Identifying Creativity in Adolescent Boys, *Journal of Applied Psychology*, *52*:1, pp. 42-48, 1968.
13. A. Anastasi and C. E. Schaefer, Biographical Correlates of Artistic and Literary Creativity in Adolescent Girls, *Journal of Applied Psychology*, *53*:4, pp. 267-273, 1969.
14. A. Roe, A Psychological Study of Physical Scientists, *Genetic Psychology Monographs*, *43*, pp. 121-239, 1951.
15. J. T. Freyberg, Increasing the Imaginative Play of Urban Disadvantaged Kindergarten Children through Systematic Training, in *The Child's World of Make Believe*, J. L. Singer (ed.), Academic Press, New York, 1973.

16. D. Feitelson and G. S. Ross, The Neglected Factor—Play, *Human Development*, *16*, pp. 202-223, 1973.
17. M. A. S. Pulaski, Toys and Imaginative Play, in *The Child's World of Make Believe*, J. L. Singer (ed.), Academic Press, New York, 1973.
18. J. W. Getzels and P. W. Jackson, *Creativity and Intelligence: Explorations with Gifted Students*, Wiley, New York, 1962.
19. P. A. Weisberg and K. J. Springer, Environmental Factors in Creative Function, *Archives of General Psychiatry*, *5*, pp. 64-67, 1961.
20. K. Dewing and R. Taft, Some Characteristics of Parents of Creative Twelve-Year-Olds, *Journal of Personality*, *41*, pp. 71-84, 1973.
21. D. W. MacKinnon, The Nature and Nurture of Creative Talent, *American Psychologist*, *17*, pp. 484-495, 1962.
22. J. E. Drevdahl, Some Developmental and Environmental Factors in Creativity, in *Widening Horizons in Creativity*, C. W. Taylor (ed.), Wiley, New York, 1964.
23. M. A. Wallach and N. Kogan, *Modes of Thinking in Young Children*, Holt, New York, 1965.
24. V. Goertzel and M. G. Goertzel, *Cradlers of Eminence*, Constable, London, 1965.
25. M. I. Stein, Creativity as Intra- and Inter-Personal Process, in *A Source Book for Creative Thinking*, S. J. Parnes and H. F. Harding (eds.), Charles Scribner's Sons, New York, 1962.
26. D. W. Bishop and C. A. Chase, Parental Conceptual Systems, Home Play Environment and Potential Creativity in Children, *Journal of Experimental Child Psychology*, *12*, pp. 318-338, 1971.
27. O. J. Harvey, J. White, M. Prather, and R. Alter, Teachers' Belief Systems and Preschool Atmospheres, *Journal of Educational Psychology*, *57*, pp. 373-391, 1966.
28. L. B. Dennis, "Individual and Familial Correlates of Children's Fantasy Play," unpublished doctoral dissertation submitted to the University of Florida, 1976.
29. D. Shmukler, Mother–Child Interaction and Its Relationship to the Predisposition of Imaginative Play, *Genetic Psychology Monographs*, *104*, pp. 215-235, 1981.
30. A. Miller, *The Drama of the Gifted Child and the Search for the True Self*, Faber and Faber, London and Boston, 1979.
31. S. Smilansky, *The Effects of Socio-Dramatic Play on Disadvantaged Pre-School Children*, Wiley, New York, 1968.
32. O. Udwin and D. Shmukler, The Influence of Socio-Cultural, Economic and Home-Background Factors on Children's Ability to Engage in Imaginative Play, *Developmental Psychology*, *17*, pp. 66-72, 1981.

CHAPTER 6

A Cognitive-Affective Theory of the Development of Imagination: Family Mediation and Television Influences

JEROME L. SINGER
AND DOROTHY G. SINGER

ORGANIZING AND INTEGRATING EXPERIENCE: THE TASKS OF INFANCY AND EARLY CHILDHOOD

A Cognitive-Affective Perspective

Throughout the first half of this century the dominant view of the origins of imagination which influenced clinical practice with children was chiefly an extrapolation of Sigmund Freud's theory of psychosexual stages. Contrasting positions, based on direct childhood observations by Vigotsky, Luria, Wallon, and Piaget were, as yet, not widely known or accepted by American developmentalists and had scarcely begun to be assimilated into child psychotherapeutic work. The model of the human being which prevailed was of a hydraulic energy system with drives such as hunger, thirst, sex, and aggression presumably pressing for overt conscious experience and discharge on what Rappaport termed a "cyclical, appetitive peremptory basis" [1]. The child's task was to develop a system for delaying and rechanneling these drives and this effort laid the basis for the ego [2]. From psychoanalysis we have gained many insights about human needs, wishes, conflicts, compromise formations, and about our inherent continuity (in the best Darwinian sense) with other animal species. We propose, however, that in the past generation we have moved well beyond such a narrow

* Research by the authors of this chapter was supported by grants from the National Science Foundation, The American Broadcasting Company, The Spencer Foundation, and the John D. and Catherine T. MacArthur Foundation.

model. Our current conception of human beings presents them as information-processing creatures, seeking continuously to organize and to give meaning to stimuli from the physical and social environment, from their own memory store or from the ongoing machinery of their bodies [3]. Indeed following upon the great insights of Silvan Tomkins [4] and the supportive empirical research of Izard, Ekman, Schwartz and others [5] we view humans as individuals whose differentiated emotional response patterns are closely intertwined with the novelty, complexity and other structural properties of the information they confront from moment to moment.

This cognitive-affective approach broadens considerably our view of human motivation. Rather than reducing all motivation to some symbolic manifestation of infantile sexuality or aggression, one can propose that the basic emotions which have been identified across human species in the work of Izard [6] and Ekman and Friesen [7] are motivating for dozens of experiences along four dimensions proposed by Tomkins [4]. We seek: 1) to reexperience or to reconstruct events, interactions or thoughts which have evoked the positive emotions of *interest-excitement* or *joy and smiling or laughter*; 2) to avoid in action or thought those situations that have evoked the specific negative emotions of *anger, fear-terror, sadness-distress* (*weeping*), or *shame-humiliation-guilt*; 3) to *express* whenever possible our felt emotions fully, and 4) to *control* emotional expression in situations where our social experiences suggests restraint is necessary. In effect situations that permit expression or experience of positive emotions or which allow for appropriate control of emotions will be intrinsically positively reinforcing while situations that have evoked fear, anger, distress or shame or which have blocked expression or socially-adaptive control of emotions will be inherently punishing or negatively reinforcing. If we consider that the emergence of basic emotions is closely tied to the fundamental human tendency to organize and integrate information, we can see how a great variety of situations can become motivating well beyond those that satisfy biological appetites or the dubious "drive" of aggression.

In Tomkins' position differentiated affects may be triggered by fairly specific variations in the information-processing tasks that one faces. For example, massive inputs of new or unassimilable information produce fear responses; moderate rates of new information generate interest or excitement which are positive affects; and the assimilation of an initially high level of seemingly ambiguous or threatening information (as in delayed recognition of an old friend, seeing the point of a joke, or finding good news upon opening a letter) leads to the positive experiences of joy or laughter. High rates of unassimilable or complex information persisting over long periods of time lead to the negative affects of anger, despair, and sadness. Thus, the flow of information, the readiness of individuals based upon their past experiences, cognitive styles, their anticipations of a situation, or their planning for the situation —all these play an important role in whether negative, punishing affects emerge or whether people experience the positive rewarding affects of interest (a moderately rising gradient of new information) or joy (a moderately declining gradient from a high level of novelty).

Inspection of Figure 1, which is drawn from Tomkins' *Affect, Imagery, and Consciousness*, will help the reader grasp what has been presented in very condensed form here [4]. Tomkins employs the term *density of neural firing*, which implies the degree to which there is a massive involvement of neural activity from various brain areas. Since such density is not an easily measured variable, we have preferred to translate it into assimilability of information into previously developed schemas. If the doorbell rings and one goes to the door and it is a child returning from school at the usual time when expected, then that information is easily assimilated since it was largely anticipated in advance. If, on the other hand, the doorbell rings and a long-lost relative, a gorilla, or two policemen

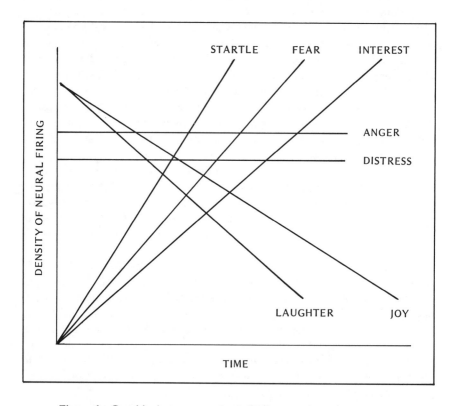

Figure 1. Graphical representation of a theory of innate activators of affect. (From Silvan Tomkins, *Affect, Image, and Consciousness*, p. 251. Copyright © 1962 Springer Publishing Company, 200 Park Avenue South, New York, New York 10003.)

are there, one is most likely to respond with a startle or fear reaction. In the first case, after the initial startle response, recognition of the relative should lead to the experience of joy and much smiling. In the cases of the gorilla and the policemen, a great deal depends on what follows from the situation; but the chances of a persisting high level of density of neural firing and, hence, negative affect are much greater.

The combining of affects and the learned patterns of manifesting affects are, of course, of great significance and depend heavily on particular cultural and family experiences. Nevertheless, as Figure 1 suggests, the innate triggering of affects is closely related to the information-processing load and patterning of environmental stimulation. One can add to this notion the possibility that one's ongoing stream of thought presents an alternative stimulus field to the material available from the external environment [8, 9].

Accommodation, Assimilation, and Early Imagery Development

With a view to understanding how the processes of imagery can be effective in the psychotherapeutic enterprise, let us take a closer look at how images and fantasies may get started. We can begin with Piaget's *assimilation and accommodation* as two fundamental processes by which a child organizes her experience [10]. The child initially is motor oriented and also perceptually attracted to moving stimuli. She attempts in some way to use her available cognitive and motor apparatus to deal with the "booming, buzzing confusion" of the novel environment that surrounds her. Her eyes follow a swinging mobile and gradually her hands, in increasingly coordinated fashion, stretch out for the objects within reach. These gross motor and perceptual activities reflect the child's attempt at accommodation to the novel environment and are associated initially with the innate arousal of the affects of interest and surprise [5].

The child also seeks to assimilate what she encounters into some kind of more permanent structure. At first, this assimilation is evident in simply grasping or, with improved dexterity, placing the objects into the mouth. Here, perhaps, Freud overemphasized the purely oral sensuality of this experience without seeing that orality itself might be just one phase of the general assimilative cognitive-affective process of dealing with the novel stimulation available to the child. We believe that a great deal more information is being organized and assimilated into the encoding system that is unrelated to specific drive satisfactions. Rather, it is related to the gradual capacity of the child to match earlier learned material with new inputs, with the resultant arousal of the affect of joy, as a high level of complex material is reduced to manageable chunks [11].

The complex stored materials begin then to be organized into various subroutines and hierarchies. In a home that affords regular care, the gratification of basic drives takes place increasingly efficiently and fairly quickly, and there is considerable time left over for active exploration. This exploration involves more than direct interaction with the physical environment. In periods of relative quiet or reduction of external cues, it takes the form of reverberation of memories with attempts at assimilating earlier experiences into available schema. The child's feedback of her own vocalisms, as well as her attempts to imitate the movements and sounds and visual characteristics of adults around her, all come into play at this point and are probably rehearsed and replayed in a variety of contexts.

We believe that much of the assimilation process has an intrinsic interest for the child since it involves the creation of a fairly novel environment by replay of the as yet unassimilated material. This "inner" environment is not so complex as to produce the negative affect of startle or fear. Instead, the child's *control* of the centrally-generated material leads to the more positive affect of interest characterized by a moderately increasing gradient of novel stimulation. This stage is followed (as the material does eventually get matched with established structures) by the affect of joy, and fairly soon is manifested in smiling and laughing on the part of the child.

The process we are describing, although probably a basic cognitive capacity, is not likely to be independent of social experience. The conscious efforts of the adults in the environment to engage the child by physical tickling or cuddling or by spoken phrases are important parts of the child's initial experiences, which she must then attempt to assimilate. To the extent that the child is able to accommodate to the adult by producing a smile, she engenders in turn a sequence of positive reactions that are generally pleasurable.

The child's attempt at assimilation of the complex novel material whether from the physical environment or from social interchange is exceedingly difficult and complex. After all, the child begins with such a limited repertory of schemas. It is at this juncture that we probably see beginnings of symbolic and fantasy or make-believe processes. The efforts at imitation of adult behaviors by the child are impeded on a number of counts: there is inadequate vocal capacity, as yet insufficiently differentiated motor skill, and, in addition, only a very limited experiential base for comprehending the nature of the adult action.

The child seeking to imitate a parent who is talking on the telephone may be able to grasp some relatively simple phrases, particularly those likely to be repeated quite frequently such as "Hi, there." The child may even get the intonation somewhat right after a while and manage to hold the telephone approximately in the right position, although it is unlikely to differentiate the speaking and listening ends of a telephone. It is much harder for a child to grasp the notion that the person to whom words are addressed may be miles away and not inside the telephone instrument itself.

A great deal of the assimilation of material from the environment for the developing child involves novel combinations that do not meet adult standards or veridicality, and, hence, may later be labeled as cute or strange or silly or bizarre. But these are the only available constructs children can store at earlier ages. These stored novel combinations do get replayed by the child time and again, and, of course, gradually many of them are tested against new inputs and modified. Probably, as psychoanalytic work suggests, original materials that form the more "childlike" images or representations also associated with rather specific childlike verbal codings may never be completely lost. They become the "objects" of interior dialogues [11, 12].

We can attempt to reconstruct the child's experience in listening on the telephone or in watching television by recalling a number of early memories and faulty assimilations that were part of our own child experiences. These include imagining that certain characters lived inside the phonograph or the radio – "Uncle Don" (a radio announcer for children) lived inside the box in the living room from which his voice emanated, or the humorous Gaelic accents of Sir Harry Lauder emerged from a quaint little man who dwelt in an aunt's mysterious Victrola record player. We suggest that the reader adopt a similar attitude for the moment and try to reestablish the mood of early childhood, choosing perhaps a particular period from one's past to see if indeed a number of comparable "faulty" assimilations and images will come back. Imagery and many of the quaint pictures that characterize childhood come almost certainly from attempts to capture strange voices and sounds in some understandable form. An Asian woman who had attended a Christian missionary school recounted that for years she was puzzled about God's interest in painting and his quaint name after having learned by rote to repeat, "Our Father, *with art* in Heaven, *Harold* be thy name." Perhaps some of these quaint assimilations were fostered even more by the radio or phonograph for which the visual component had to be actively added by the child.

Origins of Symbols and Metaphors

The early faulty assimilations of children are unquestionably very idiosyncratic in the sense that no two people have identical experience, participate in identical sets of conversations with identical parents in identical environments etc. Nevertheless, one can look to some extent for certain more universal or at least culturally widespread experiences and assimilation patterns that ultimately become the basis for the symbols and metaphors occurring in our dreams and which form the basis for our religious, cultural, and aesthetic experiences. We are not proposing archetypes in the sense of genetically established structures that take on the same symbolic meaning across cultures. Rather, there may be certain sets of experiences that all human beings have in common. Obviously these include the expression of a fairly circumscribed but differentiated set of affects and also the satisfaction of basic drives such as hunger, thirst, sex, and pain reduction, the child's contacts with adult caregivers, etc. Within certain environmental settings, the combination of environment and/or constitutional structure interact to produce certain commonalities that are found even across widely disparate cultures.

Werner and Kaplan have gone to great lengths to examine the ways in which the very nature of childhood gesture, the varieties of expressiveness of adult emotion, and certain Gestalt structures that lend themselves to our perceptual responses become incorporated with associated affects as regularities in imagery [13]. The attempts on the part of the child to mimic complex shapes of objects by particular postures have been described by Muchow and Werner [13, p. 97]. A whole host of movements and imitative actions come to symbolize complex situations within cultures and, to some extent, across cultures.

Symbolism can be seen as originating from the attempted assimilation of material in the face of limited cognitive schema or verbal encoding processes. It takes the form of imagery representation if one is alone or of imitation of sound or gesture if the attempt is to communicate to someone else. But even this imitation is subject to the limited range of experiences or organizational Gestalt properties of the objects involved. In this sense, most cultures can generate comparable patterns of imagery for certain experiences —at least, experiences of the most readily observable type. Phallic imagery that subsequently becomes incorporated into dream symbols is one obvious example clearly related to a specific natural phenomenon (penile erection) that takes the same form in all societies. The smile or the look of anger are pretty universal and can be used for symbolizing positive and negative affective conditions. The eyes shut for sleeping with the head downcast to suggest shame have also more universal characteristics and become the basis for symbols and assimilations even in early childhood [6, 7].

Early Fears and Frightening Images

We have stressed some of the more commonplace, day-to-day aspects of our environment which children try to comprehend, imitate, or assimilate into their limited cognitive repertory. Naturally one would have to view the situation in relation to different age levels and the differential cognitive capacities and environmental demands of those levels. For the preschool child and even for the somewhat later phases of childhood, there are many events and experiences particularly difficult to assimilate and to match with already established structures. Consider the situation of a child between three and six lying in bed at night and seeing the shifting play of shadows on the wall. Perhaps the lights of passing automobiles cast different patterns on the wall or perhaps the flashing of neon lights creates odd shapes in a particular apartment bedroom. There are many more noises one discerns at night that take on figural properties compared with the normal background din of the daytime. These experiences are difficult to assimilate for the child and are more likely to create conditions arousing negative affects such as fear.

Because of the reduced sensory input at the onset of sleep, the child experiences a greater awareness of the processing activity of the brain and of the images and partially assimilated materials that are the prominent part of what Freud termed the *day residue*, but which we would call the *unfinished business* – the various unresolved issues or incompletely assimilated materials of the child's day-to-day life. Klinger has elaborated on the notion of the "current concerns" that are the major characteristics of adults', as well as children's, dreams and fantasies and the ongoing stream of thoughts [14]. Breger et al. have called attention to the role of unresolved stress in generating dream and fantasy content [15].

In the preparation for sleep, the child, and later the adult, as our research suggests is confronted with a vivid replay of the major unresolved issues of the day, or of the past, and of the anticipations of the following day [8]. Most people learn simple techniques for controlling this vivid upsurge of fantasy enough so that they can fall asleep. For the child it may take a while to master this material. Even if it is not terribly threatening, it may be sufficiently complex so that, when also added to the assimilation problem of the mysterious sights and sounds of the night, the child is likely to be at a higher level of fearfulness and struggle to interpret the strange events in relation to some set of schemas. Probably, the schemas available to the child are those already presented to it by adults. These include the tales of faraway places, religious and supernatural, and the story material already provided children that is difficult to assimilate. Teasing by older children or threats of various kinds by disciplining adults must also be included. All of these probably come together at this point and make it more likely that the child will begin to form new cognitive structures around these odd shapes and sounds. Here we have the basis for the many mythological, fairy tale, and mysterious figures that occur in our fantasies and particularly in our dreams. For the television-reared child, there are also the cartoon characters, talking animals, and strange sights and sounds that cross the screen daily. These may be mixed in with the shadows in the night and become the basis for later "symbolic fantasies."

What we are proposing is that the mythological and symbolic combinations and complex metaphorical characteristics emerging in adult dreams or on the imagery trips that are encouraged during various forms of psychotherapy originate in the complexities of the assimilation process in early childhood [9]. Such a process is never completely over for any of us. We still encounter new patterns of stimulation or new social situations that are not easily matched against our well-established cogntive structures. We, therefore, must puzzle these out or at least relegate them to a category of "unfinished business" so that they are more likely to emerge in our fleeting fantasies, hypnagogic reveries, and during sleep in our dreams. By adulthood we have already many complicated sets of symbols, some of them holdovers from early childhood, but many learned as part of the various allegories and metaphors that have become a part of our culture. The historical figures who represent significant aspects of our religious and historical upbringing, as well as the methodological and supernatural aspects of our particular cultural heritage, are all now available to us for linkage to new problems or unassimilable information. Watkins has elaborated on adults' continuing use of such material in interior dialogues [12].

The complexity of symbolism available to us today is built into our language and our communication media and so surrounds us that one need really make no assumptions of a genetic coding or archetype to explain the multilayered symbolism that emerges in mental imagery techniques and psychotherapy. With advertising men actively providing us with phallic automobiles or symbolic mistresses perched within them, proposing that behind the wheel we become as powerful as cougars, or as energetic as mustangs, what need do we have to assume a racial unconscious? Symbolism pervades our lives as part of our cultural heritage and as part of the very metaphorical characteristics that humans lend to their social organizations. That these should emerge in our ongoing fantasies, once we take the trouble of *carefully attending to them*, should no longer be surprising.

The Special Role of Adults as Mediators of the Child's Environment

Our recent research has been especially directed towards examining the special ways in which parents or other adult care-givers in the family play a critical role in mediating the complexity of the child's physical and social environment [16-18]. An emerging orientation towards work with children and youth undergoing school difficulties pioneered by the Israeli psychologist, Reuven Feuerstein, has suggested that children's abilities to develop learning skills and self-directed effective use of their naturally-developing cognitive capacities depend upon the extent to which their parents have intervened early and continuously in labeling, explaining, and discussing the situations they confront [19, 20]. In our studies we have been particularly concerned with an array of possible family influences (as well as exposure to television) and their role as correlates or predictors of the preschool or early school age child's cognitive, imaginative, and behavioral tendencies. We have, for example, identified a variable based on factor analysis of a series of scales in which parents' reports of how they react to children in a number of natural daily situations (dinner table, visiting, driving) are classified. This bipolar factor score (*Discussion vs Prescription/Discipline*) predicts better cognitive development in information-acquisition, fantasy-reality discrimination, reading readiness, understanding of television etc. In other words, children whose parents describe *themselves* as engaging in more explanation, labeling, reviewing or anticipating events turn out to be showing a more differentiated and adaptive pattern of cognitive and behavioral patterns.

Of particular relevance for children's play and imagination are our findings with respect to imagination [21, 22]. We had earlier observed that, while all children show the early use of imaginative play to produce a miniaturized and hence more assimilable world (thus experiencing interest, joy and a sense of power), such a tendency needs parental acceptance at the very least, or more active encouragement for make-believe to flourish as a cognitive skill [8, 11, 16, 23]. Our own studies and independent ones conducted by Shmukler and by Tower indicate that preschool children of parents who personally value imagination, creativity and story-telling are observed as playing more imaginatively by teachers or objective raters unfamiliar with the parents' values [23-30]. In effect, one major role that parents play as mediators is to encourage and assist children to use pretending games and fantasy as tools for organizing experience. The failure to develop imaginative abilities can put the child and youth at risk of impulsivity, poor planning or limited empathetic tendencies [5, 31, 32]. Such "imagination-impoverished" children present special problems for play therapists and may require special training in fantasy prior to further treatment.

The Special Role of Television in Child Development

In many ways the television set now found in several rooms of practically every American home can be viewed as a new form of input, a part of the home environment which provides the schemas for the growing child's experience in much the same way that exposure to parents and siblings does. Considering the increasing number of families where both parents work, children may be spending more time in the rather passive type of interaction possible with the television rather than in the situation of continuous feedback that characterizes human interaction. What does it mean to grow up in an environment in which figures on a twenty-one-inch screen jump up and down, shout and pummel each other, engage in numerous car chases and crashes and urge children to buy products? The figures on TV sometimes resemble parents and "real" people but often are cartoon representations of animals who talk or superheroes who perform amazing feats. Since considerable research evidence suggests that children are watching adult programming much of the time, they are also being exposed to scenes and values that may distort their understanding of their own roles as children and produce the phenomenon of increasing concern to clinicians as well as developmental psychologists, the "hurried child" [33].

The Special Properties of Television. Research analysis have demonstrated that television in America presents specific cognitive challenges for the preschool or early elementary school age child. It is fast-paced, cuts quickly from scene to scene, and plot material is interrupted by a rapid progression of brief commercials usually backed by lively sound effects and music. A special challenge for researchers is to determine whether exposure to such pacing may have deleterious effects or may simply challenge a child to learn the codes and conventions of the medium, possibly even speeding up their cognitive grasp [34]. Experimental studies demonstrate that young children can lose track of the cause-effect sequence or moral point of an action show when there are commercial interruptions or can be so highly aroused by lively music and fast-paced presentations that they show aggressive behavior even though no aggressive material appears in the program viewed [34, 35]. Only longitudinal studies can tell us whether such effects are cumulative, however.

Family and Television Influences. Researchers increasingly recognize that the impact of television on development must be understood within the broader context of the family setting. Table 1 provides a model of the kinds of

Table 1. Home Influences (Independent Variables) as Predictors of
Cognitive or Behavioral Measures (Dependent Variables) in
Young Children—A Multiple Regression Analysis

Home Influences (Independent Variables)	Cognitive and Behavioral Patterns (Dependent Variables)

1. *Family Characteristics*
a. Parents' self-described values, e.g., Resourcefulness (imagination, curiosity, adventurousness, creativity).
b. Parents' Attitudes toward discipline and child-rearing, e.g., Power-assertive vs. Inductive methods.
c. Parental Mediation Styles: Discussion vs. Prescription.
d. Parents' belief-systems: "Mean and Scary World" test.
e. Family structure and stress level; single-parent family, etc.
f. Daily Life Style
  1. sleep patterns
  2. organized daily routines
  3. diverse cultural activities vs. limited outside activities
  4. emphasis on outdoor sports, etc.
 	
2. *The Television Environment*
a. Average weekly viewing by children.
b. Type of programming, e.g., action-adventure (realistic or fantasy), cartoons, etc.
c. Average weekly viewing by father and mother.
d. Home emphasis on TV, e.g., cable or HBO, number of sets.
e. Television Mediation (Parent report).
f. Television Rules (Child's report)
	1. *Cognition*
	a. Reading scores (Recognition and Comprehension)
	b. Language use
	c. General information
	d. Beliefs ("mean world")
	e. Reality-fantasy discrimination
	
	2. *Imagination*
	a. Inkblots, interview, block play
	
	3. *Comprehension of TV Content*
	a. Swiss Family Robinson plot
	b. Commercial understanding
	c. Television special effects
	
	4. *Waiting Ability*
	a. Spaceman; delaying ability
	b. Motor restlessness during spontaneous waiting period
	
	5. *Physical Aggression*
	
	6. *School Behavioral Adjustment*

family variables as well as television patterns that we believe must be considered if we are to estimate the long-term consequences for the child's cognitive behavioral development of the television set in the home. On the left side we see the variables that constitute the child's environment in the home. These include the parents' own personality characteristics or values, their professed and demonstrated attitudes about child rearing, their own levels of stress and pattern of daily household routine or the variety of cultural activities, emphasis on outdoor activities, requirements of adequate sleep for the child, etc. The television influences may reflect the sheer amount of viewing by the child, the specific programs viewed (which may include the more violent cartoons or action-adventure shows, the programs on public television specifically designed for children, etc.) the extent of parental viewing, the family's valuation of the medium as reflected in the expenditure of funds for more sets for cable or special services like Showtime or HBO, the effort by parents to control the child's viewing. In the right hand column we see a set of psychological functions that research suggests may be influenced by the combination of family and television influences. These include basic cognitive skills such as reading comprehension, language use, the ability to comprehend programming, capacity for imagination, basic belief-systems such as whether one's environment is dangerous or hostile, etc. Behavioral variables include motor restlessness or impulse control, aggression, school adjustment or the so-called prosocial behaviors, sharing, helping cooperation. There is now some research evidence that bears on the role of television and family factors in influencing some of the variables in the right hand column and we shall address these in turn to point out some of the constructive as well as potentially harmful influences of heavy television viewing or of viewing in an uncontrolled fashion.

Cognitive Skills and Patterns. A fairly consistent body of research suggests that children in the elementary school period who spend a great deal of time watching television may not be spending enough time practicing the skills necessary to learn reading or may be learning bad habits that impede interest or perseverance necessary for reading. This finding is especially true for children from middle-class families. For children from lower socioeconomic status backgrounds there are indications from our own research as well as large scale studies at Stanford University and at the University of Pennsylvania that moderate regular exposure to television may enhance interest in reading, especially if parents value curiosity and imagination or educational opportunity [35]. Similar findings emerge for language effectiveness. Some of our own research also suggests that children who watch a great deal of television often do not prove to comprehend the details of plots very well. There are indications that heavy viewing may be related to a tendency to adopt a global, less concentrated and critical viewing attitude. Studies by Salomon in Israel and in the United States provide indications that children invest less mental effort in watching television and hence often acquire less information from the experience than from reading which is a more difficult task [36].

Imagination and Social Reality. While one might assume that television-viewing and exposure to varied plots or characters might provide a rich and varied nutriment for the child's imagination most research evidence does not support this view. Indeed, heavy viewers have been found to be more confused about reality-fantasy distinctions and have also shown less spontaneous imagination in block play or in response to inkblots or other projective stimuli. Imaginativeness apparently requires active practice much as other cognitive skills and children who rely primarily on the television-medium to fill the human need for story-telling seem less adept at initiating their own games [37-39]. In a longitudinal study in which children were followed from ages four until age nine the best predictors of later imaginativeness were *limited* non-violent television-viewing as a preschooler and more recently, as well as a family background in which parents emphasized a diversity of cultural activities and described themselves as valuing imagination and creativity [21, 37].

Television has often been called a "window on the world." But what kind of world is it? Annual studies over almost two decades have shown that the content of television in America can be characterized by an inordinate amount of violence. Heavy viewers of television are likely to begin to incorporate the huge doses of violence and individual victimization that are presented in fiction and on news broadcasts into their own belief-systems and thus assume that their personal neighborhoods are truly "mean and scary places" [40]. Very careful studies of those segments of the population who are most likely to be victims in *fictional* television, e.g., attractive women in their twenties, lower-class men in their thirties to forties demonstrate that the heavy-viewers among them significantly overestimate the actual chances that they will be attacked or robbed in their own milieus. Our own longitudinal studies show that elementary school children who have watched a great deal of violent television, especially the "realistic" police and private eye shows, score higher on measures of belief in a dangerous world [18, 22]. The elderly who often find solace in television are also susceptible to assuming greater dangers for themselves in the streets because of the violence that is emphasized on the news as well as fictional programming [40].

Behavioral Implications of Heavy Television Viewing. There have been many complaints from teachers in the past decade which implicate heavy television viewing in what they consider the excessive restlessness of children, their unwillingness to attend to extended lectures or to sit still long enough to follow written instructions. It is assumed that television may have a consistent arousing effect (as Wright and Huston's [34] experiments suggest) or that children have become used to an entertainment pattern of the kind so frequently seen on television even in educational programs. In a study of children whose television-viewing patterns were obtained in the years from preschool to early elementary school we set up two kinds of observations to test these proposals about restlessness [22]. One measure called for children to sit still as long as possible much as an astronaut would have to do in a space capsule while awaiting blast-off [41].

The length of time the child sat quietly served as a self-control measure. Another technique involved unobtrusive observation of the amount of movement, impatient complaints and restlessness shown by a child while awaiting the beginning of an interview. In both cases heavy television-viewing by the child, especially of more violent programming predicted more restlessness and inability to sit still as much as two or three years later. A similar result, heavy viewing of television predicting poor school behavior, emerged when data were obtained from parents and report cards [22].

By far the greatest attention has been paid to the proposals that heavy viewing of television put children at risk of becoming excessively aggressive. This area has evoked considerable controversy especially since there are vocal groups that have called for boycotts of advertisers who sponsor violent programming. The contrary argument that the vicarious experience of violence may actually reduce viewers' aggressive potential through the catharsis or partial drive-reduction effect associated with early psychoanalytic theories of fantasy has been advanced by some humanists (concerned about censorship) or by some psychoanalysts. A very sizable and consistent body of experimental research pioneered by Albert Bandura with children and Leonard Berkowitz with adults have demonstrated that exposure to filmed violence *increases* subsequent aggressive behavior. Television industry representatives have doubted that laboratory experiments can be generalized to daily behavior. A number of specific longitudinal studies have therefore been carried out in addition to many correlational studies of ordinary viewing and measures of overt aggressive behavior [42].

A long-term study directed by Leonard Eron followed children from ages ten to thirty and demonstrated that heavy early television-viewing was significantly correlated with measures of adult aggressive behavior. Special care was taken in this study to eliminate alternative explanations and to use sophisticated statistical methods to support an interpretation that a causal relationship existed between viewing and aggression [43]. A careful study by William Belson in England came to similar conclusions with a sample of adolescent boys; those who reported engaging in particularly violent acts on a regular basis had also been watching more of the programming involving aggression [44]. In our own studies preschool children were observed at nursery schools over a year's time and were rated for aggressive behavior periodically. Prior heavy viewing and especially of the more violent action-adventure programming was associated with overt aggressive behavior by these children [39]. A recent report of a town in Canada in which television was introduced only relatively recently provided evidence of an increase in children's aggressive behavior *and* reduced imaginative thought [45].

No one would argue that television is the sole or even the major cause of aggressive behavior in children. What is clear is that heavy viewing along with family factors may contribute appreciably to increased aggression. Our own recent research with children observed from preschool to age nine indicates that a combination of heavy preschool viewing, more recent viewing of realistic action-adventure programs and a family pattern in which parents emphasize physical punishment and power assertive child-rearing methods predict later aggression [18, 22, 37]. These findings suggest that clinicians working with disruptive, over-active or aggressive children should look not only at family patterns but also at the home television environment as areas for intervention or for prevention.

The major conclusion that emerges from an extensive scrutiny of television is not that television is inherently dangerous. Rather, a combination of minimal available suitable programming for children, failure of parents to involve themselves early with control of viewing or with interacting to heighten the positive uses of the medium by children have brought about the situation in which heavy viewing puts children at risk for developing poor school attitudes, restlessness, excessive aggressive behavior or a frightened and hostile view of the world.

Critical Viewing Skills: A Preventive Approach

Can some steps be taken to prevent the further development of the noxious potential of television and perhaps enhance its positive use? Some approaches with parents' groups designed to raise consciousness about the medium have been found to be useful. Specific training programs teaching cognitive and imaginative games for parents to play with preschoolers may reduce involvement with television or enhance skills otherwise impeded by heavy viewing [39, 46]. Especially promising have been efforts to introduce programs into the school systems designed to educate children about the nature of the television medium. Lesson plans taught by regular teachers and videotapes for special points explain how television works, the people necessary to produce and act in a show, the way special effects are produced, why certain characters attract children, stereotypes that appear on the medium, the reason there is so much aggression and why it shouldn't be imitated, the nature of TV news as a carefully edited headline service and the functions of commercials [46, 47].

Controlled studies in a number of elementary schools have shown that such lessons do work well in helping children understand the medium and to begin to view it more critically [37]. Long-term effects have yet to be demonstrated but a large number of similar programs are now in use around the nation especially in elementary schools. As suggested earlier, Salomon's concept of amount of invested effort may be a key feature for reversing the negative impact of television. If children with the initial help of parents or teachers can approach the television medium with a critical stance, examining its method and trying to relate what they see to other sources of knowledge a more constructive outcome may emerge from what has clearly become an inherent feature of the growing child's environment.

Before summarizing our presentation of imaginative development let us consider some of the implications of the research on childhood fantasy and television-viewing for the practice of child psychotherapy. We propose that what we have learned about the cognitive-affective nature of play and also about parents' roles as mediators is directly relevant to the play therapy process.

PSYCHOTHERAPEUTIC IMPLICATIONS OF A COGNITIVE-AFFECTIVE APPROACH TO CHILDREN'S IMAGINATIVE DEVELOPMENT

Developmental Levels and Cognitive Capacities

A central assumption of most play therapy is that children, through make-believe transactions, will reveal, either directly or in some symbolic form, their conflicts, unresolved wishes, fears and internalization of parental or sibling concerns [48-51]. The research literature on imaginative development supports this view in the sense that the child will be actively playing and replaying (either overtly or in interior monologue) complex environmental issues and trying to cast them into assimilable, "miniaturized" forms in order to reduce negative effects of anger, distress-sadness or shame-humiliation. But one must realize that such imaginative reproduction will take different forms depending upon the ages, cognitive capacities or levels of imaginative development of the children. Thus, preschoolers or six-year-olds will be more open to floor play and spontaneous make-believe, verbalizing sound effects and conversations. Early school age children may also be agreeable to somewhat more structured play kits where ambiguous but human-appearing blocks such as those developed cross-nationally by Bower et al. can serve as the basis for story-telling [52].

For the middle childhood period direct inquiries about recurrent daydreams, fantasies, night dreams, favorite television shows, films, popular songs or groups, books, legends of historic figures are possible starting points. Because of the heavy dose of television and music videos to which children are exposed one can make a good entrée through asking for favorite programs, characters, or requesting them to provide sample scripts for particular shows. At this age there is also great interest in board games (such as Monopoly). Techniques such as the mutual story-telling of Gardner [53] or the even more elaborate TISKIT (Therapeutic Imaginative Story-Telling Board Game) of Kirtzberg [54] can be especially effective in eliciting recurrent concerns and conflicts from children between eight and twelve years of age.

For adolescents such more overt, "playlike" activities may appear unacceptable except when reinforced by a group process such as one finds in forms of Moreno's Psychodrama. Nevertheless, the story-telling organization of material around family conflicts persists as part of the ongoing stream of consciousness as Klos and Singer found in an experimental study with eighteen-year-olds [55]. We had these "normal" youths enact pre-developed scripts around family scenes, imagining one of their parents seated in an empty chair before them. We found strong evidence that where the artificial script we presented was one of coercive confrontation by a parent the thoughts about this simulated situation persisted strongly well after the end of the playlet. For those participants who had a history of stress in their family lives, the persistence of thoughts about our simulated situation was by far the greatest, suggesting that significant intrafamilial problems may preoccupy adolescents' stream of consciousness.

A special problem for the therapist are the preschool children or even juveniles and early adolescents who have failed to develop their basic capacities for make-believe or for private story-telling. Such is often the case where parents or other caregivers were unavailable for support of early make-believe or, indeed, were disparaging of such activities so that the child felt humiliated by the natural exercize of the imaginative function.

The capacity for daydreaming and fantasizing is a critical cognitive skill, a form of organizing and reorganizing the meanings and action-possibilities of one's experiences [8, 9, 56], a position recently also elaborated by Vandenberg [57]. The child or adolescent who is referred for therapy and who shows a deficiency in this ability may require a period of more active training in make-believe play, story-telling or fantasy (depending on age level). We have developed exercises for enhancing imagination in preschoolers [58, 59]. Techniques for older children are not yet widely available although school drama therapists are moving in this direction [60]. Joint mother–child symbolic play represents still another approach [61]. It appears that one of the major therapeutic functions of play therapy (and of many adult forms of therapy as well) is that it enhances the flexible and varied use of one's imagery capacities for daily problem solving [9].

The Therapist as a Provider of Mediated Learning Opportunities

We have already mentioned our recent studies of parental mediation patterns and their link to the child's cognitive and behavioral development [18]. The very active international movement for training under-achieving or educationally-retarded children using Feuerstein's *Learning Potential Assessment Devices* (for diagnosis) and *Instrumental Enrichment* procedures (for ongoing education) reflects a major step towards making carefully-designed mediated learning a regular feature of a school curriculum [19, 20]. We believe that therapists play such a role by their substitution for an absent, inadequate or troubled parent as the key figure who helps a child identify those features of the complex social milieu that demand attention, therapists provide approval of play efforts to miniaturize such features into assimilable form. They actually teach the child imaginative skills. Delineating key life issues, significant people, and conflicts in play helps the child to develop new schemas and scripts, knowledge structures that will reduce the ambiguity, confusion and consequent fear-terror or other negative effects that occur as new material cannot be readily organized and assimilated.

Research on training children in imaginative play has indicated that an adult needs to move cautiously into such a role. Many children need initial encouragement and "plot material." Once the children are well started, however, the evidence suggests that adults should fade back from too active involvement lest they either dominate the situation and foster passivity or, by creating an ambiguity about the delineation of adult-child role differences, only arouse further anxiety in the child [27, 37, 38].

The Affective Implications of the Therapist's Role

A key feature of the therapist's role, in our opinion, is that of providing a model for the child of a zestful, curious, lively approach to one's experience. While the therapist may often have to avoid moralizing or taking strong judgmental stands about the child's wishes, fantasies, hatreds or about parents', siblings', or the cultural patterns, this doesn't mean that no emotion should be expressed. On the contrary. We do hold values, that, at least in imagery, nothing is unthinkable and alien. A curiosity about the world and one's relationships to it, a willingness to try out in fantasy the many possibilities of human interactions is an exciting and often joyous gift with which we have been endowed. The therapist's own professional curiosity, willingness to share thoughts and play possibilities with the child conveyed in a spirit of liveliness and humor can open the troubled child to the joys of the world of introspection and fantasy. Such an approach can help change the fearful, despairing or angry child (trapped in a world of limited constructs, schemas or scripts) into one who can savor the beginning excitement of reshaping the seemingly "given" world of one's recent experience into one of innumerable possibilities. By replaying and reshaping one's schemas one can gain at least some sense of control and power within a small region of a vast and impenetrable universe. Whatever else we can offer in therapy, the enhancement of the child's ability to be curious and to play imaginatively is a major gift indeed.

A REVIEW OF THE COGNITIVE-AFFECTIVE APPROACH TO CHILDHOOD IMAGINATION

Let us try briefly to summarize the major theoretical points of our position on the origins and implications of imagery and fantasy processes. Imagery reflecting specific inputs from sensory modalities is viewed as one of several major encoding systems that the brain has for organizing and storing experience. It has the special properties of being capable of parallel processing and of providing particularly vivid ongoing reenactments of previous events with the likely arousal of greater affect than the verbal encoding system. The latter has distinct advantages in terms of labeling of material and in terms of its greater abstractness and generalizability. Optimal functioning for both child and adult requires interaction between these two systems with the possibility that interactive combinations of imagery and verbal coding may have separate properties for storage and retrieval [62].

Imagery and fantasy processes that are an extension of specific imagery into chained sequences develop originally out of the accommodation-assimilation cycle in which the child attempts to process information. As an additional feature of this cycle, the assimilated material, in its rehearsal, generates interest and related positive affects of joy as matchings are made with established cognitive schema. Indeed the special attraction of television for children may be the way the vivid imagery and music arouses moderate interest and then resolves things into the familiar without much effort for the viewer.

Much of the symbolism and the bizarre and mythical quality of our ongoing imagery stems from the "faulty assimilation" characteristic of childhood with a limited range of schemas available. Symbolism develops when children, confronted by events inexplicable to them at their levels of experience or cognitive capacity, seek to assimilate these experiences into established schemas "ready made" for them by the adult world. Thus, thunder or lightning, the vastness of the skies or the sea, all are forced into whatever religious, mythological or culturally-generated adult surrogates and forms have already been provided by parents or other adults and, nowadays, by television. Some of these rather forced "linkages" from early childhood, like events in Harry Stack Sullivan's *paratoxic mode* may appear to be forgotten, emerging if at all only in dreams or when adults find themselves in settings that to some degree mirror a childhood situation. The less verbal, generally imagery-based symbols of childhood return to mind more easily when we lie on an analyst's couch, a context comparable to the child with a parent at bedside, or if at a costume party, we dress up like children. What often seems like the "return of the repressed" may actually be a naturally-occurring retrieval of memories, fantasies or childhood symbols induced by a particular setting that lies closer on a stimulus-generalization curve to a stored but relatively poorly "labelled" child experience [9, 63].

The orientation of the individual toward awareness and special attention to his ongoing inner processes plays a key role in the degree to which materials will be elaborated in consciousness and reassimilated into other cognitive structures. The particular set of an individual toward processing and reprocessing such ongoing experiences may depend heavily on social learning within the family setting or cultural orientation toward such activities. The set toward this kind of self-awareness may take a variety of forms, some of which may be worked into a creative endeavor such as writing or painting, but which also may simply function to enhance aesthetic appreciation and, to a great extent, planning ability and role-taking capacities. As our review of the television literature suggests, heavy viewing may impede such effective self-awareness and imagination.

Early humiliation is often experienced in connection with make-believe and fantasy play by children in particular societies or subcultural groups. There is also the practical necessity of attending primarily to external environmental stimuli, including the communications of others. As a consequence of these factors, there is a sharp drop in attention to private processes with increasing age and, particularly, during a period of major adult responsibilities. For this reason, there is frequently a tendency not to pay special attention or to label one's ongoing fantasy activities as such. Hence, people may not have available a retrieval code for recalling that they actually engaged in such fantasy processes earlier in the day or in the past, even in their childhood.

Within the specific psychotherapy setting external conditions are created that are conducive to attending to one's inner processes. Whether therapists realize it or not training in attention to ongoing thought and in symbolic decoding are part of the therapeutic process [9]. In addition, the ability to produce and to report on the images is reinforced by obvious interest from the therapist, so that the individual gains not only gratification from the therapist's support, but also a more private feeling of control over these initially strange-seeming processes. This creates a considerable positive affective situation in relation to ongoing fantasy and becomes the useful part of most of the mental imagery uses for psychotherapeutic purposes [9].

The notion of control is an important one here since there is evidence, as Strupp has pointed out, that a major component of effective psychotherapy is the patient's experience of increased control over emotions and overt behavior [65]. In this sense, heightened awareness of one's ongoing fantasy processes also increases to some degree the extent of control over such processes so that they seem less strange and also can be called into service in connection with particular difficulty or momentary need of the individual. A particular advantage of imagery as a parallel processing transformation system is that it permits detailed scanning of rather specific events. Usually in the therapeutic situation, these events are of an interpersonal nature. The revival of a particular affect that was stored with the initial image also becomes possible. This gives the imagery transformational system special advantages in psychotherapy, which depends greatly upon *in vivo* reproductions of situations that are disturbing and threatening to the individual in his life outside the consulting room [9]. The frequent reference to intellectualizing, as against the advantages of true feeling experiences presented by many clinicians, probably reflects the fact that the verbal encoding system by its very sequential nature is primarily effective in communication of general events or in rapid transformation or retrieval. It is less likely however, to be stored with the special emotional context with which imagery transformations are stored and, therefore, will be less obviously generalized to outside situations. In the various behavior modification approaches to psychotherapy, consequently, the power of imagery has to do with the fact that it brings the subject closer on the generalization curve to the events that are being avoided or need to be controlled systematically as part of the therapeutic aim [9].

The emphasis here is upon the developmental sequences and capacities at particular ages and also on the available social learning and cultural demands placed upon the individual. Imagery and fantasy must be viewed as fundamental cognitive capacities of the organism which have their properties of storage through some form of active reprocessing that we can detect only when we inhibit to some extent our active processing of new external stimuli. These processes carried on privately nevertheless have the same field processes as external stimuli. To the extent to which they are readily assimilable or provide differential degrees of complexity and integration into established cognitive schemas, the private processes arouse positive affects such as interest and joy or negative affects such as anger, distress, and fear. Practical necessities of daily living call upon us to ignore much of the ongoing inner processing in order to function effectively in our relationships with others or to steer ourselves through the physical environment. Yet, it is likely that we can use a much greater share of the ongoing stimulus field provided by our own long-term memory system to establish positive affects and also to become aware of our major motivational tendencies, our significant unfinished businesses, and many other potentials for role rehearsal and advance planning.

Finally, we propose that processes of play therapy must be viewed as extensions of what we have learned from studies of imaginative development and television. The combination of repetitive play and encouragement from the therapist to try new plots or new outcomes enhances the learning of new schemas and scripts. With these cognitive changes, there eventually emerge changes in personality. For younger children therapy recreates the natural floor play of early childhood or, more often, assists the child to revive a neglected skill for pretending and make-believe. For older children board games and story-telling using plots now well-assimilated from television movies or reading are useful for reexamining rigid constructs or maladaptive schemas and forming new scripts about human interactions. Perhaps most critical is the role of the therapist as a new kind of mediator between the child its limited range of schemas and scripts and the new extrafamilial world the child must soon confront. The therapist becomes, in order, a playmate, a teacher and mediator, and finally, a new model (in Kohut's terminology, a new "selfobject"). The therapists' openness to experience, curiosities, warmth and concerns all point the way for children to try new kinds of positive emotions—surprise, excitement, joy and wonder. The intrinsic affects of joy and curiosity that our research have consistently linked to make-believe become the healing ointments that can revive in the deeply distressed child the desire to play, to explore, and to live more fully.

REFERENCES

1. D. Rapaport, On the Psychoanalytic Theory of Motivation, *Nebraska Symposium on Motivation*, *8*, M. R. Jones (ed.), University of Nebraska Press, Lincoln, 1960.

2. D. Rapaport, The Structure of Psychoanalytic Theory: A Systematizing Attempt, *Psychological Issues*, *6*, International Universities Press, New York, 1960.
3. H. Kreitler and S. Kreitler, *Cognition Orientation and Behavior*, Springer, New York, 1976.
4. S. S. Tomkins, *Affect, Imagery, Consciousness* (2 vols.), Springer, New York, 1962, 1963.
5. J. L. Singer, *The Human Personality*, Harcourt Brace Jovanovich, San Diego, 1984.
6. C. E. Izard, *Human Emotions*, Plenum, New York, 1977.
7. P. Ekman and W. V. Friesen, *Unmasking the Face*, Prentice-Hall, Englewood Cliffs, New Jersey, 1975.
8. J. L. Singer, *Daydreaming*, Random House, New York, 1966.
9. ____, *Imagery and Daydream Methods in Psychotherapy and Behavior Modification*, Academic Press, New York, 1974.
10. J. Piaget, *Play, Dreams and Imitation in Childhood*, Norton, New York, 1962.
11. J. L. Singer, *The Child's World of Make-believe: Experimental Studies of Imaginative Play*, Academic Press, New York, 1973.
12. M. Watkins, *Invisible Guests. The Development of Imaginal Dialogues*, Analytic Press, Hillsdale, New Jersey, 1986.
13. H. Werner and B. Kaplan, *Symbolic Realization*, Wiley, New York, 1963.
14. K. Klinger, *Structure and Function of Fantasy*, Wiley, New York, 1970.
15. L. Breger, I. Hunter, and R. W. Cane, *The Effect of Stress on Dreams*, International Universities Press, New York, 1971.
16. D. G. Singer and J. L. Singer, Parents as Mediators of Child's Television Environment, *Educational Media International*, *4*, pp. 7-11, 1984.
17. J. L. Singer and D. G. Singer, Psychologists Look at Television: Cognitive Developmental, Personality and Social Policy Implications, *American Psychologist*, *38*, pp. 826-834, 1983.
18. R. J. Desmond, J. L. Singer, D. G. Singer, R. Calam, and K. Colimore, Family Mediation Patterns and Television Viewing. Young Children's Use and Grasp of the Medium, *Human Communication Research*, *11*:4, pp. 461-480, 1985.
19. R. Feuerstein, Mediated Learning Experience: A Theoretical Basis for Cognitive Modifiability During Adolescence, in *Research to Practice in Mental Retardation, Vol. II: Education and Training*, P. Mittler (ed.), University Park Press, Baltimore, 1977.
20. ____, *Instrumental Enrichment*, University Park Press, Baltimore, 1980.
21. J. L. Singer, D. G. Singer, and W. Rapaczynski, Children's Imagination as Predicted by Family Patterns and Television Viewing: A Longitudinal Study, *Genetic Psychology Monographs*, *110*, pp. 43-69, 1984.
22. ____, Family Patterns and Television-viewing as Predictors of Children's Beliefs and Aggression, *Journal of Communication*, *34*, pp. 73-89, 1984.
23. D. G. Singer and J. L. Singer, Family Television Viewing Habits and the Spontaneous Play of Preschool Children, *American Journal of Orthopsychiatry*, *46*, pp. 446-502, 1976.

24. D. Shmukler, "An Investigation into Some of the Familial and Home Background Correlates of Imaginative Play in Children," unpublished Doctoral dissertation, University of Witwatersrand, Johannesburg, 1977.

25. _____, Mother-Child Interaction and Its Relationship to the Predisposition of Imaginative Play, *Genetic Psychology Monographs, 104*, pp. 205-225, 1981.

26. _____, A Descriptive Analysis of Television Viewing in South African Preschoolers and Its Relationship to Their Spontaneous Play, *South African Journal of Psychology, 11*, pp. 105-110, 1981.

27. _____, A Factor Analytic Model of Elements of Creativity in Preschool Children, *Genetic Psychology Monographs, 105*, pp. 25-39, 1982.

28. _____, Preschool Imaginative Play Disposition and Its Relationship to Subsequent Third Grade Assessment, *Imagination, Cognition and Personality, 2*, pp. 231-240, 1982-1983.

29. R. B. Tower, Parents' Self-concepts and Preschool Children's Behaviors, *Journal of Personality and Social Psychology, 39*, pp. 710-718, 1980.

30. _____, "The Influence of Parents' Values on Preschool Children's Behaviors," unpublished Doctoral dissertation, Yale University, New Haven, 1980.

31. J. L. Singer, Imagination and Make-believe Play in Early Childhood: Some Educational Implications, *Journal of Mental Imagery, 1*, pp. 127-144, 1977.

32. _____, The Powers and Limitations of Television: A Cognitive-affective Analysis, in *The Entertainment Function of Television*, P. Tannenbaum and R. Abels (eds.), Erlbaum Associates, Hillsdale, New Jersey, 1980.

33. D. Elkind, *The Hurried Child*, Addison Wesley, Boston, 1983.

34. J. C. Wright and A. C. Huston, A Matter of Form: Potentials of Television for Young Viewers, *American Psychologist, 38*, pp. 835-843, July 1983.

35. M. Morgan and L. Gross, Television and Educational Achievement and Aspiration, in *Television and Behavior: Ten Years of Scientific Progress and Implications for the Eighties*, D. Pearl, L. Bouthilet, and J. Lazar (eds.), U.S. Printing Office, Washington, D.C., 1982.

36. G. Salomon, Television Watching and Mental Effort: A Social Psychological View, in *Children's Understanding of Television*, J. Bryant and D. Anderson (eds.), Academic Press, New York, 1983.

37. J. L. Singer and D. G. Singer, Fostering Creativity in Children: Can TV Stimulate Imaginative Play? *Journal of Communication, 26*, pp. 74-80, 1976.

38. _____, Imaginative Play in Early Childhood: Some Experimental Approaches, in *Child Personality and Psychopathology*, A. Davis (ed.), Wiley, New York, 1976.

39. _____, *Television, Imagination and Aggression: A Study of Preschoolers*, Lawrence Erlbaum Associates, Hillsdale, New Jersey, 1981.

40. R. P. Hawkins and S. Pingree, Television's Influence on Social Reality, in *Television and Behavior: Ten Years of Scientific Progress and Implications for the Eighties*, D. Pearl, L. Bouthilet, and J. Lazar (eds.), U.S. Printing Office, Washington, D.C., 1982.

41. J. L. Singer, Imagination and Waiting Behavior in Young Children, *Journal of Personality, 29*, pp. 396, 413, 1961.

42. L. R. Huesmann, Television Violence and Aggressive Behavior, in *Television and Behavior: Ten Years of Scientific Progress and Implications for the*

Eighties, D. Pearl, L. Bouthilet, and J. Lazar (eds.), U.S. Government Printing Office, Washington, D.C., 1982.

43. L. R. Huesmann, L. D. Eron, M. M. Lefkowitz, and L. O. Walder, Stability of Aggression over Time and Generations, *Developmental Psychology*, *20*:6, pp. 1120-1134, 1984.
44. W. Belson, *Television Violence and the Adolescent Boy*, Saxon House, Hampshire, England, 1978.
45. T. M. Williams, *The Impact of Television. A Natural Experiment in Three Communities*, Academic Press, Orlando, Florida, 1986.
46. D. G. Singer, J. L. Singer, and D. M. Zuckerman, *Getting the Most out of Television*, Scott Foresman and Company, Glenview, Illinois, 1981.
47. _____, *Teaching Television, How to Use TV to Your Child's Advantage*, Dial Press, New York, 1981.
48. F. H. Allen, *Psychotherapy with Children*, Norton, New York, 1942.
49. V. M. Axline, *Dibs in Search of Self*, Houghton Mifflin, Boston, 1964.
50. _____, *Play Therapy: The Inner Dynamics of Childhood*, Houghton Mifflin, Boston, 1947.
51. D. Winnicott, *Playing and Reality*, Basic Books, New York, 1971.
52. E. Bower, A. Ilgaz-Conden, and K. Noori, Measurement of Play Structures: Cross-cultural Considerations, *Journal of Cross-cultural Psychology*, *13*, pp. 315-329, 1982.
53. R. Gardner, *Therapeutic Communication with Children: The Mutual Story Telling Technique*, Jason Aronson, New York, 1971.
54. N. Kritzberg, *Structured Therapeutic Game Method of (Child) Analytic Therapy*, Grune and Stratton, New York, 1975.
55. D. Klos and J. L. Singer, Determinants of the Adolescent's Ongoing Thought Following Simulated Parental Confrontation, *Journal of Personality and Social Psychology*, *41*, pp. 97-98, 1981.
56. J. L. Singer, *Daydreaming and Fantasy*, Oxford University Press, London and New York, 1981.
57. B. Vanderberg, Play, Logic and Reality, *Imagination, Cognition and Personality*, *3*:4, pp. 353-364, 1983-1984.
58. D. G. Singer and J. L. Singer, *Partners in Play*, Harper and Row, New York, 1977.
59. _____, *Make Believe*, Scott Foresman and Company, Glenview, Illinois, 1984.
60. H. S. Rosenberg and P. Picciotti, Imagery in Creative Drama, *Imagination, Cognition and Personality*, *3*, pp. 69-76, 1983-1984.
61. H. J. S. DeLoache and B. Plaetzer, *Tea for Two: Joint Mother-Child Symbolic Play*, paper presented at the meeting of the Society for Research in Child Development, Toronto, April 1985.
62. J. G. Seaman, Imagery Codes and Human Information Retrieval, *Journal of Experimental Psychology*, 1972.
63. S. S. Tomkins, A Theory of Memory, in *Cognition and Affect*, J. S. Antrobus (ed.), Little Brown and Company, Boston, 1970.
64. H. H. Strupp, Specific vs. Non-specific Factors in Psychology and the Problem of Control, *Archives of General Psychiatry*, *23*, pp. 393-401, 1970.

CHAPTER 7

Social Cognition and Social Competence in Childhood through Adolescence

LAWRENCE A. KURDEK

After a long history of studying how children reason about their physical world [1], developmentalists have begun to investigate systematically how children reason about themselves, other people, social relations, social groups, and institutions [2, 3]. The purpose of this chapter is to provide a selective overview of developmental research regarding social cognition, social competence, and the link between social cognition and social competence. Problems in these areas will be identified and recommendations will be made for future research.

THE NATURE AND DEVELOPMENT OF SOCIAL COGNITION

Social cognition is a multidimensional construct [4], and several particular dimensions of this construct have been investigated from a developmental perspective. Shantz has described these dimensions as 1) conceptions of other people and oneself as psychological organisms, 2) conceptions of relations between individuals, and 3) conceptions of social groups, social rules, and social roles [3].

One of the focuses of current work in each of these areas is charting the course of normal development. However, efforts to delineate clearly at what particular age specific skills are normally acquired have been complicated by findings of wide individual differences in group performance as well as findings that task difficulty is greatly affected by task characteristics. The broad developmental trends which will be presented below, therefore, should be regarded as tentative. (See Shantz for a detailed presentation of research in each area [3].)

Conceptions of Others and Self

Studies of how children at differing ages view other people as psychological organisms have considered how children spontaneously describe other people (person perception) [5, 6]; how accurately children infer the thoughts, visual percepts, and feelings of other people (perspective taking) [7, 8]; and how children ascribe causes to the behavior of other people (causal attribution) [9-11]. Although recent studies suggest that preschool children possess rudimentary social cognitive skills in these areas in simple situations, strong developmental trends have been consistently obtained.

A major qualitative shift in the development of social cognitive skills occurs in the early elementary school years. By about nine years of age children provide abstract/inferential rather than concrete descriptions of themselves and other people and include explanations as well as descriptions into their spontaneous accounts of what another person is like [12]. Children at this age also are able to infer the thoughts and knowledge of another person which differ from those held by the children themselves [13, 14]. Adolescents are likely to use qualifying terms when describing other people; to compare people along psychological dimensions; to be aware that specific behaviors are often evident only in special situations [5, 12]; to take the visual perspective of another person which requires coordinating left-right and before-behind spatial relations [15, 16]; and to discount the importance of a given causal attribution if other more plausible causes are also evident [9].

Conceptions of Relations Between Individuals

Investigations of children's conceptions of interpersonal relations have focused primarily on describing age-related changes in children's views of authority/leadership and friendship. Information on developmental changes in children's ideas about authority/leadership has come from interview studies of preschoolers to adolescents by Damon, Selman, Laupa and Turiel, and Tisak [17-20]. Preschoolers do not make a distinction between their own needs and wants and those of the person in authority. Rather, the two are seen as being equivalent. Six- and seven-year-olds see authority as being legitimized first by physical coercion and then by special talents or abilities. By about nine years, children hold a bilateral view of authority. Here, authority is legitimized on a reciprocal or contractual basis between the leader and those being governed. Finally, adolescents view the leader as a symbol of group concerns who structures and organizes functions of the social group. In studies of children's conceptions of peer, adult, and parent authority, children have been found not to have unitary orientations toward authority in that they evaluated the legitimacy of authority based on age and social position of the authority figure, as well as the content of the commands issued [19, 20].

Stages of children's conceptions of friendship have also been based on interview data of preschoolers through adolescents [17, 18, 21, 22]. Preschoolers perceive friends as someone with whom one can play or have fun. Friendships are based on physical proximity and are transient. By about age nine, friends are seen as providers of help or assistance in time of need. Friends are also someone whom one can trust. More reciprocal views of friendship emerge by early adolescence. Here, friendships are seen as requiring an adjustment and coordination of two persons' likes and dislikes. By about age fifteen, friendship is seen as involving the sharing of innermost thoughts and feelings, especially about peer relationship issues [23]. As such, friendship becomes a stable interpersonal process which persists in the face of geographical distance.

Conceptions of Social Groups, Social Rules, and Social Roles

Children's knowledge about social group structure and cohesion has primarily been studied from the vantage point of children's knowledge of dominance hierarchies and affective bonds between group members [3]. Preschoolers generally show low agreement among themselves in classifying peers along a dominance hierarchy. Elementary school-aged children and adolescents, on the other hand, show much greater consistency [24, 25]. Social power, then, seems to be a salient dimension of group structure among older children. Social likability, however, is an important component of group structure for even young children. There is high consensus even among preschoolers on who likes whom [26].

Research on children's understanding of social rules has been oriented around identifying sequential stages in the understanding of how social rules regulate social behavior [17, 27-29]. The social rules studied regard conventions regarding forms of address, mode of dress, cross gender behavior, sex-typed occupations, patterns of family living in different cultures, and mode of eating. Interviews with preschoolers through adults have yielded a strong developmental trend toward both seeing social conventions as one means of achieving behavioral uniformity in social situations and recognizing that social conventions are necessary for the regulation of social behavior. Moreover, reasoning about social conventions is distinct from reasoning about moral issues and issues not involving social relations [30, 31].

Most of the research on children's understanding of social roles has centered on family roles and sex roles. Even preschoolers are aware that roles can be differentiated on the basis of power and function. Thus, parents are seen as having more power than children and mothers' and fathers' actions may be perceived in terms of traditional male (instrumental) and female (expressive) modes [32]. Major developmental changes occur in children's understanding of the stability and constancy of social roles. It is only at about age seven that children recognize that a single person can occupy two or more roles (e.g., a woman can be both a doctor and a mother), and that maintaining a role is independent of superficial physical transformations (a woman retains her role as mother even when she dons the garb of doctor) [33]. Only by adolescence is a family defined in terms of two essential role relations, spousal and parent roles [34].

Developmental differences in children's understanding of social roles have been studied recently in the contexts of adoption and divorce. Brodzinsky, Singer, and Braff and Brodzinsky, Schechter, and Brodzinsky used an open-ended interview to study children's knowledge of four aspects of adoption that included the nature of the adoptive family relationship; the role of the agency as intermediary in the adoption process; motives for adopting; and motives for placing a child for adoption [35, 36]. Adopted and nonadopted four- through thirteen-year-olds were interviewed, and their responses showed clear systematic changes with development. With age, children's knowledge became increasingly differentiated and integrated into a more general matrix of social and nonsocial knowledge.

Most preschoolers, even adopted ones, were unlikely to understand much about adoption. By six years of age, most children differentiated between birth and adoption as alternative paths to parenthood and acknowledged the permanence of the adoptive family relationship. Although eight- to eleven-year-olds appreciate the uniqueness of adoptive families, they may not see them as permanent because of the biological parent's potential for reclaiming the child. By adolescence, however, adoption is viewed as involving a legal transfer of parental rights and responsibilities from the biological to the adoptive parents, and the adoption agency is seen as playing an intermediary part in this process. Generally, children's mature understanding of adoption was positively related to psychological adjustment.

Also using open-ended interviews, Kurdek found strong developmental effects in six-through eighteen-year-olds' understanding of their parents' divorces [37]. Compared to younger children, older children reasoned about parental divorce in terms that were inferential, abstract, and psychological (e.g., incompatibility and emotional distance); were aware of interparent conflict; provided balanced descriptions of both parents (i.e., provided *both* positive and negative attributes); separated the divorced status of their parents from their own peer group status; and enumerated both good and bad consequences of the divorce. Mature reasoning about the divorce has also been positively related to psychological adjustment [38].

ISSUES AND PROBLEMS IN THE STUDY OF SOCIAL COGNITION

Despite the short period of time during which social cognition has been an active area of developmental research, much has been learned about how specific social cognitive skills change with age. Future work in the area, however, needs to address some major problems of previous research [3, 7, 8, 22, 23, 39, 40] in the areas of measurement, research design, and theory.

Measurement

Much work remains to be done in constructing reliable and valid measures of social cognition that are appropriate for use with subjects across the life span. Although recent efforts have been directed at validating objective measures of social cognition (moral judgment [41, 42], attribution [43], and interpersonal understanding [44]), the fact remains that the most widely used tasks of social cognition have questionable reliability and validity [5, 8, 39, 45]. The validity issue has specifically centered around convergent validity (do similar tasks tap the same construct?) and ecological validity (do the tasks mirror children's actual real-life social situations?). Regarding the former, there have been consistent findings that similar measures of social cognition are not highly intercorrelated [3, 7, 8, 13, 45]. Such findings indicate that specific social cognitive skills such as perspective taking and person perception are themselves multidimensional constructs. The particular dimensions of these constructs need to be identified before tasks can be constructed to measure them. In short, conceptual analysis needs to precede and to provide a foundation for task construction [39, 46, 47].

Questions about the ecological validity of social cognitive assessments have been raised because many of the tasks require that children reason about hypothetical situations. While the issue of hypothetical versus real-life reasoning has been investigated [3], data are inconsistent as to whether or not one type of reasoning is more advanced than the other. Nonetheless, it is encouraging that several investigators have devised assessments of social cognition which occurs in the context of actual peer interactions [48-50].

Research Design

Given that the focus of most social cognitive developmental research has been the description of developmental change, it is surprising that few longitudinal studies have been undertaken. With the exception of the moral judgment literature, longitudinal studies of social cognition have been primarily one or two year follow-up studies (e.g.; [18, 51, 52]). More extensive longitudinal designs are needed to provide a fuller account of both age-related changes in the structure and organization of social cognition as well as the stability, consistency, and sequencing of social cognition.

Even though longitudinal studies would provide information about age changes which would complement nicely existing information about age differences derived from cross-sectional studies, experimental studies are needed to provide more insight into possible determinants of social cognitive change. To date, most experimental studies have been training studies designed to induce change in social cognition. While several studies indicate that perspective taking and social problem-solving can be advanced through training [3], two issues remain. First, naturalistic studies of social cognitive development need to be paired with experimental studies of social cognitive change in order to assess whether information about how social cognition *can* change in the laboratory setting actually mirrors how it *does* occur in a natural setting [53]. Second, intervention strategies used in training studies need to move away from a treatment package approach to an identification of what specific components (e.g., didactic training, modeling, role playing, peer conflict) lead to what specific changes [54]. Studies comparing different strategies of social cognitive change in a single study would be most informative [55]. Adding a long-term follow up assessment would provide needed information on the stability and generalizability of experimentally induced training.

Theory

The amount of research specifically devoted to the construction of developmental models of social cognition pales in comparison to the number of empirical studies [56, 57]. It could be argued that the field of social cognitive development is not yet mature enough to warrant the derivation of a general theory of social cognitive growth. This view is supported by the derivation of models of social cognitive growth in circumscribed areas such as person perception [5], perspective taking and interpersonal reasoning [18], causal inferences [9], self understanding [2], interpersonal problem solving [58], social conventions [28], and control beliefs [59]. A general theory of social cognitive growth would need to weave together common threads which run throughout these separate areas of investigation such as the nature of the relation between physical and social cognition [60]; the acquisition, sequencing, and monitoring of social information [61, 62]; the nature and explanation of gender differences [63]; the influence of family context [64] and social context [65]; and the relevance of personality and cognitive style factors [66, 67].

THE NATURE OF SOCIAL COMPETENCE

Despite some laudable attempts to provide a taxonomy of skills reflective of social competence [68], researchers have had difficulty agreeing on a single definition of social competence that is adequate for a range of developmental periods [69-72]. This problem will be dealt with in this review by focusing on a more circumscribed aspect of social competence: social status as indexed by grade school children's peer nominations and peer ratings [73]. There are two justifications for this decision. First, there is consistent evidence that children's peer relationship problems are related to and predictive of later adjustment problems [74-76]. Second, there is currently a strong interest in both providing reliable assessments of children's social status and constructing multivariate profiles of the social behaviors and social cognitive skills of children with different types of social status.

Much attention has been directed at ways of reliably assessing children's social status [77-86]. Much of the discussion has centered around 1) the relative usefulness of peer nominations versus peer ratings (i.e., having a child name his/her best friends versus having a child rate how much he/she likes each classmate); 2) the advantages of collecting both positive and negative nominations or ratings (e.g., asking a child to name classmates he/she likes as well as dislikes); and 3) the validation of social status typologies. There is some consensus on how these issues are best resolved.

Gresham has provided evidence that rating scale measures and peer nomination measures assess different dimensions of social status [85]. Based on analysis of ratings, nominations, and behavioral observations of third- and fourth-grade children, Gresham concluded that nominations tap a child's choice of high-priority playmates or best friends whereas ratings tap overall acceptability into the peer group. Thus, nominations provide a specific estimate of dyadic intimacy whereas ratings provide a general estimate of peer likability.

The fact that data relevant to children's acceptance and rejection by peers are only slightly negatively correlated indicates that the profile of the rejected child is not the direct reversal of that of the accepted child [80]. More importantly, the collection of both acceptance and rejection information allows for a more complete dimensionalization of social status. In particular, this procedure allows one to differentiate among types of nonaccepted children [86-91]. Peery first recommended that researchers combine rejection and acceptance nominations into a social impact score (the sum of both types of nominations) and a social preference score (the difference between acceptance and rejection scores) [86]. Joint consideration of high and low scores on both social impact and social preference scores allows one to categorize children into one of four mutually exclusive groups: popular (high impact, high preference), rejected (high impact, low preference), isolated (low impact, low preference), and amiable (low impact, high preference). Because the size of children's peer groups varies from grade to grade, Coie et al. have recommended that researchers standardize social impact, social preference, like, and dislike scores within grades to categorize children into the following five social status categories [80]: popular (social preference >0, like >0, and dislike <0); rejected (social preference >-1, like <0, and dislike >0), neglected (social impact <-1, like and dislike <0), controversial (social impact >1, like and dislike >0), and average (social preference between $-.5$ and $.5$).

The results of several studies clearly indicate differences among the behavioral profiles of children in these social status categories [80, 88, 90-93]. Generally, popular children are seen by other children as being cooperative, possessing leadership skills, being nondisruptive, and being unlikely either to start a fight or to seek help. Rejected children are seen as uncooperative, not possessing leadership skills, disruptive, and likely both to start fights and to seek help. Rejected children are also rated by both teachers and parents as having more problems than popular, neglected, or average children, and rate themselves as more lonely than children from these other status categories. Neglected children are seen as shy. Controversial children represent a blend of positive and negative characteristics. While they are seen as acting as leaders, they are also seen as being shy, disruptive, starting fights, and seeking help. Gender and racial effects do not appear to be pervasive, although boys are more likely than girls to be categorized as rejected, and whites are more likely than blacks to be categorized as popular but less likely than blacks to be categorized as controversial.

ISSUES AND PROBLEMS IN THE STUDY OF SOCIAL STATUS

As indicated above, recent work has begun to dimensionalize the heterogenous group of "unpopular" or "nonaccepted" children. Nonetheless, not much is known about the long-term stability and generalizability of children's social status derived from a classroom context. Two recent studies do shed some light on these issues. In one five-year longitudinal study, Coie and Dodge found moderate continuity for third- and fifty-graders' social status, with the strongest continuity being obtained for the rejected group [91]. Similar findings were obtained by Newcomb and Bukowski over a two-year period [94]. Dodge and Coie and Kupersmidt found that second- and fourth-grade boys' social status generalized to a new group of unfamiliar peers [88, 89]. Again, the generalizability was strongest for the rejected group. Thus, although the data are not extensive, there is some suggestion that children's social status derived from a classroom context is stable and generalizable to other settings. This is especially true for rejected children.

It is clear from the above that assessments of social status have become more sophisticated. Because ethical concerns over obtaining negative nominations or ratings appear unfounded [95], work in this area can be expected to advance vigorously (e.g., [96]). Several directions are promising. First, methodological improvements in assessments are likely to continue. Bukowski and Newcomb suggest that measures of peer relations include how *variably* a child is regarded by peers [97], and Hymel cautions that the stability of peer acceptance and rejection may partially be a function of affective bias in peer perceptions (e.g., giving liked peers the benefit of the doubt) [98]. Second, our understanding of how social status is derived or maintained has been increased by studies with a process orientation that enables an examination of reciprocal effects. For example, Coie and Dodge note that aggressive rejected boys may develop a reputation for being aggressive which contributes to reactions among these boys' peers which in turn facilitates the likelihood of future aggressive interactions [91]. Clearly, the relation between labeling and social status and the possible adaptive function of negative peer status deserve close study. Third, given the importance of contextual linkages, it is also of interest to investigate the extent to which children's classroom social status generalizes to non-classroom settings such as the family, neighborhood, and community. Kurdek and Lillie found that popular and neglected children had more neighborhood friends than either rejected or average children, and that neglected children had more younger neighborhood friends than did average children. These findings suggest that the neighborhood context might buffer some of the negative characteristics of the classroom context, at least for neglected children [99]. Finally, developmental changes in the nature, stability, and generalizability of children's social status need to be more comprehensively studied in children both younger and older than the elementary school-aged children already studied.

THE RELATION BETWEEN SOCIAL COGNITION AND SOCIAL STATUS

One of the most complex areas of current social cognitive developmental research is the nature of the link between social cognition and social behavior. From a basic science standpoint, the study of social cognition is worthy of investigation in and of itself. From an applied standpoint, however, the study of social cognition gains in importance if it can be shown to be reliably related to actual social behavior. In this section of the chapter, two questions are of interest: Do children of varying types of social status have differing levels of social cognitive skills? and Can children's social cognitive deficits be remedied so that their actual social behavior is changed? Research related to these two questions will be reviewed in turn.

Social Cognitive Correlates of Social Status

Identifying social cognitive correlates of social status has been approached from complementary quantitative and qualitative strategies. From the quantitative perspective, one correlates children's social status scores (such as number of positive/negative nominations or peer-rating score) with their scores obtained on tasks of social cognition. The results of these kinds of studies have been consistent with a skills deficit position: Children with unfavored peer status have poorly developed social cognitive skills. In particular, children with favored peer status relative to children with unfavored peer status are more adept at knowing how to initiate a friendship, communicating effectively, integrating themselves into a group conversation, knowing peer norms and values, inferring and vicariously experiencing others' affective states, constructing effective alternative interpersonal goals, monitoring their social impact, matching their social skills to the demands of a particular situation, assessing their own level of social competence, and reasoning about interpersonal relations [44, 69, 100-106].

Two qualitative approaches to identifying the social cognitive correlates of social status have been used, but neither has been used extensively. One approach builds on the above quantitative approach by comparing the social cognitive skills of children from differing social status categories. Six studies have used this approach, and have generally found that popular children have well-developed social-cognitive skills. Rubin compared the social problem-solving skills of isolated, sociable, and normal groups of children [107]. Compared to sociable children, isolated children were found to use more aggressive and defensive strategies and were more likely to seek adult intervention in resolving peer conflict. Dodge, Murphy, and Buchsbaum found that rejected and neglected children were less accurate than popular children in detecting prosocial and accidental behavior, and that the errors made by rejected and neglected children were biased toward hostile attributions [108]. Peery compared the affective perspective taking skills of popular, amiable, isolated, and rejected children [86]. The highest scores on this task were attained by the popular children, the lowest scores by the rejected children. When differences among the other groups were examined, isolated childrens' scores were not significantly different from those of popular children, and amiable children's scores were not significantly different from those of rejected children. Kurdek and Lillie found that popular children had better developed compromising skills than rejected or average children [99], and Stiefvater, Kurdek, and Allik found that popular children had higher social problem-solving scores (means-end thinking) than rejected, neglected, or average children [109]. On the basis of behavioral observations which focused on social interactions with both a best friend and a stranger, Gottman divided his sample of three- to six-year-olds into two groups: one in which children "hit it off" with a stranger and the other which children did not [106]. Compared to children in the second group, children in the first group were more likely to clarify messages, to employ weak forms of demands in conflict resolution, and to reciprocate humor with their best friends.

The second qualitative approach utilizes the clinical case study. Here, isolated or aggressive children's social cognitive skills are studied in depth. The few reports available consistently indicate that isolated or aggressive children have markedly delayed self-reflection, perspective taking, and interpersonal reasoning skills [18, 50, 110-112].

Social Cognitive Interventions with Negative Social Status Children

Based on the above studies, one can conclude that children with negative social status (isolated or rejected children) are deficient in their level of social cognition. Because the above studies are correlational, the causal relation between social cognition and social status cannot be assessed. Such a relation can be assessed, however, in intervention studies where training in social cognitive skills is provided to children experiencing relationship difficulties. The general effectiveness of social cognitive intervention has been critically evaluated by Ladd [113], Ladd and Mize [58], Schneider and Byrne [114], Urbain and Kendall [115], and Weissberg [116]. Its use with isolated or withdrawn children has been discussed by Conger and Keane and Wanlass and Prinz [73, 117]. These reviewers agree that training children, especially isolated or withdrawn children, on social problem-solving skills is a promising intervention strategy. They also point out, however, that work in this area is flawed on both conceptual and methodological grounds.

The major conceptual problem has been the definition of social cognitive skill and social competence. While each of the reviewers acknowledges the diversity of definitions used, they exhort future researchers to define clearly the terms to be used and to present a conceptual justification for the choice of one skill or behavior over another. Bierman's work in the area of conversational skills training is an excellent illustration of this approach [118, 119]. The methodological issues involve the use of clinical versus nonclinical samples, choice of an appropriate control group, the need for multiple outcome measures and overt measures of behavioral adjustment, the need for refined measures of social cognition, the need to specify the process of intervention, the need to begin comparing the relative effectiveness of various treatment strategies (e.g., operant, structured activity, modeling, coaching, and peer socialization), the necessity of building long-term follow-up assessments into the design of the study, and the use of post-intervention measures which are not identical to those used in either pre-testing or intervention to assess the generalizability of effects.

ISSUES IN STUDYING THE RELATION BETWEEN SOCIAL COGNITION AND SOCIAL STATUS

Issues in the study of the relation between social thought and social behavior have been previously discussed particularly in reference to the relation between moral judgment and moral behavior [67, 120], empathy and aggression [3], and perspective taking and prosocial behavior [40, 121, 122]. The intent here is to expand on issues raised in these reviews in the context of the study of the link between social cognition and social status.

Most of the research done in the area of social cognitive development is derived from a cognitive-developmental model. Consequently, the focus of study centers on how children's social reasoning is structured and organized, how that structure and organization undergoes qualitative shifts with age, and whether or not these changes follow a progressive, hierarchical, invariant developmental sequence. From this structural perspective, the link between social cognition and social status could be examined from a "necessary but not sufficient" viewpoint. That is, levels of social cognition set the stage for certain types of social status, but additional factors interact with social cognition to influence or to determine the nature of social status. Staub, for example, states that while helping behavior is related to one's ability to assume the perspective of the person needing help, the actual execution of helping behavior is also influenced by the degree of need for help, the extent to which providing help can be diffused among group members, the amount of decision making and initiative required, the perceived costs of helping, and positive or negative consequences associated with helping behavior undertaken or observed in the past [123]. More recently, Eisenberg has presented a model of prosocial action that is directed at alleviating another's need. The components of the model include attention to another's need; motivational factors; hierarchies of personal goals; the intention to assist; the link between intention and behavior; and the consequences of prosocial behavior [67]. Similarly, Ford identifies several governing processes involved in the attainment of social goals [52]. These include directive processes (goal directedness, interest in social goals), regulatory processes (empathy and consideration of consequences), and control processes (social and nonsocial goal capabilities, goal improvement ideas, and means-end thinking). Staub's, Eisenberg's and Ford's multivariate models can be viewed as expansions of Flavell's information processing model of interpersonal inference [124]. According to this model, one must first recognize the existence of covert psychological processes in others, recognize that the current situation elicits the need for inferring what that process is in another person, accurately carry out the inferential process, and then apply the information gleaned to the situation at hand. The critical point addressed by each of these models is that social cognition is *only one* of many components involved in the production of social behavior. From a bivariate standpoint, then, one should not expect strong correlations between social cognition and social status because social status is too complex and varied a phenomenon to be explained by a single factor or even a single set of factors. On the other hand, from a multivariate standpoint, one should expect social cognition to explain some variability in social status that is not explained by other factors. Simply put, social cognition is a necessary but not sufficient condition for social status.

It is clear from the above review that some progress has been made in justifying the use of social cognitive interventions with children experiencing interpersonal difficulties. However, much work needs to be done in identifying which children will and will not benefit from a social cognitive intervention. Given that social cognition is only one cog in the large wheel of factors related to social competence, it is likely that not all children with social difficulties will benefit from an intervention which focuses exclusively on the building of social cognitive skills. A better type of intervention would be one which is preceded by assessments of children's abilities at each of Flavell's levels of existence, need, inference, and application [124]. Such a diagnostic procedure would help pinpoint what skill or set of skills need to be engendered or strengthened. A case in point is the differential effectiveness of social cognitive intervention with isolated versus aggressive children [73, 117]. Isolated children might need to bolster the development of particular social cognitive skills whereas aggressive children might have well developed social skills but tend to use them ineffectively or in inappropriate situations.

One final issue to be highlighted in the study of social cognition and social status is how to pinpoint the nature of the relation between these two constructs. As noted above, much of the research in this area has been correlational and even the intervention studies provide no guarantee that social cognition plays a causal role in the development of social status in a natural setting. We have seen significant strides made in the dimensionalization of both social cognition (e.g., perspective taking, person perception, interpersonal reasoning, reasoning about social conventions, causal attribution) and social status (e.g., popular, rejected, isolated, and controversial children). What are needed are research programs which attempt to tie together the dimensions of the two areas. Such an enterprise requires multivariate model building, the use of complementary research methodologies (experiments, correlational studies, naturalistic observations, and case studies), the construction of psychometrically sound measures of both social cognition and social status, an analysis of reciprocal relations rather than unidirectional causal pathways, and a strong developmental focus (from cross-sectional, longitudinal, or sequential standpoints). For a young area of study such as social cognitive development, the above program is an exciting challenge. The outcomes are not only an understanding of how and why social cognition develops and social status is acquired and maintained, but also how children who are isolated or rejected can avoid the short- and long-term consequences of negative social status.

ACKNOWLEDGMENT

The author would like to thank the late J. Patrick Schmitt for his critical reading of an earlier version of this chapter. It is with great fondness and sadness that I dedicate this chapter to him. I would also like to express my appreciation to Delmont Morrison for his helpful comments, and to Tina Farley and Cyndi Dawson for typing the manuscript.

REFERENCES

1. J. H. Flavell, Concept Development, in *Carmichael's Manual of Child Psychology*, P. H. Mussen (ed.), John Wiley, New York, pp. 983-1060, 1970.
2. W. Damon and D. Hart, The Development of Self-understanding from Infancy Through Adolescence, *Child Development*, *53*:4, pp. 841-864, 1982.

3. C. U. Shantz, Social Cognition, in *Carmichael's Manual of Child Psychology*, P. H. Mussen (ed.), John Wiley, New York, pp. 495-555, 1983.
4. H. A. Marlowe, Social Intelligence, *Journal of Educational Psychology*, *78*:1, pp. 52-58, 1986.
5. C. Barenboim, The Development of Person Perception in Childhood and Adolescence, *Child Development*, *52*:1, pp. 129-144, 1981.
6. R. N. MacLennan and D. N. Jackson, Accuracy and Consistency in the Development of Social Perception, *Developmental Psychology*, *21*:1, pp. 30-36, 1985.
7. M. E. Ford, The Construct Validity of Egocentrism, *Psychological Bulletin*, *86*:6, pp. 1169-1188, 1979.
8. H. S. Waters and V. S. Tinsley, Evaluating the Discriminant and Convergent Validity of Developmental Constructs, *Psychological Bulletin*, *97*:3, pp. 483-496, 1985.
9. A. J. Sedlak and S. T. Kurtz, A Review of Children's Use of Causal Inference Principles, *Child Development*, *52*:3, pp. 759-784, 1981.
10. C. J. Dalenberg, K. L. Bierman, and W. Furman, A Reexamination of Developmental Changes in Causal Attributions, *Developmental Psychology*, *20*:4, pp. 575-583, 1984.
11. T. R. Shultz, G. W. Fisher, C. C. Pratt, and S. Rulf, Selection of Causal Rules, *Child Development*, *57*:1, pp. 143-152, 1986.
12. W. J. Livesley and D. B. Bromley, *Person Perception in Childhood and Adolescence*, Wiley, London, 1973.
13. L. A. Kurdek, Structural Components and Intellectual Correlates of Cognitive Perspective Taking in First- through Fourth-Grade Children, *Child Development*, *48*:4, pp. 1503-1511, 1977.
14. J. Gnepp and M. E. Gould, The Development of Personalized Inferences, *Child Development*, *56*:6, pp. 1455-1464, 1985.
15. L. A. Fehr, Methodological Inconsistencies in the Measurement of Spatial Perspective Taking Ability: A Cause for Concern, *Human Development*, *21*:5, pp. 302-315, 1978.
16. A. J. Nigl and H. D. Fishbein, Perception and Conception in Coordination of Perspectives, *Developmental Psychology*, *10*:6, pp. 858-866, 1974.
17. W. Damon, *The Social World of the Child*, Jossey-Bass, San Francisco, 1977.
18. R. L. Selman, *The Growth of Interpersonal Understanding*, Academic Press, New York, 1980.
19. M. Laupa and E. Turiel, Children's Conceptions of Adult and Peer Authority, *Child Development*, *57*:2, pp. 405-412, 1986.
20. M. Tisak, Children's Conceptions of Adult Authority, *Child Development*, *57*:1, pp. 166-176, 1986.
21. T. J. Berndt, The Features and Effects of Friendship in Early Adolescence, *Child Development*, *53*:6, pp. 1447-1460, 1982.
22. J. Youniss, *Parents and Peers in Social Development*, University of Chicago Press, Chicago, 1980.
23. F. T. Hunter, Adolescents' Perception of Discussions with Parents and Friends, *Developmental Psychology*, *21*:3, pp. 432-440, 1985.

24. F. F. Strayer and J. Strayer, An Ethological Analysis of Social Agonism and Dominance Relations among Preschool Children, *Child Development*, *47*:4, pp. 980-989, 1976.
25. G. E. Weisfeld, D. R. Omark, and C. L. Cronin, A Longitudinal and Cross-sectional Study of Dominance in Boys, in *Dominance Relations*, D. R. Omark, F. F. Strayer, and D. G. Freeman (eds.), Garland, New York, 1980.
26. S. R. Asher, L. C. Singleton, B. R. Tinglsey, and S. Hymel, A Reliable Sociometric Measure for Preschool Children, *Developmental Psychology*, *15*:4, pp. 443-444, 1979.
27. G. Furth, *The World of Grown Ups*, Elsevier, New York, 1980.
28. E. Turiel, Social Regulations and Domains of Social Concepts, in *Social Cognition*, W. Damon (ed.), Jossey-Bass, San Francsico, pp. 45-74, 1978.
29. T. Stoddart and E. Turiel, Children's Concepts of Cross-gender Activities, *Child Development*, *56*:5, pp. 1241-1252, 1985.
30. J. G. Smetana, Children's Impressions of Moral and Conventional Transgressions, *Developmental Psychology*, *21*:4, pp. 715-724, 1985.
31. M. S. Tisak and E. Turiel, Children's Conceptions of Moral and Prudential Rules, *Child Development*, *55*:3, pp. 1030-1039, 1984.
32. W. Emmerich, Family Role Concepts of Children Ages Six to Ten, *Child Development*, *32*:3, pp. 609-624, 1961.
33. M. W. Watson and K. W. Fischer, Development of Social Roles in Elicited and Spontaneous Behavior During the Preschool Years, *Developmental Psychology*, *16*:5, pp. 483-494, 1980.
34. M. W. Watson and T. Amgott-Kwan, Development of Family Role Concepts in School-age Children, *Developmental Psychology*, *20*:5, pp. 953-959, 1984.
35. D. M. Brodzinsky, L. M. Singer, and A. M. Braff, Children's Understanding of Adoption, *Child Development*, *55*:3, pp. 869-878, 1984.
36. D. M. Brodzinsky, D. Schechter, and A. B. Brodzinsky, Children's Knowledge of Adoption, in *Thinking About the Family*, R. D. Ashmore and D. M. Brodzinsky (eds.), Erlbaum, Hillsdale, New Jersey, pp. 205-232, 1986.
37. L. A. Kurdek, Children's Reasoning About Parent Divorce, in *Thinking About the Family*, R. D. Ashmore and D. M. Brodzinsky (eds.), Erlbaum, Hillsdale, New Jersey, pp. 233-276, 1986.
38. _____, Cognitive Mediators of Children's Adjustment to Divorce, in *Children of Divorce: Perspectives on Adjustment*, S. Wolchik and P. Karoly (eds.), Gardner, New York, in press.
39. R. D. Enright and D. K. Lapsley, Social Role-taking: A Review of the Constructs, Measures, and Measurement Properties, *Review of Educational Research*, *50*:4, pp. 647-674, 1980.
40. B. Underwood and B. Moore, Perspective Taking and Altruism, *Psychological Bulletin*, *91*:1, pp. 143-173, 1982.
41. R. D. Enright, A. Bjerstedt, W. F. Enright, V. M. Levy, D. K. Lapsley, R. R. Buss, M. Harwell, and M. Zindler, Distributive Justice Development: Cross Cultural, Contextual, and Longitudinal Evaluations, *Child Development*, *55*:2, pp. 527-536, 1984.

42. J. C. Gibbs, K. D. Arnold, R. L. Morgan, E. S. Schwartz, M. P. Gavaghan, and M. B. Tappan, Construction and Validation of a Multiple-choice Measure of Moral Reasoning, *Child Development*, *55*:2, pp. 527-536, 1984.

43. J. P. Connell, A New Multidimensional Measure of Children's Perceptions of Control, *Child Development*, *56*:4, pp. 1018-1041, 1985.

44. L. A. Kurdek and D. Krile, A Developmental Analysis of the Relation between Peer Acceptance and Both Interpersonal Understanding and Perceived Social Self Competence, *Child Development*, *53*:6, pp. 1485-1491, 1982.

45. K. H. Rubin, Role Taking in Childhood: Some Methodological Considerations, *Child Development*, *49*:2, pp. 428-433, 1978.

46. M. O. Landry and K. Lyons-Ruth, Recursive Structure in Cognitive Perspective Taking, *Child Development*, *51*:2, pp. 386-394, 1980.

47. K. A. Urberg and E. M. Docherty, Development of Role-taking Skills in Young Children, *Developmental Psychology*, *12*:3, pp. 198-203, 1976.

48. W. Damon and M. Killen, Peer Interaction and the Process of Change in Children's Social Reasoning, *Merrill-Palmer Quarterly*, *28*:3, pp. 347-368, 1982.

49. R. L. Selman, M. Z. Schorin, C. R. Stone, and E. Phelps, A Naturalistic Study of Children's Social Understanding, *Developmental Psychology*, *19*:1, pp. 83-102, 1983.

50. R. L. Selman and A. P. Demorest, Putting Thoughts and Feelings into Perspective, in *Thought and Emotion*, D. J. Bearison and H. Zimiles (eds.), Erlbaum, Hillsdale, New Jersey, pp. 93-128, 1986.

51. W. Damon, Patterns of Change in Children's Social Reasoning: A Two-year Longitudinal Study, *Child Development*, *51*:4, pp. 1010-1017, 1980.

52. L. A. Kurdek, Developmental Relations among Children's Perspective Taking, Moral Judgment, and Parent-Rated Behaviors, *Merrill-Palmer Quarterly*, *26*:2, pp. 103-122, 1980.

53. R. B. McCall, Challenges to a Science of Developmental Psychology, *Child Development*, *48*:2, pp. 333-344, 1977.

54. A. E. Kazdin, *Research Design in Clinical Psychology*, Harper and Row, New York, 1980.

55. L. J. Walker, Sources of Cognitive Conflict for State Transition to Moral Development, *Developmental Psychology*, *19*:1, pp. 103-110, 1983.

56. M. J. Chandler, Social Cognition and Social Structure, in *Social-Cognitive Development in Context*, F. C. Serafica (ed.), The Guilford Press, New York, pp. 222-239, 1982.

57. M. Feffer, Developmental Analysis of Interpersonal Behavior, *Psychological Review*, *17*:3, pp. 197-214, 1970.

58. G. W. Ladd and J. Mize, A Cognitive-social Learning Model of Social Skill Training, *Psychological Review*, *90*:2, pp. 127-157, 1983.

59. E. A. Skinner, Action, Control Judgments, and the Structure of Control Experience, *Psychological Review*, *92*:1, pp. 39-58, 1985.

60. D. P. Keating and L. V. Clark, Development of Physical and Social Reasoning in Adolescence, *Developmental Psychology*, *16*:1, pp. 23-30, 1980.

61. K. W. Fischer, A Theory of Cognitive Development, *Psychological Review*, *87*:6, pp. 477-531, 1980.
62. J. H. Flavell, Monitoring Social Cognitive Enterprises, in *Social Cognitive Development*, J. H. Flavell and L. Ross (eds.), Cambridge University Press, Cambridge, pp. 272-287, 1981.
63. N. Eisenberg and R. Lennon, Sex Differences in Empathy and Related Capacities, *Psychology Bulletin*, *94*:1, pp. 100-131, 1983.
64. D. J. Bearison and T. Z. Cassell, Cognitive Decentration and Social Codes, *Developmental Psychology*, *11*:1, pp. 29-36, 1975.
65. M. Hollos and F. A. Cowan, Social Isolation and Cognitive Development, *Child Development*, *44*:3, pp. 630-641, 1973.
66. R. D. Peters and G. A. Bernfield, Reflective-impulsivity and Social Reasoning, *Developmental Psychology*, *19*:1, pp. 78-81, 1983.
67. N. Eisenberg, *Altruistic Emotion, Cognition, and Behavior*, Erlbaum, Hillsdale, New Jersey, 1986.
68. S. Anderson and S. Messick, Social Competency in Young Children, *Developmental Psychology*, *10*:2, pp. 282-293, 1974.
69. M. R. Ford, Social Cognition and Social Competence in Adolescence, *Developmental Psychology*, *10*:2, pp. 323-340, 1982.
70. E. Waters and L. A. Sroufe, Social Competence as a Developmental Construct, *Developmental Review*, *3*:2, pp. 79-97, 1983.
71. F. M. Gresham, Conceptual and Definitional Issues in Reassessment of Children's Social Skills, *Journal of Clinical Psychology*, *15*:1, pp. 3-15, 1986.
72. K. A. Dodge, Facets of Social Interaction and the Assessment of Social Competence in Children, in *Children's Peer Relations*, B. H. Schneider, K. H. Rubin, and J. E. Ledingham (eds.), Springer-Verlag, New York, pp. 3-22, 1985.
73. J. C. Conger and S. P. Keane, Social Skills Intervention in the Treatment of Isolated or Withdrawn Children, *Psychological Bulletin*, *90*:3, pp. 478-495, 1981.
74. E. L. Cowan, A. Pederson, H. Babigian, L. D. Izzo, and M. A. Trost, Long-term Follow-up of Early Detected Vulnerable Children, *Journal of Consulting and Clinical Psychology*, *41*:3, pp. 438-446, 1973.
75. L. Kohlberg, J. LaCrosse, and D. Ricks, The Predictability of Adult Mental Health from Childhood Behavior, in *Manual of Child Psychopathology*, B. Wolman (ed.), McGraw-Hill, New York, pp. 1217-1286, 1972.
76. D. Panella and S. W. Henggeler, Peer Interactions of Conduct-disordered, Anxious-withdrawn, and Well-adjusted Black Adolescents, *Journal of Abnormal Child Psychology*, *41*:1, pp. 1-11, 1986.
77. S. R. Asher, R. A. Markell, and S. Hymel, Identifying Children at Risk in Peer Relations, *Child Development*, *52*:4, pp. 1239-1245, 1981.
78. S. Beck, R. Forehand, R. Neeper, and C. H. Baskin, A Comparison of Two Analogue Strategies for Assessing Children's Social Skills, *Journal of Consulting and Clinical Psychology*, *50*:4, pp. 596-597, 1982.
79. W. M. Bukowski and A. F. Newcomb, Variability in Peer Group Perceptions, *Developmental Psychology*, *21*:6, pp. 1032-1038, 1985.

80. J. D. Coie, K. A. Dodge, and H. Coppotelli, Dimensions and Types of Social Status: A Cross-age Perspective, *Developmental Psychology*, *18*:4, pp. 557-570, 1982.

81. S. L. Foster and W. L. Ritchey, Issues in the Assessment of Social Competence in Children, *Journal of Applied Behavior Analysis*, *12*:4, pp. 625-638, 1979.

82. D. C. French and T. F. Tyne, The Identification and Treatment of Children with Peer-relationship Difficulties, in *Social Skills Training*, J. P. Curran and P. M. Monti (eds.), Guilford Press, New York, pp. 280-312, 1982.

83. K. D. Green and R. Forehand, Assessment of Children's Social Skills: A Review of Methods, *Journal of Behavioral Assessment*, *2*:2, pp. 143-159, 1980.

84. K. D. Green, R. Forehand, S. J. Beck, and B. Vosk, An Assessment of the Relationship among Measures of Children's Social Competence and Children's Academic Achievement, *Child Development*, *51*:4, pp. 1149-1156, 1980.

85. F. M. Gresham, Validity of Social Skills Measures for Assessing Social Competence in Low-status Children, *Developmental Psychology*, *17*:4, pp. 390-398, 1981.

86. J. C. Peery, Popular, Amiable, Isolated, and Rejected: A Reconceptualization of Sociometric Status in Preschool Children, *Child Development*, *50*:4, pp. 1231-1234, 1979.

87. J. R. Asher and V. A. Wheeler, Children's Loneliness, *Journal of Consulting and Clinical Psychology*, *53*:4, pp. 500-505, 1985.

88. J. D. Coie and J. B. Kupersmidt, A Behavioral Analysis of Emerging Social Status in Boys' Groups, *Child Development*, *64*:6, pp. 1400-1416, 1983.

89. K. A. Dodge, Behavioral Antecedents of Peer Social Status, *Child Development*, *54*:6, pp. 1386-1399, 1983.

90. K. A. Dodge, J. D. Coie, and N. P. Brakke, Behavior Patterns of Socially Rejected and Neglected Preadolescents, *Journal of Abnormal Psychology*, *10*:3, pp. 389-410, 1982.

91. J. D. Coie and K. A. Dodge, Continuities and Changes in Children's Social Status, *Merrill-Palmer Quarterly*, *29*:3, pp. 261-282, 1983.

92. V. L. Cantress and R. J. Prinz, Multiple Perspectives of Rejected, Neglected, and Accepted Children, *Journal of Consulting and Clinical Psychology*, *53*:6, pp. 884-889, 1985.

93. D. C. French and G. A. Waas, Behavior Problems of Peer-neglected and Peer-rejected Elementary-age Children, *Child Development*, *56*:1, pp. 246-252, 1985.

94. A. F. Newcomb and W. M. Bukowski, A Longitudinal Study of the Utility of Social Preference and Social Impact Sociometric Classification Schemes, *Child Development*, *55*:4, pp. 1434-1447, 1984.

95. M. Hayvren and S. Hymel, Ethical Issues in Sociometric Testing, *Developmental Psychology*, *20*:5, pp. 844-849, 1984.

96. A. S. Masten, P. Morrison, and D. S. Pellegrini, A Revised Class Play Method of Peer Assessments, *Developmental Psychology*, *21*:3, pp. 523-533, 1985.

97. W. M. Bukowski and A. F. Newcomb, Variability in Peer Group Perceptions, *Developmental Psychology*, *21*:6, pp. 1032-1038, 1985.

98. S. Hymel, Interpretations of Peer Behavior, *Child Development*, *57*:2, pp. 431-445, 1986.

99. L. A. Kurdek and R. Lillie, The Relation Between Classroom Social Status and Classmate Likability, Compromising Skill, Temperament, and Neighborhood Social Interactions, *Journal of Applied Developmental Psychology*, *6*:1, pp. 31-41, 1985.

100. S. R. Asher and P. D. Renshaw, Children Without Friends, in *The Development of Children's Friendships*, S. R. Asher and J. M. Gottman (eds.), Cambridge University Press, Cambridge, pp. 273-296, 1981.

101. J. M. Gottman, J. Gonso, and B. Rasmussen, Social Interaction, Social Competence, and Friendship in Children, *Child Development*, *46*:3, pp. 709-718, 1975.

102. G. W. Ladd and S. Oden, The Relationship Between Peer Acceptance and Children's Ideas about Helpfulness, *Child Development*, *50*:2, pp. 402-408, 1979.

103. R. F. Marcus, Empathy and Popularity of Preschool Children, *Child Study Journal*, *10*:3, pp. 133-145, 1980.

104. D. S. Pellegrini, Social Cognition and Competence in Middle Childhood, *Child Development*, *56*:1, pp. 253-264, 1985.

105. K. H. Rubin and T. Daniels-Beirness, Concurrent and Predictive Correlates of Sociometric Status in Kindergarten and Grade One Children, *Merrill-Palmer Quarterly*, *29*:3, pp. 327-352, 1983.

106. J. M. Gottman, How Children Become Friends, *Monographs of the Society For Research in Child Development*, *48*:3, Serial Number, 1983.

107. K. H. Rubin, Social and Social-cognitive Developmental Characteristics of Young Isolate, Normal, and Sociable Children, in *Peer Relationships and Social Skills in Childhood*, K. H. Rubin and H. S. Ross (eds.), Springer-Verlag, New York, pp. 353-374, 1982.

108. K. A. Dodge, R. R. Murphy, and K. Buchsbaum, The Assessment of Intention Cue Detection Skills in Children, *Child Development*, *55*:1, pp. 163-173, 1984.

109. K. Stiefvater, L. A. Kurdek, and J. Allik, Effectiveness of a Short-term Social Problem Solving Program for Popular, Rejected, Neglected, and Average Fourth-grade Children, *Journal of Applied Developmental Psychology*, *7*:1, pp. 33-44, 1986.

110. D. A. Jaquette, A Case Study of Social-cognitive Development in a Naturalistic Setting, in *The Growth of Interpersonal Understanding*, R. Selman (ed.), Academic Press, New York, pp. 215-242, 1980.

111. R. L. Selman, D. R. Lavin, and S. Brion-Meisels, Troubled Children's Use of Self-reflection, in *Social-Cognitive Development in Context*, F. Serafica (ed.), Guilford Press, New York, pp. 62-99, 1982.

112. N. J. Cohen, J. Kershner, and W. Wehrspann, Characteristics of Social Cognition in Children with Different Symptom Patterns, *Journal of Applied Developmental Psychology*, *6*:3, pp. 277-290, 1985.

113. G. H. Ladd, Documenting the Effects of Social Skill Training with Children, in *Children's Peer Relations*, B. H. Schneider, K. H. Rubin, and J. E. Ledingham (eds.), Springer-Verlag, New York, pp. 243-269, 1985.

114. B. H. Schneider and B. M. Byrne, Children's Social Skills Training, in *Children's Peer Relations*, B. H. Schneider, K. H. Rubin, and J. E. Ledingham (eds.), Springer-Verlag, New York, pp. 175-192, 1985.

115. E. S. Urbain and P. C. Kendall, Review of Social-cognitive Problem Solving Intervention with Children, *Psychological Bulletin*, *88*:1, pp. 109-143, 1980.

116. R. P. Weissberg, Designing Effective Social Problem-solving Programs for the Classroom, in *Children's Peer Relations*, B. H. Schneider, K. H. Rubin, and J. E. Ledingham (eds.), Springer-Verlag, New York, pp. 225-241, 1985.

117. R. L. Wanlass and R. J. Prinz, Methodological Issues in Conceptualizing and Treating Childhood Social Isolation, *Psychological Bulletin*, *92*:1, pp. 39-55, 1982.

118. K. L. Bierman and W. Furman, The Effects of Social Skills Training and Peer Involvement on the Social Adjustments of Preadolescents, *Child Development*, *55*:1, pp. 155-162, 1984.

119. K. L. Bierman, Process of Change During Social Skills Training with Preadolescents and Its Relation to Treatment Outcome, *Child Development*, *57*:1, pp. 230-240, 1986.

120. A. Blasi, Bridging Moral Cognition and Moral Action: A Critical Review of the Literature, *Psychological Bulletin*, *88*:1, pp. 1-45, 1980.

121. L. A. Kurdek, Perspective Taking on the Cognitive Basis of Children's Moral Development, *Merrill-Palmer Quarterly*, *24*:1, pp. 3-29, 1978.

122. R. J. Iannotti, Naturalistic and Structured Assessments of Prosocial Behavior in Preschool Children, *Developmental Psychology*, *21*:1, pp. 46-55, 1985.

123. E. Staub, *Positive Social Morality*, Academic Press, New York, 1979.

124. J. H. Flavell, The Development of Inferences about Others, in *Understanding Other Persons*, T. Mischel (ed.), Rowman and Littlefield, Totown, New Jersey, pp. 66-116, 1974.

PART IV

The Uses of Imagination

CHAPTER 8

Process and Change in Child Therapy and Development: The Concept of Metaphor

SEBASTIANO SANTOSTEFANO

INTRODUCTION

This chapter proposes a model of metaphor construction, as one approach to the study of process and change in child therapy and development.[1] Metaphor construction is defined operationally as the continuous fitting together of action, fantasy and language behaviors with representations and imagery. The heuristic value of the model is illustrated by summaries of the psychoanalytic therapy of two children and a sample of research studies. While integrating aspects of psychoanalytic, developmental and cognitive theories, the model also attempts to take into account major issues each of these theories brings to the topic of process and change. Therefore we begin by outlining a frame of these issues within which the proposed model is then located.

Contributions and Issues from the New Cognitive Science

Over the past twenty-five years, American psychologists interested in process and change in human behavior have gradually shed a mechanistic model of human functioning, initially advocated by Watsonian behaviorists, and embraced an organismic model [2-4]. The mechanistic model views an individual as reactive, passive, and inherently at rest, and provoked to thinking, perceiving, feeling, and wishing only when stimulated by external forces. In contrast the organismic model views an individual as inherently and spontaneously active, approaching avoiding and selecting stimulation, constructing meaning of stimulation, and initiating behaviors, whether thoughts, feelings, fantasies, or overt actions [5].

---

[1] This chapter incorporates and elaborates a previous publication [1].

With this shift in point of view, clinicians and theoreticians have been seeking ways to understand how a person's active perceiving, thinking, wishing, feeling, and behaving are interrelated and how these interrelated domains change. Their efforts have produced a massive and diversified body of observations and concepts which have been referred to as "cognitive science" [3, 4, 6], as "the mind's new science" [2], and as responsible for creating a "cognitive revolution" in psychology and psychotherapy [2, 4, 7, 8].

Cognitive science is defined as empirically based efforts concerned with the nature, components and sources of human knowledge, how knowledge develops and changes, and how knowledge relates to what we feel and do [2, 4]. Although cognitive science has yet to evolve a family of theories sharing common assumptions, its perspectives have influenced both psychoanalytic and behavioral therapies [9], and have stimulated therapists from both camps to construct an interface between the two approaches using cognitive concepts and techniques [10]. Most recently the perspectives of cognitive science have been emphasized in addressing the issue of process and change in psychotherapy [3, 4]. Further, while critiques acknowledge gains made by cognitive science in reforming psychotherapeutic concepts and techniques, they also articulate a number of problems and needs [11-13]. A few are sketched here because they relate to the focus of this discussion.

With Regard to the Components of Human Knowledge: The Inappropriate Emphasis on Words and Beliefs. Although a variety of cognitive behaviors have become the target for therapeutic intervention, there is an overwhelmingly narrow focus on self statements and beliefs a person expresses during treatment. This emphasis leads to several related issues. For example, the beliefs a person holds (e.g., "I'm not very good at what I try") may not be isomorphic with the way the person behaves; and different statements may carry the same meaning while a single verbal statement may have several, different underlying meanings.

With Regard to the Source of Human Knowledge: The Need to Include Deeper Unconscious Structures. The issue of multiple meanings underlying a single statement suggests that thoughts and beliefs may be surface cognitive behaviors with ties to deeper cognitive structures. What a person says may be the tip of an iceberg influenced by unconscious processes rarely accessible to awareness. Further, some beliefs may not be accessible to language expression because a belief could have been formed before the full development of language or because a belief is more accessible to other behavioral forms of expression. As Mahoney notes, unconscious processes have been disregarded or overlooked whenever therapists have emphasized a cognitive perspective. "We should be careful not to over-rationalize a developing system (the person) that contains powerful and primitive prerational modes of knowing and adapting to his world" [13, p. 14].

With Regard to the Development of Knowledge: Irrational Beliefs May be as Useful and Adaptive as Rational Ones. When integrating a cognitive perspective within psychotherapy, clinicians have tended to view what a person says as either irrational or rational, unrealistic or realistic, and task irrelevant or task relevant. Underlying these dichotomies is the assumption that it is better to be rational, realistic and task relevant than it is to be irrational, unrealistic and task irrelevant. Some so-called irrational beliefs may be adaptive, while rational beliefs may be maladaptive as guides to behavior, depending upon the meaning of the thoughts for the individual and the functions they serve.

With Regard to How Knowledge Changes: Old Knowledge is Not Eradicated by New Knowledge and the Principle of Epigenisis. Because self statements and beliefs are dichotomized as either good or bad, adaptive or maladaptive, when therapists attempt to promote change, they tend to emphasize techniques that help patients identify bad thoughts and replace them with good ones. Mahoney is particularly critical of these techniques. "I do not believe that the simple cueing, recitation, or reinforcement of positive self statements or the rationalistic reconstruction of explicit beliefs are optimal or sufficient approaches for facilitating significant and enduring personal development" [13, p. 14]. Along with rejecting the approach of replacing one behavior with another, reviewers take the position that whenever change is effective, earlier forms of knowledge or behavior must be consolidated into later forms, rather than eliminated. Further, in order to change later knowledge or surface behavior, it is necessary first to change the deeper structures tied to it. Last, techniques that produce change must also address resistance to change [12].

One Proposed Solution by Cognitive Science: Constructivist/Transactional Models of Process and Change. In order to address these several issues, constructivist-transactional models of therapeutic process and development have been proposed. From this vantage point, each person actively constructs a model of his/her world that continuously incorporates earlier structures. The person's model is influenced by the environment and at the same time actively shapes the environment the person engages, both by interpreting and giving meaning to it and by leading to actions that select particular stimulation (e.g., [11, 13, 14]).

While constructivist/transactional perspectives of human process and change have been suggested for at least two decades, more recent proposals stand out because they center on the meaning a person gives to stimulation. For example in Arnkoff's model, meaning is the "ultimate issue" [11]. Similarly Mahoney assigns meaning a position of "primacy," and accepts the proposition that human experience is imbued with the pursuit, construction, and alteration of meanings that guide a person's transactions with the environment [13].

If the meaning a person gives stimulation is placed at the center of adaptation and development, it would follow that therapeutic process and techniques intended to stimulate change should focus on the meanings a person constructs. Thompson takes this position in recommending, "the challenge now is to discover the types of meanings that can be used (by a person) and to explore how to help individuals develop the ability to assign meanings that will be most beneficial to them" [15, p. 99]. Along the same line, Mahoney proposes that "one major task

as therapists and theorists lies in the realm of identifying the structures and processes through which our clients construct and construe their everyday existence
[15, p. 18] . . . the heart of change is found in how meanings change" [15, p. 26].

The position that meaning is the ultimate issue and at the heart of change
converges with Gardner's conclusion that the major accomplishment of cognitive
science has been to demonstrate that the constructs of mental representation
and meaning are valid in explaining a range of phenomena [2]. Whereas forty
years ago, at the height of the behaviorist era, few scientists dared to speak of
schemas, images, and transformations, these representational concepts are now
taken for granted and permeate the cognitive sciences.

If we are interested in further operationalizing how meaning is constructed and
how patients could be helped to develop the ability to change meaning, where
can we turn for assistance? There are two obvious directions. One leads to
research, theory and clinical application of imaginal processes, the other to
psychoanalytic theory and therapy, both of which have focused on the meaning
persons give behavior.

Contributions and Issues from
the Camp of Imagery

The camp of imagery has also exploded with research and theoretical
reports ever since its return from being ostracized by behaviorism [16]. Yet, while
critiques of this work show that much has been learned about the significance of
imagery in the areas of memory, learning, thinking, perception, motivation, and
emotion [17], there is little agreement about the most useful way of thinking
about imaginal processes and the therapeutic roles they play [18]. In a review of
definitions and types of imagery reported in the literature, Richardson elaborates
this lack of agreement [19]. Is imagery a mental picture that arises from a memory
of some event, or a verbal abstraction or both? Are action and play a form of
imagery? How should we understand imagination imagery, that is a fantasy the
ingredients of which appear to have no connection with a person's experiences in
reality? How do we distinguish between conscious and unconscious imagery? And
what information do images make available and how do images undergo change?

Gardner wonders whether there are several systems involved in constructing
images, analogous to the one described for the visual system, but capturing and
transforming other kinds of information [2]. He believes there is a need to
learn more about the various vehicles used in the process of representing and
giving meaning to stimulation and whether and how these "(different) modes of
representing relate to one another" [2, p. 5]. (See also [11, 13].)

Contributions and Issues from Psychoanalysis

At this point we turn to psychoanalysis, a school of thought which has
paid almost exclusive attention to deeper personality structures and the meaning

a person gives experiences. To conceptualize the meaning a person gives his/her world, Freud coined the term "psychic reality" in a 1913 publication, a notion which to that point had not been articulated explicitly in Continental philosophy [20]. The concept of psychic reality included the wishes, memories, fantasies, and dreams which a person injected, usually without awareness, into his/her day-to-day stimulation. Psychic reality, for Freud, defined the world as it is experienced and understood by the individual. It is a person's private sense of reality, "the inner world" and through which he/she experiences. To articulate the concept, Freud juxtaposed the notion of psychic reality and the notions of "external," "factual," or "material," reality.

But the concept of psychic reality contains problems and limitations. In post-Freudian literature, psychic reality has been viewed usually as distorting external reality and often equated with psychopathology [20]. The mentally disturbed (neurotic or otherwise) lives in psychic reality while the normal lives in "objective" reality. The person suffering from a neurotic symptom such as a fear of dirt, or of going to school, is dominated by his/her psychic reality, and when free of such symptoms, as functioning in objective reality. Resembing the rational versus irrational dichotomy of cognitive therapists, the dichotomy of psychic and objective reality, when operationalized, requires a two-part view of the process of constructing meaning: one as "real" and the other as distortions of the real or as "imagined." One consequence of this split can be seen in the psychoanalytic view that there are two types of symbols used in constructing meaning, images and words with each a part of a different mental process. Images are typical of the more primitive "primary process" mode of thought which is characterized by irrationality and close ties to instinctual tensions. Words are typical of the preferred "secondary process" mode of thought which is characterized by rationality and a reality orientation [18].

In part because of this two-part view of mental activity, deeper structures consisting of repressed wishes and fantasies are treated clinically and theoretically in psychoanalysis as self-perpetuating, more or less static systems which give meaning to experiences and influence how reality is construed. In this notion reality is considered primarily as a source of triggers capable of activating different parts of already formed deep structures (e.g., [21]). Here psychoanalysis is guilty of ignoring the significance of surface structures and of assuming that repressed memories and wishes (the deeper structures) can be reached only through the layers of the past. Wachtel proposes that equal attention must be paid to surface structures by considering how the past is perpetuated in the present both by the person's behaviors in the present and by the behaviors the person evokes in others [21]. In short, there is need for psychoanalysis to give more attention to the actions a person takes in the present. This need is emphasized by those who integrate behavioral and psychoanalytic concepts [14, 21], and converges with developmental studies of the relations between action and thought: that at every point from infancy, representations lead to actions and actions lead to representations [22].

It would follow that by subordinating the role of action and emphasizing mediating processes, psychoanalysts have neglected interpersonal processes involved in constructing meaning—the back and forth, give and take, between the demands of the person's psychic reality and those of his/her external environments. Exceptions are found in interpersonal models which extended Freud's theories (e.g., the concepts of Adler, Sullivan, Horney, Erikson, Arieti), but these are only now beginning to be appreciated as contributing to the propositions of cognitive science (see Chapters in [4]).

At this point we have completed the frame surrounding the main theses of this Chapter and the concepts and data to be shared. To recapitulate, as clinicians and theoreticians pursue the task of interrelating the ways in which a person actively thinks, feels, fantasizes, and behaves in changing environments, and while negotiating development, they have placed in the center the need to understand how meaning is assigned to experiences, the ways in which different behaviors are coded and represented in terms of the past, the role these meanings play in the actions a person takes in the present, and, in turn, how actions taken change the original meanings. What we need, then, is a model that defines how multiple behavioral modes both construct meaning and take action at both surface and deep levels, the relationships among these modes, and how changes in meaning and related actions take place in the treatment process and development.

A MODEL OF METAPHOR AS MEANING AND ACTION

To introduce the model consider the following vignettes. One concerns a child behaving in his neighborhood and the other a child behaving in the treatment situation.

First Vignette. Spotting a jogger, a three-year-old leaned his body forward, and with each exhuberant "Choo! Choo!," vigorously thrust his right arm forward and back as he playfully ran along side of the jogger for a few moments. Later he spotted the same jogger. This time the toddler scampered behind a tree and crouched low, his facial expression and body posture clearly suggesting he was viewing something to be feared.

While it seems clear that the child is imaging and assigning meanings to each encounter with the same person, we are left with questions. Why was the jogger assigned one meaning at one time (the jogger as a powerful train engine) and a very different one at another (the jogger as a monster)? And is there significance to the actions the child took for the meanings constructed and for possible changes in those meanings?

Second Vignette.   In the professional playroom a child marched with sober, measured steps, holding a stick overhead and posturing strength and determination. When asked what she was playing, she did not reply. In another session she sat on the floor and nudged a pig hand-puppet against a doll while narrating an elaborate fantasy about a giant animal swallowing a person. In still another session, slouched in a chair, she laughed as she described a birthday present her brother received. "His cork gun was a plop."

This vignette articulates the issue of multiple modes involved in imaging and meaning. How can we understand the significance of why at one moment the child enacted being a confident, powerful figure without speaking a word, at another engaged in minature actions while elaborating a vivid fantasy of one figure engulfing another, and at another verbally described the memory of a gift without emphasizing actions or fantasies in her behavior?

To approach these questions, and the issues raised in the introduction, a model of metaphor construction has been developed, which departs from typical uses. Therefore a sketch of metaphor as presented in the psychological literature is a necessary preamble.

Current View of Metaphors[2]

It is generally accepted that metaphor (along with its close relatives, simile, and analogy) involve the transfer of meaning; that is, something is described in terms of properties that belong to something else. Our toddler provides us with an example of a linguistic metaphor. In exclaiming, "Choo choo!" he is saying, "The man is a powerful train engine." At an older age this same child could provide examples of a simile and an analogy with the respective statements, "That man is running like a powerful engine," and "That man runs as if he is a powerful engine."[3]

How is meaning transferred from one thing to something else? With the "comparison/substitution" view a referent and its substitute are classified together and compared on the basis of a shared attribute. In our example, the attribute of power is the basis for the comparison between the referent (jogger) and its substitute (train engine). With the "interaction" view a metaphor achieves a new meaning, that goes beyond the objects compared and substituted, and synthesizes present and past experiences with them, a view which bridges the proposed model. Considering our example from this view, the jogger is assigned a new meaning by the toddler that transcends particular properties of both

---

[2] Because a review of the psychological literature on metaphor falls outside the scope of this chapter, this discussion is highly condensed and selective; for reviews see [23, 24].

[3] Current investigators tend to see the distinction between metaphor, simile, and analogy made in terms of the presence or absence of words such as "like," "as if," not useful [25].

the jogger and a train engine and within which both are no longer what they once were.

What functions are served by metaphor? A variety have been proposed. Aristotle viewed metaphor as ornamental and useful in rendering discourse less dull. Later writers agreed with Aristotle but concluded that these ornaments of language obscure or distort meaning since language should convey only facts, or, at best, serve to coin terms for new concepts. In contrast, Ortony proposed that metaphors serve functions valuable to communication such as condensing many facts, depicting events which by their nature are not describable, and reconstructing experiences [25]. Others have emphasized that metaphors supply language with flexibility [23].

Methods used to study metaphor construction and comprehension have included, for example, asking subjects: to describe their understanding of sentences (e.g., The prison guard is a hard rock); and to select one of several statements judged to be the most appropriate continuation of a story (e.g., The bicycle is a charging horse; The bicycle goes very fast). Yet, in spite of numerous studies, reviews conclude that findings are contradictory and theory incomplete [23]. One source of these contradictions comes from child studies which report both that the capacity to produce metaphors does not appear until adolescence and can be observed in four-year-olds.[4]

In dealing with these inconsistencies, workers have articulated issues which also bridge the present proposal. There is excessive emphasis on the metaphorical use of words which assumes that a verbal expression is the exclusive locus of a metaphor.[5] A less restrictive definition of metaphor must be adopted if research is to advance [24, pp. 930, 937]. Billow implies a less restrictive definition in underscoring the need to study the relationships between metaphor and the processes of play and imaging and in wondering if metaphor is an example of imaged thinking and not simply spoken language [23]. Along the same line, Verbrugge and McCarrel propose that metaphors invite pretending and imaging, as well as reasoning by analogy, and "may be basic to all growth in understanding, whether in the playroom, the psychotherapeutic setting, the scientific laboratory, or the theater" [28, p. 495].

The reformulation proposed here frees the definition of metaphor from its traditional locus in words and expands it by integrating play action, imaging, language, emotions, and cognition in metaphor construction. Our earlier anecdotes set the stage for this expanded definition. When the nine-year-old girl noted her brother's cork gun was a plop, she provided an example of a familiar linguistic metaphor. But, when she marched about the playroom with a stick

---

[4] For an excellent examination of variables involved in children's understanding of metaphors see [26].

[5] Mounoud similarly criticizes studies of symbol formation in early childhood for their excessive reliance on words [27].

overhead posturing power, was meaning being transferred from a sword to a stick without a word being spoken? And when the pig puppet swallowed the doll, is a metaphor at work in this fantasy?

A Reformulation of Metaphor

We begin with the proposition that the reality with which a child nego-tiates and copes is constructed by the child's representational activity. This proposition maintains the broader, more basic usage of the term "psychic reality" as detailed by Barratt,[6] and ignores the distinction made in the post Freudian literature between psychic reality and objective reality [20]. In this broader usage, a child's psychic reality makes up *all that is real for the child*, defining what the child experiences and understands, whether or not these fit with the conventions of the family/community in which the child lives. What the child knows and does is what the child represents [20].

To operationalize how a child constructs his psychic reality, I propose the following definition of metaphor and of part-processes involved in metaphor construction.

A Definition of Metaphor.   Phenomenologically, a metaphor is a per-sistent, habitual organization (pattern) of behaviors that *simultaneously* repre-sents past experiences, construes present situations, and prescribes actions/ emotions to handle them. A metaphor may include the following behaviors: images, symbols, words, thoughts, emotions, postures, and physical actions. This pattern of behavior condenses, conserves and represents past experiences and integrates these into present situations fundamental to a person's *negotiating key developmental issues vis-a-vis* the self, other persons, objects and situations. Examples of these issues are: attachment-trust-love, loss-detachment, separation-individuation, controlling-being controlled, dependence-autonomy/independence, initiating-reciprocating, ambition/dominance, and assertiveness-aggression-com-petitiveness.

The Process of Metaphor Construction.   The process of constructing metaphors is the same as that outlined for the formation of a symbol [29, 30]. But metaphor construction is a more elaborate process in that a metaphor consists of a *pattern* of *behaviors* involving a *cluster of symbols* the organization of which enacts and rehearses a *key developmental issue.*

To illustrate recall the toddler who encountered the jogger. In slouching his body and throwing his arm back and forth, the child constructed a symbol by representing the action of one attribute of a train (the large metal strip that con-nects the wheels of the engine) with the action of his arm. In contrast, a twenty-month-old authored and repeated over many weeks a particular "game" consisting of a pattern of symbols. He sat on his father's lap, asked father to

---

[6] The reader interested in a comprehensive discussion of the concept of psychic reality as used here is referred to Barratt [20].

button his shirt around his (the boy's) body, enveloping him; then he asked that the shirt be unbuttoned, he slid off father's lap, and darted off, with father looking for him. Here a metaphor is at work negotiating the key developmental issue of attachment (being enveloped by father's shirt and at one with his body) and separation (running off with father looking for him).

In both symbol formation and metaphor construction the meaning a person experiences is termed the "referent," and the behavioral expression of that meaning, "the vehicle" [30]. For the first toddler, the referent of power and strength was conveyed by the vehicle of body posture and arm movements. For the second toddler the meaning of attachment—separation was conveyed by an organization of many vehicles (e.g., having father's shirt buttoned and unbuttoned around his body, running off, etc.). This contrast emphasizes that unlike symbol formation, a metaphor always involves a pattern of actions/words/thoughts/emotions/images (i.e., a configuration of symbols), and *is always repeated for an appreciable period of time in different contexts* before phasing out or undergoing significant modification. One symbol does not make a metaphor.

Metaphor Construction and the Centrality of Action and Cognition.[7] When constructing a metaphor, the person *simultaneously* constructs a referent, and an organization of vehicles, and then actively fits the two together, a notion which follows the view of Werner and Kaplan and converges with constructivist/transactional models [30]. The dynamic interaction of referent and vehicles emphasizes the role of cognition and the centrality of action in metaphor construction. The form a metaphor takes depends on: a) the material things and persons available in the child's environment; b) the requirements, opportunities and limitations of these things and persons; c) the child's cognitive capacity to perceive these opportunities and limitations; d) the requirements of the referent or meaning; and e) the child's freedom to take action so that vehicles and meaning are fitted together in a form which enacts, rehearses, and changes the meaning (developmental issue) in the service of growth.

To illustrate, consider the toddler who played the "shirt game" with his father. The child's *perception and understanding* of both the enveloping and disengaging properties of a buttoned shirt developed from perceiving and experiencing various shirts being buttoned around, and unbuttoned from, his body as well as the bodies of others. On the one hand, father's body and shirt were available as opportunities for an "enveloping—disengaging game." On the other, the child perceived the unique requirements of the meaning of separation/individuation. The child's understanding of the self, both as one with the father and as separate from the father, became clear gradually as the child repeatedly enacted having his body enveloped by father's shirt, detached from father's shirt and with father chasing him.

---

[7] See Santostefano for a more detailed discussion of the critical role of cognition in registering and coordinating the requirements of external stimuli with meaning [31].

Referents and Vehicles are Nested: The Concept of Action, Fantasy, and Language as Developmentally Ordered and Interrelated Modes. While various behaviors can represent the meaning of a metaphor (referent), and be combined to convey that meaning (vehicles), developmental principles (which derive from research by the writer [32-34]) operationalize which particular vehicles are selected, organized, and fitted with a meaning in the process of metaphor construction. Acting, imaging (fantasying) and verbalizing are conceptualized as alternative coding systems (modes of representing meaning) as well as alternative modes of behaving. A physical object could be represented by a verbal label, an image, or an action, and one can engage a physical object by imaging, verbalizing, or acting. For example, a five-year-old could represent a wooden block as a bomb by racing behind a barrier to protect himself from it, by imaging a bomb exploding, or by verbalizing, "It's a bomb!" Similarly, the child could engage the block by tossing it at a friend's fort, by sitting and imaging the block hurling toward the fort, or by verbalizing, "I threw a bomb at you."

While all three coding systems and modes of behaving are potentially available, younger children are more likely to represent things/events with the action coding system and to behave with the action mode. (A child runs about, stick in hand, being a soldier and fighting the enemy). With age, representing and behaving in the action mode are subordinated by and integrated within the fantasy mode (imaging) which emerges as dominant (the same child later moves a small plastic toy soldier a couple of inches across the floor fantasying the soldier in a vigorous attack against an imagined enemy). With further development the language (verbal) mode subordinates and integrates action and fantasy (the same child says "I'm a soldier in the good army").

Although subordinated in the course of development, early modes are not replaced but remain potentially active so that under certain conditions they could temporarily represent and express meaning (regression). In this hierarchical view the language mode is nested within the fantasy mode which in turn is nested in the action mode. For similar views, see Werner and Kaplan's proposed shift from "things of action" to "objects of contemplation" [30] and Kosslyn's "representational development hypothesis" [35].

The progression from one mode to the next is conceived as an ontogenetic shift from concrete processes (direct-immediate) to abstract ones (indirect-delayed). The action mode is most concrete and involves physically manipulating an object here and now. The fantasy mode is less concrete since an image is manipulated rather than the object itself, both in the here and now and beyond in space and time, and since delay of gross motor action is required at least for the duration of the fantasy. The language mode is most indirect and delayed representing the greatest distance from referents and physical action.

Within each mode, levels are also nested in terms of concrete-abstract processes. Initially actions are immediate and tied to a narrow set of goals (direct), (e.g., a four-year-old strikes his infant brother with his hand and strikes his brother's crib and high chair with a toy hammer). With development, actions become tied to a wider range of goal objects and are more delayed (e.g., a six-year-old topples various animal dolls belonging to his infant brother, obstructs the progress of an ant by laying a series of sticks in its path, and "decorates" his brother's crib with water colors). Similarly, fantasies are initially more concrete (e.g., a boy imagines his baby brother being attacked by a giant warrior) and gradually become more indirect and delayed (the boy imagines winning a bicycle race against a younger neighbor). Words also shift from concrete to more abstract forms (e.g., from "I'll smash you! to "I'll win the game!").

With the progressive shift from concrete to abstract, both within modes and from one mode to the next, the child gradually develops the capacity to employ alternative means to achieve the same end and to utilize alternative ends to satisfy the same mean. The capacity for increasing delay and for multiple means-ends alternatives results in a range of representations and vehicles from highly personal to socially shared, thereby permitting adaptive, flexible responses to changing opportunities and prohibitions (e.g., the second grader in the playground tackles a classmate in a game of King of the Mountain, and in the classroom tackles math problems to get the best grade).

The Origin and Development of Metaphor.[8] The first metaphors are constructed in infancy with roots primarily in body and sensory representations [36], a proposition that has received support from laboratory findings [22, 26, 27]. These first metaphors, coupled with cognitive and physical-behavioral structures determine the infant's negotiations with caretakers and the pace and complexity of stimulation unique to the infant's environment [39].

How is an existing metaphor reformed? Revolving continuously on a horizontal plane, and standing ready to be expressed, an existing metaphor construes stimuli and prescribes actions in response to a range of available contexts. In this process, during normal development, a metaphor assimilates particular environments, experiences and actions taken and then accommodates to these. Now in its modified form the metaphor is ready to construe more complex stimuli and to require more complex actions on them. In horizontal revolutions, then, the environment plays a specific role in restructuring existing metaphors. To illustrate, the child who played the shirt game with his father eventually abandoned this activity and gradually phased in a new "game" in which, for several weeks, the child and father sat side-by-side at dinnertime and compared fingers, noses, hair, shoes etc. while also taking turns with each directing the other to perform a particular act (e.g., touch your nose; raise your arms), a game cast in the familiar format of *Simon Says*. Here the earlier metaphor enacting attachment-separation gave way to a metaphor now negotiating autonomy and control.

How is a new metaphor constructed? A metaphor spirals from one develop-

---

[8] The formulation of metaphor developed here integrates Mounoud's [36] model of revolutionary periods in development, writings on metaphor [37], Piaget's [38] conceptualization of the process of equilibration and equilibrium states, and new psychoanalytic views of psychic reality [20].

mental level to another and takes on a new organization with the emergence of new coding systems and the dominance of new modes of behavior. Here environment and experience play a non-specific role relative to maturational influences. Examples from psychoanalytic theory would be a shift in dominance from oral to anal to genital sources of excitation which code experiences; and from the concept discussed above, a shift from the dominance of action, to fantasy, to language modes of coding and behaving. In this process, when a new coding system emerges, a new stage is defined by the particular behaviors which dominate (e.g., soiling-controlling, imaging). But as noted earlier previous stages, though subordinated, are not replaced but remain potentially active in determining behaviors.

The following illustrates how the same event could be experienced through early metaphors which construe and prescribe diadic encounters in terms of nuture and control, as well as through a developmentally later metaphor which construes triangular relationships in terms of genital coding. In the treatment situation, a seven-year-old gradually articulated the following. While listening to mother read her a story, the child at one moment construed the experience as mother giving her as much milk as her baby brother received; at another moment, she construed the experience as mother controlling her since she had to go to bed after the story was read, and, at another moment, she construed mother as jealous and reading to her as a way of keeping her away from daddy's lap and "special time" she spends with him.[9]

The Role of Internalizing Behaviors of Idealized Models. The changes that take place within and between modes occur as a function of the child's imitating, identifying with, learning from and internalizing real and idealized standards of parents and other significant models. The content and timing of the behavior of idealized models are especially critical ingredients in restructuring metaphors. While the action mode dominates, the actions of idealized adults and peers are centered by the child and become especially potent, when assimilated, in differentiating the range of action responses available (from concrete to abstract). As one example, an extremely impulsive and aggressive boy revealed in treatment that his metaphors about assertion and aggression included memories/representations constructed when three years old, of his father suddenly exploding in anger, hurling a car wrench across the driveway, and on another occasion angrily chasing his mother with a kitchen knife. In like manner, when the fantasy mode spirals as dominant, the fantasies expressed by models, when internalized, become especially potent in restructuring the child's fantasy metaphors, and when the language mode dominates, verbalizations by models now play a more critical role in the restructuring of language metaphors.

The Issue of Past-Present, Conscious-Unconscious, and Dreams. Metaphors may or may not be at work when a child is experiencing stimuli in the

---

[9] The metaphors stated by these three experiences are respectively: reading is milk; reading is you make me do with my body what you want my body to do; and reading is you keep me from the man I love because you want him for yourself.

present or reliving the past. For example, if a child describes a trip the family took last summer, the details forming a photocopy of the event, no metaphor is at work. If the same child slithers a long stick toward the therapist as if the stick were an attacking snake, repeating this behavior over many weeks, a metaphor is construing and prescribing the here and now. Similarly, a dream is not automatically a metaphor. A child could describe a dream (e.g., a tall building) as he/she would a picture and not yet show evidence that the dream is part of a metaphor construing information. In contrast, while describing the dream, the same child could stack and topple blocks, suggesting one meaning imposed on the dream.

Metaphors are not synonymous with unconscious. A person could be aware or unaware of a metaphor at work. For example, while modeling clay an encopretic boy did not reveal he was conscious of the possible meaning of his activity. Then, at one point, he oozed the clay between his fingers, grinned, and said, "A BM," suggesting he is becoming aware of his equation between clay and feces. Still later he angrily hurled pieces of clay at the wall. While aware that clay now equaled bullets, he was not yet conscious of the possible equation in his metaphor between defecation and destruction.

The Issue of Pathological Metaphors. In abnormal development metaphors do not accommodate to nuances in stimuli and experiences but remain fixed, nearly always constructing the same dynamic fit between the meaning (issue) experienced and the behaviors used to enact that meaning. A metaphor is pathological whenever its representation and associated calls for action: 1) result in behaviors that are highly idiosyncratic, inappropriate for, and/or rejected by the context, resulting in, personal suffering (anxiety, guilt, conflict with significant others); 2) have failed over an extended period of time to accommodate to available contexts/experiences which contain ingredients (especially from models) suitable for restructuring; and 3) do not fit with developmental expectations.

For example, if a three-year-old repeatedly covers the bathroom wall with water colors, this behavior would not be viewed as prescribed by a pathological metaphor but would be if displayed by a ten-year-old. In terms of context, if a ten-year-old repeatedly smears paint on the walls of his bedroom and the family accepts this behavior, the metaphor prescribing this behavior in the home would not be pathological, but would be if prescribed in school. The following illustrates how the same metaphor construction can cycle into different situations but not accommodate to experiences. During the course of treatment, a ten-year-old child revealed that she construed a number of encounters in terms of a metaphor of herself as "an empty basket" which others pass by, refusing to place something in it. When this metaphor was constructed in various situations, she behaved with the same action (running off) and emotion (crying), e.g., in a restaurant with her family, the waiter happened to take her order last; in the classroom she was standing second to last in line waiting to receive worksheets from the teacher; and at a birthday party she happened to receive a balloon containing less air than most.

Metaphor Construction in the Therapeutic
Process: The Principle of Psychic Continuity

We conclude our discussion by bringing the model into the treatment process. We considered how metaphor construction consists of a person actively fitting together a meaning and a set of organized vehicles in order to repeatedly rehearse-negotiate a key developmental issue. When enactments are assimilated and the issue is successfully negotiated, the person constructs another metaphor that enacts-negotiates the same developmental issue with more elaborate and different behaviors or constructs a metaphor dealing with a new developmental issue. In day-to-day living, and at any phase of development, a person could be creating his/her psychic reality in terms of several metaphors dealing with more than one developmental issue, one perhaps completing the negotiating of attachment-love, and another introducing autonomy-independence. For our purposes it is important to emphasize that since metaphors deal with key developmental issues, it would follow that in daily living, metaphor construction focuses on and recruits persons who play significant roles as *construed by the child* with regard to these issues: e.g., parents, relatives, teachers, sibs, peers, and the material things surrounding them.

Towards whom are metaphors directed in therapy? In the therapy process the child substitutes the therapist for one or another of these significant figures and recruits the therapist to play a part in constructing metaphors and in negotiating developmental issues. The roles assigned to the therapist, and the therapist's participation in constructing metaphors and negotiating issues, are conceptualized in psychoanalytic therapy as transference and relate to a fundamental assumption termed "psychic continuity" by Rapport [40]. This concept deserves our attention because it helps us operationalize the purpose of metaphor construction in child therapy and the therapist's efforts to help the child change meanings contained in his/her psychic reality which are responsible for maladaptations.

The concept of psychic continuity proposes that when remembering a past experience as construed and when expressing and/or enacting its meaning, this meaning and expression are integrated and fitted into the total context and continuity of the rest of the child's experiences, both past and present. In this view, then, the meaning of a developmental issue expressed in therapy does not derive from a photograph of a past experience, so to speak, which has been stored in the mind's library, recovered in therapy, and passively examined for information it contains in the service of understanding present problems. Rather, the meaning of a developmental issue is actively constructed *anew in the present therapeutic relationship* in ways that make it continuous *both* with the child's past and present life experiences with other persons and things as construed, and with the child's past and present "life experiences" *with the person of the therapist*, and things in the treatment room, as construed.

These two lines of continuity are different in one critical aspect. The persons and things in the child's environment have participated in the child's metaphor construction in ways that have resulted in unsuccessful negotiations and static metaphors which continually construe situations and prescribe behaviors that lead to psychic pain and developmental failure. In contrast, the therapist and materials in the playroom are willing and prepared to participate in negotiating these incomplete developmental issues and to construct new meanings and vehicles to enact them, resulting in new transactions between the child and another person that eventually relieve suffering and promote developmental advances.

By embedding metaphor construction within the principle of psychic continuity, the process of child therapy could be operationalized as consisting of four broad phases. First, the child negotiates trust and alliance with the therapist which enables the child to construe the therapist as a person who will not evaluate or punish any part of his/her psychic reality, who is not uncomfortable participating in constructing and enacting metaphors, however primitive and idiosyncratic, and who at the same time has the strength to challenge, and find ways of changing, the child's core pathological metaphors and therefore rescue the child from his misery. Once trust and alliance are negotiated, the child, in the second phase, recruits the participation of the therapist to organize vehicles that enact and negotiate aspects of pathological metaphors in the present *for the therapist* as the person entrusted to find a way to change these maladaptive meanings. In this phase of therapy, the metaphors the child introduces concern various issues nearer to the surface which require negotiating if the child is to reach the deeper, core pathological metaphor.

If the child and therapist are successful in negotiating these initial metaphors, the child in the third phase of therapy eventually expresses a developmental issue, from the deeper part of his/her psychic continuity of life experiences, which is a major source of the child's psychological troubles. This developmental issue initially was negotiated in ways that resulted in a core pathological metaphor. That is, a meaning was constructed which prescribed maladaptive behaviors, which remained fixated, unresponsive to subsequent experiences, and which was integrated into later metaphors and their negotiations. The third phase of therapy is devoted to changing the meaning of this core pathological metaphor. In the fourth phase, freed from the pathological and fixated core metaphor, the child reenacts, renegotiates, and restructures the meanings of metaphors introduced earlier in therapy but now coded at more advanced, developmental levels, and tied more closely to the child's current world and its requirements and opportunities.

If process and change in therapy are viewed as child and therapist constructing and negotiating metaphors, sequenced within the child's psychic continuity, what of the content and form of the therapist's interventions (e.g., play acting, fantasy, interpretations) that are intended to change the meanings of metaphors and behaviors they prescribe in ways that are growth fostering? From the view proposed here, the broad goal of interventions by the therapist is twofold: help the child articulate meanings of significance to him/her; and help the child locate vehicles (including the person of the therapist as well as material) which enable the child to construct a metaphor that successfully enacts and negotiates the issue and meaning in question.

Beyond this broad goal, the model proposes that ideally when constructing, negotiating and changing the meaning of a metaphor (especially the core pathological metaphor) the therapist should sequence his/her interventions following a progression from action to fantasy to language behaviors. In this way the meaning and vehicles of the metaphor constructed are gradually changed and nested to include concrete (developmentally lower) and abstract (developmentally higher) coding systems. By helping the child nest meanings within a hierarchy of behavioral modes, the child acquires multiple means-ends alternatives to negotiate the issue in daily living ranging from actions without thought to thought without actions (see earlier discussion). While a given child may prefer to sit at a table and draw pictures, or move toy figures about and talk, this view proposes that the therapist initially should help the child use the action mode as much as she/he is capable. To emphasize the point, the therapist initially would refrain from explaining or interpreting the meaning of some current behavior or a memory of past experiences as sources of present difficulties and would facilitate constructing the meaning in action metaphors and then restructuring the meaning in fantasy metaphors before introducing language metaphors (explanations, interpretations).

OBSERVATIONS OF METAPHOR CONSTRUCTION IN CHILD THERAPY

At this point we turn to consider observations of metaphor construction and restructuring made during the psychoanalytic treatment of two children. While perhaps saying little about the development of normal metaphors, the observations provide insights that may serve normative studies. Further, the treatment situation presents advantages for the study of metaphor not made available by other settings. Once child and therapist establish unconditional trust and a working alliance, the child gradually reveals his/her unique metaphors, however, primitive and idiosyncratic, which guide pathological behavior and the child reveals the course of change these metaphors follow.

Narrative descriptions of each session were recorded, and once the treatment was completed, processed to address several questions. When examined for repeated organizations of physical actions, fantasies, symbols, and spoken words, does the child's activity suggest phases, each involving the construction of a metaphor (i.e., a representation and associated vehicles) that dominates and sustains over a period of time? Does the progression of metaphors constructed eventually lead to a core pathological metaphor which construes and deals with present situations and persons in maladaptive ways that block development? As the core pathological metaphor is repeated, does it undergo restructuring, following the developmental progression of action, fantasy and language, and is it associated with internalizing behaviors of standards (superego)? Does each restructuring change the meanings of the child's concepts of self and others resulting in less pathological behavior? When reformed, does the pathological metaphor undergo a spiraling revolution, as new coding capacities emerge, associated with developmentally more advanced meanings and more adaptive behavior?

To answer these questions the identified configuration of activity and its associated metaphor were noted as well as the time span over which they were repeated. The metaphor was viewed as having been restructured whenever changes occurred in the meaning and vehicles fitted together as revealed by a shift in play theme, the roles assigned to child and therapist (e.g., a shift from mythical to human figures), and the behavioral mode dominating (e.g., action to fantasy).

In the material to follow, the child alone initiated and authored the configurations of play and metaphors. As the activity and metaphor repeated, the therapist initiated behaviors within the ongoing metaphor, and its particular behavioral mode, in the hope that the child would assimilate these to restructure the metaphor and change its meaning in the service of growth. Last, this discussion is not intended to address psychoanalytic technique as such but to serve the purpose of this chapter, namely, the construction and reconstructing of metaphors when a child is given the freedom to do so. While available space permits only a highly condensed description of each case, the sequence of metaphors constructed and negotiated by each child was preserved.

THE FIRST CLINICAL CASE

Harry was referred at the age of four years when preschool personnel observed extreme hyperactivity and that each day he spit at, bit, or hit other children and teachers without obvious provocation. At home parents, grandparents and a sibling (eighteen-months-old) were targets of the same aggressive behaviors. Harry began a therapeutic analysis (four sessions per week) which took place over a period of three years except for summer vacations.

Metaphor: The Body Has No Control (Three Months)

Harry initially manipulated and threw materials about, focused activity sustaining for only a minute or two (e.g., he formed globs of clay and licked and bit them; scribbled crayons on paper; threw clay balls against the wall). Then Harry organized and repeated one activity. He toppled puppets and dolls one by one from the shelf to the floor, exclaiming anxious confusion with each fall.

The therapist occasionally imitated this activity, toppling himself to the floor and expressing distress. Harry seemed to assimilate the therapist's intervention. Calling himself "Mr. Fall," Harry repeatedly fell to the floor, arms waving in confusion. After each fall, he asked the therapist to surround Mr. Fall with furniture so he could remain stable. The therapist complied. Harry then replaced this game with another which repeated the theme with a hand puppet, also named Mr. Fall, which Harry tried to prop up with toy furniture, assisted by the therapist. By experimenting with various props and showing that Mr. Fall continued to fall no matter what was used, the therapist conveyed, within the metaphor, that Mr. Fall needed more than props to keep himself stable and avoid distress and that the therapist was ready to find out what this would be.

Metaphor: Establishing An Alliance With the Therapist (One Month)

At this point, Harry initiated a metaphor which suggested he was beginning to trust and ally himself with the therapist in order to discover the source of his difficulties. Asking the therapist to lie on the floor, and while listening to his chest with a toy stethoscope, Harry asked, "What's the matter puppy?" The therapist enacted he was scared and mixed up. Each time Harry would exclaim, "You mean your mother spanks you?" or "The teacher yells at you!" etc. Each time the therapist agreed, puzzled that there were other things troubling the puppy and asked the doctor (Harry) to help him. Another theme developed. Harry threw himself on the floor yelling "Help I'm sinking!" The therapist grabbed Harry and pulled him onto a newspaper, "a raft." As Harry and therapist sat on the raft, the therapist enacted what else could be used from the playroom to keep Harry from sinking and to learn what makes Harry sink.

Metaphor: A Boy "Flips Out" Unless His Body Is Tied Down (Twelve Months)

Harry repeated and restructured the previous metaphor of body control now within the mode of microaction accompanied by increasingly differentiated fantasies involving the hand puppet, Mr. Fall, now renamed "Alvin." With this game, exclaiming fear and excitement, Harry flipped his wrist sending Alvin soaring across the playroom. ("He flips out!") Each time the therapist retrieved the puppet, and Harry repeated the action. Harry elaborated playing that Alvin could not sit still, sometimes was hurt when crashing against the wall, and sometimes disappeared and needed to be found. The therapist struggled to prevent Alvin from flipping out, worried about the harm that might befall Alvin, and became weary because he could not hold him down. Harry related Alvin's inability to control himself ("flip out") to Mr. Fall's and tied one end of a string around Alvin's head and the other to a knob. But, without the string, Alvin could not control himself.

Metaphor: Bite And Stab/My
Brain Is Crazy (Two Months)

Following a few sessions of diffuse agitation, Harry became violent, showing no evidence of pretending, and replicating behaviors he displayed at school and at home. Screaming, "I hate you!," "I wish you were dead!" Harry bit, hit, and spit at Alvin and the therapist and sometimes tried to stab them with scissors. During these outbursts, he exlaimed, "My brain is crazy!" The therapist restrained Harry, and when Harry was calm, imitated aspects of Harry's behavior (e.g., moving his arm as if to stab, exclaiming with fear/confusion, "This is crazy!" "I can't stop my hand!" "I am flipping out!") Introducing activity from an earlier phase, the therapist also tied a string around his head and Harry's head in search of a way to stop the brain from flipping out and going crazy ("Like you tied one to Alvin.")

Metaphor: The Police Station (Rules and
Standards) Controls Crazy (Two Months)

Harry asked the therapist for several padlocks and located a "police station" under the playroom table. Hanging a lock on a string around his neck and another around his waist, he introduced the "trapping" game. For example, he hung one lock on a knife and another on scissors. The police station (played by the therapist) decided when and what to unlock and how the released item would be used, instructing Harry or Alvin, for example, to cut paper with scissors. Once the item was used, the lock was secured again. As the police station, the therapist enacted that what Harry and Alvin now do was under control and followed what the policeman wanted. But sometimes when unlocked their hands still did crazy things (e.g., Harry threw an item against the wall), so they should find out what had that power in Harry and Alvin and how they could lock it up.

Metaphor: The Bad Force Is Fought
And Conquered (Ten Months)

Harry transformed the area under the table from a police station to a fort, barricading the area with chairs behind which sat Harry, *wearing the therapist necktie*, Alvin, and the therapist. The fort was repeatedly attacked by "Mr. Bad" (cylindrical punching bag) who attempted to capture us and take us to monster land. Harry fought back in various ways (e.g., whipping the bag *with the therapist's belt*; shooting rubber bands with a gun constructed by Harry and the therapist). Mr. Bad repeatedly commanded us by name to perform "bad things" (e.g., throw a toy). With each command, Harry flexed his muscles and screamed (e.g., "You can't make us do that!"), shouted that the therapist was, "The president of the world!" "stronger than you," and cautioned Alvin when commanded , "Don't do it; hold back!" Harry concluded this theme by "setting fire" to Mr. Bad, cheering, "Now all the monsters of the world are dead!"

Metaphor: I Am Mastering My Aggression
And Discussing Current Problems (Six Months)

Harry challenged the therapist to race toy cars in contests, engaged the therapist competively in form board games, and spontaneously discussed current difficulties he experienced playing and competing with classmates. He also reported that he had wet his pants at school on several occasions (confirmed by parents), and elaborated he did not use school toilets because the flushing sounded like "thunder" and frightened him. In the office bathroom he repeatedly flushed paper cups down the toilet exclaiming, "Help! I'm sinking!" activity which enabled us to relate his wetting to Mr. Fall's and Alvin's sinking and loss of control, and how they had established strength and control.

Harry also introduced behaviors suggesting the emergence of new coding capacities which construed aggression now in terms of the phallic stage. He brought, played, and discussed a phonograph record about a giraffe with a short neck who wished the neck would grow longer, and a record about a small train engine that wanted to be powerful. He crawled about the floor playing "snake." When doing so he sometimes commented about the good feelings he experienced when his penis rubbed along the carpet, and he discussed that at home he put a piece of toilet paper on his penis which also gave him good feelings.

Critique

Following the therapist's imitating, with his total body, puppets falling out of control (off the shelf), Harry initially constructed a metaphor of loss of body control (Mr. Fall) playing the part himself in macroaction, and then in microaction, employing a hand puppet. Although a relevant beginning, this metaphor was nearer the surface and not yet connected with the meaning of violence that caused Harry's difficulties. When props failed to aid Mr. Fall, Harry negotiated alliance and trust in the therapist, a development which permitted the core pathological metaphor to emerge gradually. First the metaphor of loss of control was restructured and elaborated with the fantasy mode dominating, as many imagined injuries befell Harry, and as the character shifted closer to a representation of Harry (Alvin, a mythical boy). Further the activity of a falling body was now construed as "flipping out," the first comprehension of mental loss of control, with Harry attempting to aid Alvin by tying a string to the puppet's head.

At this point, Harry revealed his core pathological metaphor: hate and violence toward others, a state he construed as "mind going crazy," and which Harry enacted on the therapist as well as a puppet. By tying a string around his head, and Harry's head, as Harry had previously done with Alvin, the therapist employed an action metaphor integrating work from a previous phase and conveying the possibility that the crazy mind could be controlled.

Having enacted his core pathological metaphor and assimilated that crazy could be controlled, Harry constructed the first metaphor of standards of conduct (police station) which he assigned to the therapist, repeating and stabilizing the ingredients of "trapping" and controlling bad impulses. While Harry could exercise control when prescribed by another person (therapist), he also continued to experience the impulse to aggress. Accepting the policeman's invitation to discover and conquer this impulse in Harry, Harry constructed a metaphor of an evil force (Mr. Bad) which was subdued by resources internalized from an idealized model (symbolized by Harry's wearing the therapist's necktie, using the therapist's belt to fight Mr. Bad and construing the therapist as powerful president of the world).

With control over impulse established, Harry's pathological metaphor dissolved and aggression spiralled to a higher level of coding (competition, phallic excitation, fantasies and wishes to become bigger and stronger). Significantly, Harry could now use reflective thought with a focus on his current difficulties (e.g., wetting accidents; difficulties competing with classmates).

What was the relationship between this process of restructuring metaphors and Harry's behaviors at school and home? During the first year of analysis, Harry completed preschool, his violence gradually attenuating. By the second year of analysis, he had completed kindergarten, having shown significant improvement in academic readiness and social adjustment (no violence was observed during the last half of the school year). As a result, he was promoted to an accelerated program of first and second graders which he successfully completed at the conclusion of treatment.

THE SECOND CLINICAL CASE

Mary was referred when six-years-old and a first grader because she was withdrawn, nervous, sensitive to correction, stubborn and demanding (especially of mother), and refusing to attend school, weeping uncontrollably if pressed. Parents made clear that her younger sibling, John, (four-years-old) was favored by them and grandparents, and that his pulmonary problems (resulting in multiple hospitalization during infancy) had required much of their time and attention. Mary was seen in a therapeutic analysis for two years (four sessions per week) during which a series of metaphors, including one at the core of her pathological behavior, were constructed and restructured.

Metaphor: The Girl Craves Nurture/
The Boy Gets It All (Six Months)

Initially, Mary busied herself drawing numerous pictures of flowers, suggesting her attempts to avoid and deny conflicts and pain which plagued her.

Then at one point, she began each session by arranging real furniture in the playroom to construct a house, particular pieces defining kitchen, living room, etc. Sitting primarily in the kitchen (space under the table), she repeated two themes, now using baby talk. One involved engaging the therapist in the form board game, *Candyland*, in which she labeled one game piece a girl and the other a boy. Mary modified the rules to insure that the boy always reached the candy house first, whereupon he devoured it, while the girl pleaded for "crumbs" and struggled to get some. Sometimes when playing the boy, Mary placed her mouth on the form board vigorously licking and "eating" the candy house and instructed the therapist to do the same when playing the boy. The second theme involved a boy doll who stepped into a refrigerator for food, the door shut behind him, he screamed, and parent and grandparent dolls rushed to rescue him, ignoring the girl doll nearby. During both activities Mary angrily hurled the boy game piece or doll across the room. When playing the parts of the girl game piece, or girl doll, the therapist enacted their anger and frustration and puzzled that there must be a way to reach the candy house and to get things from parents and grandparents.

Metaphor: Establishing An Alliance With The Therapist (Two Months)

Mary interrupted these themes, sometimes becoming withdrawn and sullen (she sat in the waiting room refusing to join the therapist), or agitated and aggressive (she barricaded herself in the playroom, excluding the therapist, and pounded on the playroom door shouting, "It's locked! Let me in!" The therapist play acted he wanted to help her get her share of the candy house but closed doors kept them apart. Following this Mary again rearranged the real furniture as a house and assigned herself the role of an ill baby and the therapist the role of a doctor who made house calls to treat her. The therapist enacted that until the baby's sickness came out for the doctor to see, he could help her only a little.

Metaphor: The Girl Feeds The Boy Dirt (Feces/Anger) And Is Guilty Of Making Him Sick (Six Months)

Mary occupied herself for almost two months repeatedly sloshing mushy clay from one pan to another and then carefully covering each pan with a cloth. She followed this "game" with dripping glue and finger paints on drawings of volcanos which were exploding and spewing mud that covered "everything." Throughout, she was sullen, irritable and provocative. The therapist busied himself initially helping prepare mushy clay and cloth covers and later by scraping away the "mud" that spewed from volcanos, wondering what was it that had to be covered up, and showing interest in finding out.

Arranging play furniture on the table top, and using miniature actions, Mary gradually evolved the fantasy play of a boy doll who always drinks milk when hungry, while a girl doll not only drinks from the toilet but is blamed for the "messes" he makes, a predicament which enrages her. Then the girl repeatedly gives the boy dirt to eat and each time the boy "gets spots of mud on his chest" and is rushed to the hospital in a car or ambulance with parents and others rushing about and searching for ways to help the boy. Within the metaphor, the therapist introduced and enacted a doctor who gradually explains to all the characters that the spots on the boy's lungs were not caused by dirt but by germs. After numerous hospitalizations and treatments the boy recovers.

Metaphor: The Girl Gets Nurture By Reciprocating/Girls Are As Good As Boys (Five Months)

Next Mary constructed clay bowls filled with clay fruit, set the table, prepared and served meals to the therapist, and asked the therapist to prepare and serve meals to her. She made items with a toy sewing kit and drew pictures of boys and girls in various situations (e.g., playground), differentiating activities boys and girls enjoy and do well. She also drew pictures of cows and bulls, comparing physical differences including genitalia.

Metaphor: I Enjoy Industry And Can Now Discuss Past Trauma (Five Months)

Mary began bringing homework assignments to the sessions, inviting the therapist's participation, and played a form board game of careers for women, (*What Shall I Be*), discussing her ambitions (e.g., being a nurse, housewife, ice skater). During these activities, she spontaneously paused, discussing memories of brother John's first two years of life, his illness, multiple hospitalizations, and her parents' preoccupation with him, clarifying a number of details (e.g., at one time she construed raisins she gave John as globs of dirt).

She reported a dream of "a baby carriage," it cost eight dollars, and was filled with candy in a store, and a lot of children were trying to get it." As she decoded its meaning she connected eight dollars with her current age (eight years), she discussed her current apprehension with having to negotiate with mother to obtain nurture in competition with brother, and she reviewed ways she could go about this and the pitfalls that caused her difficulties. In terms of the latter, she gradually developed the understanding that she did not cause her brother's illness (recalling with humor her earlier fantasy of feeding a boy dirt who then got spots on his chest), that she refused to go to school last year because she was furious with and jealous of her brother but also afraid something would happen to him if she did not keep him in her view, and that she no longer needed to approach mother with the conviction that she is too busy with John because John is no longer ill.

Critique

The first metaphor Mary constructed made use of microaction and fantasy and consisted of a mythical boy receiving boundless nurture (candy house, milk) and a mythical girl unworthy, deprived and craving. While this metaphor appeared to relate to her demanding, stubborn, sullen behavior and sensitivity to correction, further developments indicated this metaphor was relatively near the surface and tied to deeper meanings. Mary established an alliance with the therapist by enacting being barricaded from the therapist as an interested caretaker, a metaphor which was restructured to define a sick child allowing herself to be cared for by a doctor.

Once an alliance was established, Mary gradually constructed and elaborated a core pathological metaphor which seemed to be at the base of her difficulties. Initially behaving in terms coded by the anal stage, she enacted soiling, rage, and guilt, at first in the mode of macroactions (sloshing and covering up mushy clay) and then with more attenuated action and differentiated fantasy (dripping mud that explodes from pictures of volcanos and covers everything). These ingredients were then integrated with previous ones to restructure and elaborate the first metaphor and issue (i.e., the boy receives endless supplies, the girl is undeserving). Now while the boy receives milk, the girl must drink from the toilet and is blamed for his messes. With further restructuring, "the mess," the crime for which the girl is blamed, is differentiated, and the construction of a core pathological metaphor is completed. The girl feeds dirt (for Mary the symbol for feces=anger) to the boy causing chest illness. This meaning was changed when the metaphor was elaborated to include that germs caused the illness not dirt (anger) and the boy recovers.

Freed from the pathological metaphor, Mary constructed metaphors of nurture in terms of reciprocating and mutuality, (feeding and being fed by the therapist) and of girls as deserving and as worthy as boys. With this redefinition, Mary spiralled from earlier metaphors coded primarily in terms of deprivation, envy, soiling—(oral and anal stages) to a metaphor coded in terms of pride, ambition, and industry (phallic stage). At the same time, she was equipped to make spontaneous use of self reflection and insight in interrelating present and past events especially those concerning her view of brother's illness and of the availability of parents then and now.

How did the restructuring of metaphors in the therapeutic process relate to Mary's behavior at home and school? Birthday parties provide one convenient measure because, as chance would have it, brother's birthday fell on the day before Mary's. Prior to and during the first year of treatment Mary had been especially sullen and withdrawn at her own and her brother's birthday parties, protesting as usual, "He always comes first!" At the close of the second year of treatment when the birthdays arrived, Mary enjoyed both occasions and noted with pride to her grandparents "John's birthday comes first but I got here four years before him." In addition, Mary's refusal to attend school declined steadily during the first grade. At the close of treatment her second grade reported that her academic performance shifted from below grade level to adequate and most notably, that she involved herself in peer activities.

Comments on the Clinical Cases

The observations made in the treatment situation lend support to the heuristic value of the proposed formulation of metaphor. Each child revealed a core pathological metaphor consisting of a pattern of actions, fantasies and words which condensed and represented the child's past unsuccessful negotiations with one or another issue critical to development. Harry's core metaphor concerned one of the earliest developmental issues defining the body-self as highly unstable and lacking regulation (falling is crazy) and defining others as indiscriminate targets of aggression coded in oral terms (biting). Mary's core pathological metaphor involved a later developmental issue defining the self as deprived by parents, in contrast to her brother's boundless supplies, and as guilty of causing his illness, all coded in both oral and anal terms (feeding brother dirt=feces=rage). Further each core metaphor contained prescriptions for habitual behavior that converged with the maladaptations observed in each child's environment.

With repeated restructuring the meaning of each core metaphor and the associated vehicles changed from representations and behaviors dominated by the action mode then by microaction with elaborated fantasy, then by language (words, thoughts, beliefs). Comprehension of present and past realities were eventually articulated with the language mode and involved integrating metaphors from earlier levels within the child's continuity of life experiences. During this course, the content of metaphors shifted from highly idiosyncratic to socially shared symbols, and the child's internalizing an idealized model played a critical role in each major reconstruction. For each child, restructuring and resolving the core metaphor was associated with conscious awareness (insight) of his/her unique difficulties and with significant developmental advances.

These observations suggest a principle that relates to how deep and surface changes in meaning and associated behaviors are brought about in the treatment process. Ideally, in the course of treatment, the therapist should intervene progressively with action, fantasy and language, symbols and metaphors so that metaphors constructed primarily with words eventually establish deep and widespread roots within the fantasy mode (which casts the same meanings in images), as well as within the developmentally earlier action mode (which casts the same meanings in actions and gestures). Without these shared roots, integrating and nesting meanings within the three modes, words and concepts float detached as intellectualizations having little power to steer behavior, fantasies are deprived of the benefits of rehearsal and fulfillment in reality experiences, and actions are robot-like lacking the breadth, psychological economy, and comprehension provided by language and fantasy.

LABORATORY RESEARCH SUGGESTED
BY THE PROPOSED MODEL OF METAPHOR

This section briefly illustrates research approaches to normal and pathological functioning suggested by the proposed model. In metaphor construction, we considered that the child fits together, within his/her psychic continuity, representations of past experiences with vehicles provided by present stimuli. This notion raises the question as to whether children, when constructing their psychic realities, differ in how they construe stimuli and whether such differences relate to psychological functioning and adaptation.

I have conceptualized and operationalized this issue with a variable variously termed, "cognitive coordination," "cognitive-affective balancing," and "cognitive orientation" [31, 33, 41, 42]. The concept defines a continuum of ways children give meaning to information, ranging from one child who maintains an outer, cognitive-orientation, construing stimuli as they are and introducing very little of his/her personal world when constructing the meaning of something, to another child who maintains an inner, cognitive-orientation, giving meaning to stimuli in terms that are highly personal and distant from (or unrelated to) attributes of the stimuli.

To assess a child's cognitive orientation, a hierarchy of test methods have been developed ranging from those which emphasize imaging imbedded in action to those which emphasize imaging imbedded in fantasy. For example, with one test, the child assumes body postures and performs body movements while describing what they bring to mind; with another demonstrates and describes the possible "usual" and "unusual" uses of a stick and paper clip; with another describes what ambiguous shapes bring to mind when the shapes are examined only by touch; and with another makes up a story to the blank card of the Thematic Apperception Test (TAT).

The possible value of investigating how children assign meaning to stimuli is illustrated here by the results of two studies which used the blank card of the TAT. Following traditional TAT administration, the child is handed a blank, white card, asked to imagine a scene, and to tell a story about it. The story is rated in terms of an eleven-point continuum. When physical attributes (e.g., the whiteness of the card, a smudge on the card, the number on the back of the card) are used in the story in some concrete way, an outer cognitive-orientation is inferred (e.g., "All I can think of is coffee was spilled; see the spot here," the child points to a smudge on the card; "It's snowing and white polar bears are walking around.") At the other end of the continuum, when meaning given to the stimulus card consists of highly personal symbols that depart from concrete attributes available, an inner, cognitive-orientation is inferred (e.g., "There is a rainbow and on each side of it there are two bolts of lightning; the rainbow is the queen and the lightning are the soldiers guarding the queen.")

In one study, sixty-six children, successive admissions to a psychiatric facility because of adjustment problems and school failure, were administered the blank card of the TAT along with other routine tests. On the basis of the story told to the blank card, each child was assigned to an Outer-Oriented or Inner-Oriented group, each reflecting the tendency either to construe a stimulus as it is or in personal terms.

The two groups were comparable in several respects except for their performance with the TAT blank card. Outer-Oriented Group: $\bar{x}$ Coordination Score = 3.3; $\bar{x}$ age = 148 months; $\bar{x}$ I.Q. = 99; males = 15; females = 15; Inner-Oriented Group: $\bar{x}$ Coordination Score = 7.6; $\bar{x}$ age = 152 months; $\bar{x}$ I.Q. = 101; males = 16; females = 20.

As one probe into the possible significance of types of cognitive orientation, the efficiency with which each group recalled the content of two paragraphs was compared. One paragraph presented a brief story of a family in a plane crash; the other story of a person in charge of a town's water works. After reading each paragraph the child was asked to recall the details. The examiner recorded details whether correct or invented by the child and introduced into the story. The two groups did not differ significantly in the number of correct details recalled to the more emotional paragraph vs. the more neutral one. However, the inner-oriented children produced significantly more invented details to the emotional paragraph than to the neutral one ($p = .04$). This finding suggested that cognitively inner-oriented children, when reading emotional, provocative material, introduced more personal meanings into the story than when reading neutral material. In contrast outer-oriented children took the emotional material as it was in much the same way as they experienced the more neutral material.

In a second study, adolescent boys hospitalized in a psychiatric facility were assigned to a High-Violence group (admitted because of arson, assault with a dangerous weapon) or Low-Violence group (admitted because of runaway, shoplifting). The High-Violence group consisted of twenty-six adolescents, $\bar{x}$ age, 187 months; mean I.Q., 105. The Low-Violence group consisted of twenty-three adolescents, $\bar{x}$ age 190 months; mean I.Q., 99. The Cognitive Orientation mean scores of the two groups were compared and found to be significantly different ($p = .05$). The High Violence group was characterized more by an inner cognitive-orientation, tending to assign highly personal meanings to the scene imagined in response to the blank stimulus card. In contrast, the Low Violence group was characterized more by an outer cognitive-orientation, assigning meanings consisting of conventional symbols and/or symbols which construed the stimulus in terms of its actual attributes.

Other studies have examined the adaptive significance of shifts in cognitive orientation observed when individuals deal with each of two molar environments, one more emotionally provocative than the other (e.g., at home and at the airport before executing a parachute jump; at home and at the hospital before undergoing surgery) and when individuals deal with each of two molecular environments represented by test stimuli, one depicting aggressive and the other non-aggressive information to be processed cognitively [42]. In each study significant shifts in cognitive orientation occurred in directions, from inner to outer, or vise versa, consistent with theoretical expectations.

The results of these studies support the value of exploring further ways of assessing how persons assign meaning to stimuli, how these meanings undergo change, and the significance of the flexibility of a person's cognitive orientation for adaptation and learning, whether when in the larger environment or in the treatment situation.

CONCLUDING COMMENTS

We began by noting that the camps of cognition, imagery, and psycho-analysis, in addressing the issue of process and change, converge on the need to interrelate the ways in which a person fantasies and behaves, and to conceptualize how experiences are coded at surface and deep levels, and how these meanings influence and are influenced by the actions a person takes. As one approach to these issues, a model of metaphor construction was outlined, the heuristic value of which was illustrated by changes in metaphor observed in the treatment situation and by studies exploring the significance of individual differences in the way meanings are constructed. While resembling other constructionist/transactional/contextualist models, the proposed model is also distinguished by the position it takes on several issues concerning process and change, a few of which are highlighted here.

1. *Action, fantasy and language as alternative coding systems.* In contrast to the proposed model, Paivio, for example, proposes two alternative coding systems, verbal and imaging, both of which operate when a situation is concrete with the verbal system dominating when a situation is abstract [43]. Further the verbal system is considered as more useful because verbal codes are more concise, a view emphasized by the approaches of Bandura and Meichenbaum [18].

   While Horowitz proposes that three types of representations are available for the conscious expression of meaning (inactive, imaging, and lexical), the motoric mode is defined as skeletal, kinestetic and visceral behaviors, in contrast to purposeful, instrumental acts and gestures proposed here [44]. Moreover, the present model conceptualizes the three modes as available for unconscious as well as conscious coding.

2. *Metaphor as a pattern of developmentally ordered and nested action, fantasy and language symbols which guides negotiations of key developmental issues.* This conceptualization elaborates and locates the process of symbol formation within day-to-day learning and adaptation. At each stage of development, the child constructs alternative relationships between

developmental issues (meanings) and possible behavioral expressions of them (vehicles) which are built upon and nested within previous metaphors and which equip the child to cope with and learn from a widening range of environments. Which level of metaphor the child "sees" and enacts at the moment is a function of the context, as well as the personality and developmental state of the child [29]. For example, while modeling sausage-like clay shapes in transactions with an adult, a child, at one stage could be expressing clay as food, at another clay as feces, at another clay as bullets, at another, clay as an artistic activity, and at another, clay as any one of these. In like manner, as discussed earlier, a single developmental issue (meaning) could be expressed by different patterns of vehicles. From the view of multiple vehicles and meanings flexibly fitted together in a dynamic process of metaphor construction, change is operationalized as occurring in *both* the meaning and the vehicles used to express that meaning.

3. *Constructing metaphors in the treatment situation and changing metaphors by transacting and negotiating.* If a child requires treatment, it is assumed the child's environment and caretakers did not permit particular meanings to be expressed and/or did not make available materials and persons necessary to enact, negotiate and transform these meanings. Therefore, the therapist initially insures a context within which the child trusts that meanings, however bizarre and idiosyncratic, will not be prohibited or criticized when expressed. The therapist also makes available a variety of vehicles in the form of play materials and his/her person as willing to play various identities. Using these materials and the person of the therapist, the child forges metaphors (meanings and vehicles) expressing core developmental issues that have taken pathological forms and which child and therapist enact and negotiate. Through repeated negotiations, the meaning and vehicles of the pathological metaphor are gradually transformed to include representations and prescriptions for action that are not dangerous to the child or others, and growth fostering. The notion that metaphors change as the child repeatedly enacts them in negotiations with the therapist converges with cognitive psychology's recent emphasis on the role instrumental actions play in all cognitive activity [13] and with the Piagetian concept of figurative and operative functions interacting throughout cognitive development [38].

4. *When attempting to change metaphors, verbalizations (interpretations-clarifications) are saved for last.* When negotiating and transacting with the child, the therapist introduces behaviors, within the child's metaphor, which follow a progression from those dominated by action to those dominated by fantasy. Spoken words *as vehicles* and as linguistic metaphors are introduced last and nested within already formed action and fantasy metaphors and thereby develop power to steer behavior and generate

understanding (insight). Saving verbal interventions until the last, until change has taken place in action and fantasy behaviors/metaphors, contrasts sharply with the emphasis cognitive therapies give to verbal behavior as the vehicle of change (e.g., replacing maladaptive beliefs; self-verbal instruction) and with the emphasis given by psychodynamic therapy to "understanding" as the vehicle for change [45].

5. *Resistance to change.* When the child construes the therapist and the treatment situation as unable or unwilling to negotiate, replicating his/her experiences with significant others, the child resists change. As one example, recall Mary, discussed earlier, who barricaded herself behind closed doors construing the therapist as unavailable and not understanding. To overcome resistance to change the therapist introduces, within the child's metaphors, idealized standards and representations of psychological strength which are played out and internalized by the child. These metaphors of standard and strength in turn contribute to the resolution and transformation of core pathological metaphors.

6. *What if a child lacks the capacity to construct symbols and metaphors?* In order to promote change in meanings and vehicles of metaphors within the non-directive treatment process, the child should come equipped with stage-adequate capacities to construct symbols and metaphors. But symbol formation and metaphor construction call for a complex set of cognitive functions [42]; for example, copying (reproducing) static, moving, and anticipated information; inferring relationships between perceptions and images and between actions and outcome; approaching the same information from different points of view; transforming information with conventional and personal symbols and by using different vehicles; perceiving standards of behavior permitted and prohibited by various environments. For children who have not adequately developed these cognitive functions, a cognitively oriented, directed form of treatment is indicated either as preparation for non-directed therapy or as an alternative. One such method has been proposed which rehabilitates cognitive functions, promotes symbol formation and then provides the child with experience in metaphor construction with a method of directed fantasy [42].

7. *Cognition and emotion.* With the model of metaphor construction proposed, cognition plays a pivotal role as a highly mobile set of functions which determine whether and how a child perceives the requirements and prescriptions of internal meanings and those of external opportunities and limitations, integrating these and influencing the type of correspondence possible between them. Emotions are conceptualized as an integral part of the behaviors a metaphor prescribes and represents and not as a separate behavioral system (see [31] for a detailed discussion). In this view, a single

meaning or vehicle could include different emotions and different meanings could be connected with the same emotion. For example, in the treatment of Mary discussed earlier, she experienced and expressed agitation and anger while manipulating clay (as a metaphor of explosions and dirt) and later she experienced pleasure, pride and affiliation while manipulating clay in a metaphor of serving and receiving meals.

If we consider Aristotle's view that mastery of metaphor is a sign of originality and genius [23, p. 83] then all children are original artists, representing past victories and defeats with developmental battles, revealing unique conceptions and distortions of present situations, and following plans of actions which result in new victories as well as fresh wounds. Whether working in the psychological laboratory or treatment situation, the challenge, following Thompson [15], is to continue learning about the types of metaphors children construct throughout development in order to negotiate key developmental issues, how the meanings and vehicles of these metaphors undergo change, and how children can be helped to develop the capacity to construct and negotiate metaphors that foster development, learning from experience and successful adaptation.

REFERENCES

1. S. Santostefano, Metaphor: Integrating Action, Fantasy and Language in Development, *Imagination, Cognition and Personality*, 4:2, pp. 126-146, 1985.
2. H. Gardner, *The Mind's New Science: A History of the Cognitive Revolution*, Basic Books, Inc., New York, 1985.
3. M. J. Mahoney (ed.), *Psychotherapy Process: Current Issues and Future Directions*, Plenum Press, New York, 1980.
4. M. J. Mahoney and A. Freeman (eds.), *Cognition and Psychotherapy*, Plenum Press, New York, 1985.
5. H. W. Reese and W. F. Overton, Models of Development and Theories of Development, in *Life-Span Developmental Psychology*, L. R. Goulet and P. B. Baltes (eds.), Academic Press, New York, pp. 115-145, 1970.
6. P. C. Kendall (ed.), *Advances in Cognitive-Behavioral Research and Therapy Vol. 1*, Academic Press, New York, 1982.
7. M. J. Mahoney, Reflections on the Cognitive Learning Trend in Psychotherapy, *American Psychologist*, 32, pp. 5-13, 1977.
8. W. N. Dember, Motivation and the Cognitive Revolution, *American Psychologist*, 29, pp. 161-168, 1974.
9. S. Garfield and A. Bergin, *Handbook of Psychotherapy and Behavior Change: An Empirical Analysis* (2nd Edition), John Wiley, New York, 1978.
10. M. Marmor and S. M. Woods (eds.), *The Interface Between Psychodynamic and Behavioral Therapies*, Plenum Press, New York, 1980.
11. D. B. Arnkoff, Psychotherapy from the Perspective of Cognitive Theory, in *Psychotherapy Process: Current Issues and Future Directions*, M. J. Mahoney (ed.), Plenum Press, New York, pp. 339-361, 1980.

12. D. C. Arnkoff and C. R. Glass, Clinical Cognitive Constructs: Examination, Evaluation, and Elaboration, in *Advances in Cognitive-Behavioral Research and Therapy* (Vol. 1), P. C. Kendall (ed.), Academic Press, New York, pp. 1-34, 1982.
13. M. J. Mahoney, Psychotherapy and Human Change Processes, in *Cognition and Psychotherapy*, M. J. Mahoney and A. Freeman (eds.), Plenum Press, New York, pp. 3-48, 1985.
14. R. N. Sollod and P. L. Wachtell, A Structural and Transactional Approach to Cognition in Clinical Problems, in *Psychotherapy Process: Current Issues and Future Directions*, M. J. Mahoney (ed.), Plenum Press, New York, pp. 1-27, 1980.
15. S. C. Thompson, Will It Hurt Less If I Can Control It? A Complex Answer to a Simple Question, *Psychological Bulletin, 90*, pp. 89-101, 1981.
16. R. Holt, Imagery: The Return of the Ostracized, *American Psychologist, 19*, pp. 254-264, 1964.
17. A. A. Sheikh (ed.), *Imagery: Current Theory, Research and Application*, Wiley, New York, 1983.
18. M. P. Anderson, Imaginal Processes: Therapeutic Application and Theoretical Models, in *Psychotherapy Process: Current Issues and Future Directions*, M. J. Mahoney (ed.), Plenum Press, New York, pp. 211-248, 1980.
19. A. Richardson, Imagery: Definition and Types, in *Imagery: Current Theory, Research and Application*, A. A. Sheikh (ed.), John Wiley, New York, pp. 3-42, 1983.
20. B. B. Barratt, *Psychic Reality and Psychoanalytic Knowing*, Analytic Press, Hillsdale, New Jersey, 1984.
21. P. L. Wachtel, *Psychoanalysis and Behavior Therapy: Toward an Integration*, Basic Books, New York, 1977.
22. G. E. Forman (ed.), *Action and Thought: From Sensorimotor Schemes to Symbolic Operations*, Academic Press, New York, 1982.
23. R. M. Billow, Metaphor: A Review of the Psychological Literature, *Psychological Bulletin, 84*, pp. 81-92, 1977.
24. A. Ortony, R. E. Reynolds, and J. A. Arter, Metaphor: Theoretical and Empirical Research, *Psychological Bulletin, 85*, pp. 919-943, 1978.
25. A. Ortony, Why Metaphors Are Necessary and Not Just Nice, *Educational Theory, 25*, pp. 45-53, 1975.
26. E. Winner, W. Wapner, M. Cicone, and H. Gardner, Measures of Metaphor, *New Directions for Child Development, 6*, 1979.
27. P. Moumoud and C. Hauert, Development of Sensorimotor Organization in Young Children: Grasping and Lifting Objects, in *Action and Thought: From Sensorimotor Schemes to Symbolic Operations*, G. E. Forman (ed.), Academic Press, New York, pp. 3-36, 1982.
28. R. R. Verbrugge and N. S. McCarrell, Metaphoric Comprehension: Studies in Reminding and Resembling, *Cognitive Psychology, 9*, pp. 454-533, 1977.
29. N. R. Smith, Developmental Origins of Structural Variation in Symbol Form, in *Symbolic Functioning in Children*, N. R. Smith and M. B. Franklin (eds.), Lawrence Erlbaum Associates, Hillsdale, New Jersey, pp. 11-26, 1979.

30. H. Werner and B. Kaplan, *Symbol Formation*, John Wiley, New York, 1963.
31. S. Santostefano, Cognitive Controls, Metaphors, and Contexts: An Approach to Cognition and Emotion, in *Thought and Emotion: Developmental Perspectives*, D. J. Bearison and H. Zimiles (eds.), Lawrence Erlbaum, Hillsdale, New Jersey, pp. 175-210, 1986.
32. ____, Action, Fantasy, Language: Developmental Levels of Ego Organization in Communicating Drives and Affects, in *Communication Structures and Psychic Structures*, N. Freedman and S. Grand (eds.), Plenum, New York, 1977.
33. ____, *A Biodevelopmental Approach to Clinical Child Psychology: Cognitive Controls and Cognitive Control Therapy*, Wiley, New York, 1978.
34. ____, Cognition in Personality and the Treatment Process: A Psychoanalytic View, *Psychoanalytic Study of the Child*, *35*, Yale University Press, New Haven, pp. 41-66, 1980.
35. S. M. Kosslyn, *Image and Mind*, Harvard University Press, Cambridge, 1980.
36. P. Mounoud, Revolutionary Periods in Early Development, in *Regressions in Mental Development*, T. G. Bever (ed.), Lawrence Erlbaum, Hillsdale, New Jersey, 1982.
37. A. Ortony (ed.), *Metaphor and Thought*, Cambridge University Press, New York, 1979.
38. J. Piaget, The Role of Action in the Development of Thinking, in *Knowledge and Development*, W. F. Overton and J. M. Gallagher (eds.), Plenum Press, New York, 1977.
39. L. W. Sander, Regulation and Organization in the Early Infant-Caretaker System, in *Brain and Early Behavior*, R. Robinson (ed.), Academic Press, London, 1969.
40. M. M. Gill (ed.), *The Collected Papers of David Rapaport*, Basic Books, New York, 1967.
41. S. Santostefano and C. Reider, Cognitive Controls and Aggression in Children: The Concept of Cognitive-Affective Balance, *Journal of Consulting and Clinical Psychology*, *52*, pp. 46-56, 1984.
42. S. Santostefano, *Cognitive Control Therapy With Children and Adolescents*, Pergamon Press, 1985.
43. H. Paivio, *Imagery and Verbal Processes*, Holt, New York, 1971.
44. M. J. Horowitz, *Image Formation and Cognition*, 2nd Edition, Appleton-Century-Crofts, New York, 1978.
45. L. Luborsky, *Principles of Psychoanalytic Psychotherapy: A Manual for Supportive/Expressive Treatment*, Basic Books, New York, 1984.

CHAPTER 9

The Paracosm:
A Special Form of Fantasy

ROBERT SILVEY[1] AND
STEPHEN MACKEITH

> Almost any man may like the spider spin from
> his own inwards his own airy citadel
>
> *John Keats* [1]

What do Thomas de Quincey, Anthony Trollope, Friedrich Nietzsche, Robert
Louis Stevenson, Claes Oldenbourg, C. S. Lewis, and W. H. Auden have in
common? The answer is that each one of them, in childhood and/or youth,
experienced a particular and uncommon form of imaginative activity, the
"paracosm,"—a spontaneously created, but maintained and elaborated, imaginary
private world. The classical examples of this psychological phenomenon are
"Angria" and "Gondal," the imaginary private worlds of the Brontë children,
Charlotte and Branwell, Emily and Anne. This chapter, based on an unpublished
monograph first drafted in 1980, is about paracosms; but we will begin with
some more general comments.

OUR GENERAL APPROACH

There are many different approaches to the study of imagery and the
imagination. Some concern themselves with the processes of imagery; we, on the
other hand, are chiefly interested in the form and content of imaginings. Our
studies are chiefly directed to the imaginative activites of healthy and "normal"
children and young people. Our approach is non-clinical, and only cautiously
interpretative. It is mainly explorative and descriptive, classificatory and developmental. Our interest is "humanist" and literary, as well as psychological. Our
prime concern is with the *mental* aspects of the imagination of children and

---

[1] Now deceased

young people. We are concerned hardly at all with their graphic arts and their writing of stories. Those subjects demand, and have widely received, separate attention. We assume that the development of spontaneous fantasy follows continuously on from the development of imaginative play in young children. That individual children can vary widely in their degree of imaginative potential is well known. Nonetheless, we can trace some typical threads of the development of the imagination through successive age-stages. Our three main age periods are three to six years, seven to twelve years, and thirteen to eighteen years.

There are, in childhood and youth, numerous differing *sorts* of imaginative activity. These can, with great advantage, be classified. One of us (S.M.) has worked out a useful classification into four main divisions and fifteen subdivisions. Here, however, we are limiting ourselves to one particular sort of imaginative activity, viz. paracosms, as defined above. As long ago as 1966 Jerome L. Singer briefly mentioned these "repeated, self-consistent and elaborate fantasies" [2]; but we cannot trace any proper investigation of the subject. The useful specific term, "paracosm," was devised for us by a friend, Ben Vincent, who later in this chapter himself figures as an ex-paracosmist, under the pseudonym "Dan." The additional terms, "ex-paracosmist," "paracosmist," and "paracosmic" are self-explanatory.

REASON FOR STUDYING PARACOSMS

At this point we should explain why paracosms aroused our special interest and provoked the present study. Most of the fantasies of childhood and youth are fleeting and ill remembered. Paracosms, by contrast, are remembered remarkably well, often for decades and usually in considerable detail. They are the "flies in amber" of fantasy. Moreover, written or pictorial documents about them are sometimes preserved for many years. Thus, quite apart from their intrinsic fascination, they constitute valuable material for the study of the imagination and of the general mental development of children. In fact, the variety of the forms of imagining found in children is, at first sight, so bewildering, and the various types so tend to merge into one another, that we were happy to be starting our explorations with paracosms only. Even so, we found it necessary to delimit our field of study with some care.

We assumed that a "true paracosm" has three essential characteristics, as follows:

1. The child distinguishes clearly between what he has imagined and what really exists.

2. His interest in his private world is sustained over an appreciable length of time.

3. His private world is important to him, and *matters* in his life; and he really cares about it.

A common additional feature is that the child takes a pride in his private world being systematized and attaches importance to it being internally consistent; but this does not always apply in the earlier half of the age-span from three to eighteen years.

SOURCES OF OUR MATERIAL

This study was originally begun by one of us (R.S.) on his own. He himself was an ex-paracosmist, having had, between the ages of ten and fifteen years, an elaborate imaginary private world, and he had preserved many of its documents. He retained an interest in this experience. In February of 1942 he gave, on the "Children's Hour" of the British Broadcasting Corporation, a series of three radio broadcasts about it. (For many years he was head of Audience Research for the B.B.C.). After his retirement, from about 1976, he developed further his interest in the subject. He set out to find other adults who had had paracosms in childhood or youth. He did this by making various enquiries, and by publishing letters and short articles in journals, such as *The Author*, and in newspapers, such as the *Observer*. In 1979 he invited S.M., an old friend, to share in the investigation. S.M. himself had never had a paracosm in childhood or youth; but he had a special interest in various related fields of study. He started to collect additional cases of paracosm. This he has done mainly by making personal enquiries of friends and acquaintances. The collaboration continued for two years, i.e., until Silvey's death in 1981. Since then S.M. has carried on, on his own. Indeed, he has extended the study to cover, in outline, all the main types of spontaneous imaginative activity in "normal" children and young people.

These informal methods of exploration, though pursued assiduously over more than a decade, and supplemented later by a diligent search for examples in published autobiographies, have yielded less than a hundred paracosmists and ex-paracosmists in all. This gives us a strong impression that the paracosm is an uncommon phenomenon (much less common than, say, imaginary companions). We are, however, well aware that we are in no position to offer any reliable evidence of its incidence or prevalence. We are vividly conscious of the fact that ours is by no means a random sample. It is an arbitrarily collected and self-selected group, probably heavily biased towards the middle socioeconomic class. In composition, it is Western, predominantly English-speaking, and largely British in nationality. Nonetheless, we are confident that the main results of our study are worthy of presentation, together with such examples as there may be space for.

METHOD

We were determined to analyze as carefully as possible our group of cases, such as it was. We wanted to know, not only about the private worlds created in childhood, but also about the circumstances of their creation and about the creators themselves. In 1978 one of us (R.S.) had, with the help of the late Dr. Vladimir L. Kahan, devised a suitable questionnaire. This had thirty-nine questions, arranged in four sections, as follows:

Section I — Your Private World Itself — Eight questions

Section II — Yourself and Your Private World — Fourteen questions

Section III — Yourself as a Child — Seven questions

Section IV — Your Home and Your School — Ten questions

The questionnaire was usually distributed by post; only in a small number of cases were we able to interview our subjects face to face. The questions were simplified and reduced in number for our three *child respondents*.

Why only three? The reason is that we did not seek them out. Our attitude to the *continuing* imaginary private world of a child or young person is one of "instinctive" respect. We are loth to meddle with the chrysalis while it is still developing. It seemed to us to be quite a different thing to invite mature adults to tell us, if they so chose, about the paracosms of their past childhood. In four exceptional instances, however, parents or teachers, who heard about our investigation, brought us cases where a particular extroverted child had spontaneously shared with them an imaginary private world, and these we accepted.

We present below some of the findings of our analysis of the replies of our first fifty-seven respondents. (In addition, we occasionally refer to one or another of our more recent cases to illustrate a particular point.) Thereafter, we present summary descriptions of eight of the sixty-four separate paracosms reported to us by those fifty-seven respondents. Our selection of examples aims to convey some idea of their variety.

FIRST IMPRESSIONS OF OUR PARACOSMIC MATERIAL

We have been surprised and impressed by the obvious delight of our respondents at finding someone actively interested in their paracosmic activities as children. Creating an imaginary private world is clearly a long-term emotional investment. We have been struck by the frank, detailed and seemingly accurate answers to our questionnaire. In a few instances, we have been able to check against each other the reports of two respondents who had shared a joint paracosm.

Within our paracosmic sample, we have found a wide range of variation in the attitude adopted by the paracosmist — as regards, at one extreme, communicativeness and sharing of the imaginary private world, and, at the other extreme, privacy or even complete secrecy. Many of our respondents reported having shared their paracosms with one or more friends, or with one or more siblings, or with the whole family. By contrast, quite a number stated that, until they wrote to us, they had kept their private world entirely to themselves. Often their frank and detailed answers to our questionnaire hinted clearly at the reasons for this. It seems that for some children, at certain times, secrecy about a paracosm has a high symbolic value. Occasionally an attitude of privacy, or even of secrecy, about a paracosm may be found in an adult who has willingly admitted creating in childhood one or more imaginary private worlds. An American friend, an Episcopalian priest, readily answered all our questions about a paracosm which he had between ten and fifteen; but he merely *mentioned* another paracosm which he had between ten and fifteen, saying that it was "so private I cannot share it." Such reactions, however, are very uncommon. The usual pattern of response combines delight at our interest in the subject with complete openness and a generous outpouring of detailed information about the paracosm and the childhood of the ex-paracosmist.

In our analysis of the sixty-four paracosms collected from the first fifty-seven respondents, an obvious point of interest was the age at which each particular child began to imagine his or her private world. In the case of any paracosm which was shared by two or more children, we have allotted it in our records to the age, at that time, of the particular ex-paracosmist who is reporting to us. Our analysis reveals that 19 percent of the respondents began to create their (first) paracosms during the three to six age period, 74 percent did so in the seven to twelve age period, and 7 percent between the ages of thirteen and sixteen. We prefer to use percentages, even though our numbers are small. Since such a high proportion of the children began their paracosms during the seven to twelve age period, it seemed worthwhile to break down that age-period into successive years. Results are listed in Table 1.

We are well aware that our collection of cases is not a proper "random sample." Nonetheless, we feel that we cannot totally ignore the peak of paracosm-commencements in the ninth year (between eight and nine). At first, this finding rather surprised us. Now, however, we realize that it is highly compatible with the concurrent increase, reported by J. L. Singer [3], in imaginative responses to the Rorschach test. By contrast, there has occurred, during the seventh or eighth year, a decline of the *overt* expression of fantasy in action [4].

Table 1. Age at Which Paracosms
Had Started

Birthday	Percent
Eighth	31
Ninth	53
Tenth	63
Eleventh	77
Twelfth	82
Thirteenth	93

VARIATION OF CONTENT IN PARACOSMS

We have been impressed by the remarkable variety of the content of the imaginary private worlds of childhood. They fall, as regards their main focus, into five Content-Groups, as follows: 1) Toys, animals, and family groups; 2) Particular places and communities; 3) Islands and countries, and their peoples; 4) Systems, documents and languages; and 5) Unstructured, shifting and idyllic worlds.

PARACOSMS STARTING BETWEEN THREE AND SIX

Of most paracosms it can be said that each has its own individuality and its own intrinsic fascination. For each of the first sixty-four we collected, we hold a full dossier, with a detailed description of the paracosm, and much information about the paracosmist and his/her childhood. (The numbers of males and females in the group, were as it happens, almost exactly equal.) Here we shall need to restrict ourselves to just a few fairly typical examples of paracosms. Moreover, we shall be able to draw only very briefly on the relevant case summaries. In each case quoted, the "first name" given is a pseudonym. (Our selection does *not* represent the total incidence or the gender-distribution in any particular age-period.)

Paracosms beginning between the ages of three and six tend to belong to Content-Groups 1 and 2 (see above), and to originate from, for example, domestic animals, favorite soft toys, or particular places. They usually have a large element of direct wish-fulfillment. There may also be a considerable element of physical "acting out" of events in the imaginary private world. As compared with the paracosms of the later age-periods, paracosms starting between three and six years tend to be more shifting and more loosely structured, less consistent internally, and less clearly differentiated from imaginative stories of other kinds. Following is just one example.

Holly. For "several years" before the age of six, Holly's private world was a country called Branmail, to which "access could only be attained by scaling a height called Bumpety Banks. Apart from myself, all the inhabitants were cats. Within this nation was one family, who were my especial friends, consisting of father, elder daughter Kitty and younger offspring. Kitty was a sort of antiheroine . . . the perpetrator of any offence I had myself committed." Holly's was a solitary preoccupation of which, however, her parents were aware and in which they encouraged her. She would act out stories about it. (Subsequently, between the ages of seven and thirteen, Holly created other worlds.)

PARACOSMS STARTING BETWEEN SEVEN AND TWELVE

We have shown above that the inception of imaginary private worlds is mainly a phenomenon of the seven to twelve age-period. In addition, most of the paracosms begun between three and six persist at least some way into the seven to twelve age-period, so that the total prevalence is increased. Over the six years of this age-period, there are gradual changes in imaginative activities *generally*. For example, the content of the child's ordinary free-floating *day-dreams* alters gradually, according to whether his or her age is seven to eight, nine to ten, or eleven to twelve [5]. There is a similar gradual shift, over the seven to twelve age-period, in the form and content of imaginary private worlds.

Like the pre-sleep serial stories and daytime stories, in which they seem to have their roots, the paracosms of this period tend gradually to become more detailed, more sophisticated, more elaborate and more systematized. Actual favorite soft toys, etc., which are often prominent in the paracosms of the three to six age-period, now figure less often (though that trend is sometimes delayed when a child of, say, ten or eleven shares a private world with a sibling who is several years younger). On the other hand, there tends to be increasing use of incidents and characters from the child's favorite reading material or television program, especially when a paracosm is being *started*. With regard to the *main focus of content* in the commencing paracosm, we detect, as we progress through the six years of the seven to twelve age-range, an increasing tendency towards the lower groups of the list of Content-Groups. The content of a paracosm seems, however, to be heavily influenced by the particular child's individual temperament, special interests and knowledge. In this seven to twelve age-period, therefore, we shall give one typical example for each of the five Content-Groups.

Content-Group 1: Toys, Animals and Family Groups

Alice. Alice has one sibling, a brother three years younger than herself (both are now artists). When she was ten and he was seven, they began to create together an imaginary private world. It reached its zenith a few years later. Although its character changed when they reached adolescence, their joint enjoyment of it has never really stopped.

To begin with, the paracosm was toy-based, mostly paper dolls, but "Once we realized we could draw and write about the characters, we were emancipated from the toys." The physical setting of their "world" resembled the northern industrial area in which they lived. The milieu of their imaginary widely-ramifying principal family was similar to the children's own. They gradually built up a wealth of picturesque characters, partly drawn from radio series they had heard and books they had read. As time passed, their paracosms developed increasing internal consistency. Alice lists the satisfactions they derived from it. It gave them "symbolic power over their environment." It generated a "relaxing and recreative humour." There was the pure pleasure of "what Tolkein calls 'the joy of sub-creating'," and "the special joy" of an intimate sibling relationship.

Content-Group 2: Particular Places and Local Communities

Jim. The whole of Jim's adult life has been bound up with the drama, which he has served in a variety of capacities. He describes himself as "an incurable romantic." He came, in his childhood, from a working-class family, whose members, he says, on the whole got on well together, and at times of need were mutually supportive. However, there were seven of them, including three generations, and since their home had only four and a half rooms, they were on top of one another. Jim deeply felt the lack of any physical privacy. His "private world entity" came into being when he was about nine. It took the form of an imaginary theater. He wrote down virtually nothing, made no models and drew no designs. "It was set in the here-and-now . . . and was almost entirely interior." He was concerned with both "back stage" and "front of the house"; with mentally designing and building sets, choosing the plays for his imaginary company of players, casting and finally producing them. He would identify with all his actors, none of whom were based on people he knew. It was a solitary pursuit. He had no other hobbies. He says: "I think I was born with an instinctual conception of the disciplines of the drama." He explains that his private world was "the kind of escapism judiciously necessary to keep people sane." He sees it as having provided him with a way of withdrawing from the real world, in which he felt controlled, often unpredictably.

Content-Group 3: Islands and Countries, and Their Peoples

Miriam. Miriam (now a professional writer of fiction) had one sibling, a younger brother to whom she was close. Their parents had married late, so "we children lived an almost separate life." When Miriam was eight, she and her brother created a race of very small people, called the Minaturians, for whom cart-tracks were streets. She edited and illustrated a magazine for them. When she was about eleven, she and her friend Mary created imaginary islands — Insula for Miriam, Prosperito for Mary, and, later on, an enemy island, a dictatorship called Urilia. Their joint enterprise continued well into their adolescence, reaching a peak when they were fifteen to seventeen. Mary, Miriam's collaborator, has supplied us with her separate evidence, which at all points confirms Miriam's description of their private world. Mary makes the point that, since both girls led sheltered lives as children, their paracosm gave them "the chance to have adventures and experiences that we could not have had and, indeed, were not ready for. . . . In fact I think it was when things really happened to *us* that the thing started to fade."

Miriam reports that, as well as maps, there were "notebooks of historical dates, dynasties, wars, major writers with titles of plays, etc., legends, orders of chivalry and patron saints. . . . Our people were not children but grown-ups, leading adventurous lives with love affairs to match. We got interested in the love affairs a bit later than the adventures, but they soon became important. . . . The people were the most important part of our world." The girls did not identify with their characters; "they were like the characters a novelist uses."

Content-Group 4: Systems, Documents and Languages

Dan. Dan's paracosm, shared with his slightly younger cousin Peter, ran continuously from five to thirteen, developing all the time. We have obtained separate evidence from Peter. Both of them became senior civil servants. Dan was the only child of a socialist middle-class couple. He was a very happy child. He and Peter, when they were five, created the mythical state of Possumbul, which eventually grew into a contemporary island-state. The two boys shared the throne, on the precedent of William-and-Mary. At first they used their toy soldiers as citizens. They invented a neighboring state, called Possumbile, on which they made war. Possumbul was a democracy, but the elections were always won by the Socialists with a thumping majority. The language, Possumbulese, was English with a modified spelling, and a beautiful script based on Tamil, a primer of which Dan's father had brought back from India. The boys invented a religion, with an evil God and a good God, a small Victorian phrenological bust being the good God's image. They also devised an appeasement ritual. For the fine cities of Possumbul, the boys at first used their bricks; but later Dan transferred his interest to making elaborate maps and plans of the capital, Padington. There were timetables of the regular bus and tram services, and great trouble was taken in the designing of uniforms and medals. There were no miracles or magic; plausibility was essential.

Content-Group 5: Unstructured, Shifting and Idyllic Worlds

Francis. Francis, as an adult, had a distinguished military career, attaining the rank of major-general. As a child, he had two different private worlds which overlapped in time. The first was "a Walter Mitty affair in which I had much success." In it, he "identified with military heroes." Its events were implausible and largely inspired by books and stories. In fact, it barely ranks as a "true paracosm." The second private world was quite different. It was created spontaneously when he was about seven. Its zenith came about four years later. He was about eighteen when it began to pall, though spasmodically, he says; it is real to him even now. He drew maps of it, though it had no precise location. "In it I saw, touched and felt things. Other beings, human or animal, came and went without any particular effect on me." He felt that the imagining of this second world was subject to "some form of limitation which, if broken, would ruin it." He cannot define this "beyond that it was intangible and somewhat strange. . . . No conscious effort by me was necessary to enter this world." In it he "was very happy, did nothing in particular but just loved being there. . . . It was a happy, enjoyable, un-evil place." In retrospect, Francis wonders whether its serenity had not something Utopian about it. He feels that his second world satisfied his life-long deep sense of order and his hatred of destruction. "In my private world all was clean, tidy and undamaged."

PARACOSMS STARTING BETWEEN THIRTEEN AND EIGHTEEN

Among the first sixty-four paracosms we collected, only 7 percent began between the ages of thirteen and eighteen. (Actually, in that series there was none after the seventeenth birthday). Occasionally, an imaginary private world begun in this age-period will combine the display of remarkably detailed knowledge of a pet subject with an element of rather self-conscious facetiousness. We have selected, however, a more ordinary example.

Jack. Jack was an only child. In childhood he was often lonely, but he was usually happy and never lacked a feeling of security. He writes: "From early teenage years I created an imaginary island in the North Sea. . . . It was supposed to be in all respects realistic, with roads, railways, towns, hills and other geographical features. At first it was called Saxonland, but I soon changed the name to Cwayland. From the start the people of the island spoke their own language, with hardly any words like English. . . . It was fun inventing an old religion, like the Greek or Norse. . . . I've kept all the maps and almost everything I ever wrote or drew about the island, including, for example, lists of local radio and TV programmes. . . . As an adult, I confess to you that I still have an island in the North Sea. It is a descendant of Cwayland, and very occasionally I draw a new map of it. . . . It is reassuring to think that my unusual pastime is maybe not so strange after all."

HOW PARACOSMS USUALLY COME TO AN END

This selection of examples of imaginary private worlds has demonstrated the wide variety in the age-stages at which they are initiated. There is a similar variability in the ages at which they come to an end. Quite a lot stop during the last third of the seven to twelve age-period, viz. at eleven or twelve. Many more cease in the first half of the thirteen to eighteen age-range, and most of the rest in its second half.

The manner of the ceasing is not always the same. In most instances, it seems, the private world is merely called to mind less and less often, with the paracosmist barely noticing the change. In a few cases, however, the paracosmist makes a more conscious and deliberate decision about the matter. Here is an example.

Holly (one of the cases selected above) "decided in the space of one afternoon that I could not go on living in a childish world of non-existent people. This was a distressing decision, and I found that I continued to talk to figments of my imagination at times when I was not concentrating on anything else . . . to some extent I still do so."

Of the small number of paracosms which last up to the age of eighteen, some, to some extent, continue until nineteen, twenty or even later before they finally lapse. More rarely, an imaginary private world begun in childhood or youth may persist, fitfully but quite vividly, throughout adult life. In our group, of the first fifty-three (adult) respondents to our questionnaire, five told us that, at the time of their writing to us, their paracosms still, in some degree, persisted. Of those five, four are included among the case summaries selected for quotation earlier in this chapter. These four are Holly, Alice, Jack, and Francis. But, what about imaginary private worlds *beginning* after the age of eighteen? These seem to be very rare and to happen only to unusual persons in special circumstances. There was none in the group of our first sixty-four cases. However, further paracosm reports kept trickling in. One which we recently received concerned an imaginary private world which began when the paracosmist was about twenty-one.

Darius. Darius is a retired academic scientist. He was a bookworm from the early days of his childhood. During the Second World War he was in the British Army. From 1940, when he was about twenty-one, he was under training in the United Kingdom. Of this period, he writes: "I was bored much of the time, for the Army has a slogan 'Hurry up and wait' which was very characteristic of my service at that time. . . . It was the amount of idle time that Army training regimes provided that was the opportunity, as well as possibly some cause." Darius at that time created the imaginary private world of Pacifia, "an island state, a country with a small, highly educated and intelligent population. . . . This high I.Q. enabled the community to overcome numerical deficiency by high-tech, mostly imagined, but deriving from the real world. . . . It was loosely based on the configuration of Tierra del Fuego. . . . I was certainly present within the community, but not a leader, rather a No. 2. . . . There were no individual characters in my world, only groups of people. . . . Much time was spent in creating an armed forces structure, totalling a brigade with units down to section, and appropriate badges, etc. This obviously was a direct reflection of life in the training units. . . . My paracosm was an ideal of the real world, and therefore operated within the same constraints. . . . It really was exploratory rather than compensatory." Darius describes his private world as a "mental Meccano." This first-phase paracosm was active during his 1940-42 period of training. "Once I went on field service, Pacifia went into the shadows; but after the war, when I finished a second degree here, . . . it resurrected as a 'just' society, still of highly intelligent small population, in which the ideals of social justice, and equality, a rather vague social democracy, with meritocracy overtones, took over. The military faded away. Again, it filled in time when I was hanging around, waiting for something." Darius thinks that "the most intense interest, and probably the fullest scenario" was in that phase 2, about thirty years ago, when he was thirty-five. That went into decline about five years later.

In this context we must refer, if only briefly, to another example, about which we have read, of a true paracosm occurring in adult life. In the U.S.S.R. Vladimir Bukovsky was a well known dissident. He was repeatedly imprisoned in circumstances of deprivation and severe pressure; he experienced long periods of solitary confinement. In his autobiographical book, he vividly describes how he used, as an instrument of survival, an elaborate paracosm—the imaginary building, furnishing and enjoyment of a magnificent castle [6]. He was about thirty-four at the time.

THE FOUR MAIN "DIMENSIONS" OF PARACOSMS

Careful study of the sixty-four paracosms reported to us by our first fifty-seven respondents showed us that there are four main dimensions, in terms of which private worlds can vary among themselves. These are as follows:

I —Fantastic-Naturalistic
II —Idealistic-Realistic
III—Degree of Personal Interaction
IV—Degree of Egocentricity

Such terms deserve some explanation. In the *fantastic* paracosm—as in the traditional fairy story—natural laws and normal conventions of behavior can be set aside. There may be trees with the power of speech or gnomes or mythical beasts. Holly's world is an example. On the other hand, children who create *naturalistic* private worlds often give the impression of striving to make their worlds as normal as possible. The events in naturalistic private worlds may be improbable, but they will always be possible—at least in the opinion of the creator. Examples include Jim's repertory company.

We have called the second major variable *Idealism-Realism*. In the *idealistic* paracosm, everyone is happy, and nothing can go wrong. It may even be intended to be a model of perfection, as was that most famous of all adult imaginary worlds, More's Utopia. Francis' paracosm is an example. On the other hand, in a private world which is, in our terminology, *realistic*, the patterns of behavior correspond to real life; moral dilemmas can arise, and sins can be committed. Indeed, blood-thirsty warfare is quite frequent in some realistic paracosms. Such is Jack's private world.

The third variable relates to the extent for which the paracosm is, for the child, primarily a setting in which imaginary characters can act out their lives, and in which the interplay of personality can take place. We have called this the *Personal Interaction* variable. In the private worlds in which *personal interaction* is *maximal*, the imaginary characters may loom so large that their setting is quite shadowy, being limited to the bare necessities. The islands of Miriam and her friend exemplify this. In those paracosms in which *personal interaction* is *low*, their creators seem to be preoccupied with the act of creation, with impersonal events in the world created or with both. In such cases, the setting is likely to be highly elaborate, whereas the people, if any, are likely to be present only in a functional capacity. The world shared by Dan and his cousin illustrates this pattern.

Finally, the fourth variable, *Egocentricity*, has to do with the way in which the child him/herself relates to his/her private world. When the child himself is the central figure in it, either as himself or as a character with whom he identifies, obviously there is a *high* degree of *egocentricity*. *Egocentricity* is, equally obviously, *low* when the child stands outside his private world, detaching himself from it, or, if he participates in the action at all, does so only in some minor role. Darius provides an example of this attitude.

Further, to illustrate our classification we may cite Angria, the imaginary country of Charlotte and Branwell Brontë. For both children, this paracosm was naturalistic and realistic; and, since neither figured within it, it was also nonegocentric for both of them. But in terms of the personal interaction variable, we must distinguish between Angria's significance for Branwell and its significance for Charlotte. Branwell was preoccupied with its geography, history, and institutions, and above all with its political events; whereas Charlotte, loyally accepting the scene provided by her brother, concentrated on writing stories about Angrian characters. Thus from Charlotte's point of view Angria was personalized, whereas from Branwell's it certainly was not. This is a reminder that, when more than one child "plays with" the same paracosm, it does not necessarily have the same significance for each child.

To a particular child, the significance of a private world which lasts a long time may well change in the course of the life of the paracosm. For example, if it is started when the child is seven years old, it may well be fantastic at first, but as the child develops, that fantastic character is likely to satisfy him less and less and to be gradually shed. In a few years' time the paracosm may become wholly naturalistic, even though in loyalty the child may retain the names of places in it to which he has become attached.

ANALYSIS IN TERMS OF VARIABLES AND GENDER

Although our sample (of sixty-four paracosms described by our first fifty-seven respondents) was self-selected, there is some interest in seeing how the paracosms distribute themselves in terms of the four variables discussed above. Analysis in terms of the gender of the child-creator is included. The smallness of groups compelled us to limit ourselves to either/or assessments, seeking

Table 2. Fantastic-Naturalistic Variables by Sex

	Created by		
	Boys	Girls	All
Fantastic	5	12	17
Naturalistic	24	21	45
Mixed	2	0	2
Total	31	33	64

to assign ambiguous cases to where they seemed "on balance" to belong. The distinction between "fantastic" and "naturalistic" was sometimes blurred among the younger children.

We compiled the figures for Variable I (*Fantastic-Naturalistic*) in the sixty-four paracosms in Table 2. These figures show that, where their creators were boys, naturalistic private worlds outnumbered the fantastic in our sample by nearly five to one. But where their creators were girls, though the naturalistic did substantially outnumber the fantastic, the disparity was not nearly so great.

Similar tables were compiled for the three other variables, but in this short chapter they need not be set out in detail.

As regards Variable II, *Idealistic-Realistic*, the overwhelming majority of our samples of paracosms were realistic, whether created by boys or by girls. It may be noted at this point that an examination of the interrelationships of Variables I and II reveals that, although virtually all the naturalistic paracosms are realistic, the converse does not hold; nearly one in four of the realistic private worlds is fantastic.

The distribution of the girls' and boys' paracosms in terms of Variable III, *Degree of Personal Interaction*, reveals a sharp contrast. Those in which personal interactions is high account for only one in ten of the boys', whereas they account for two-thirds of the girls'.

As regards Variable IV, *Degree of Egocentricity*, two-thirds of the private worlds in our sample are not egocentric; but among the eighteen which *were* classified as egocentric, more were created by girls than were created by boys.

Finally, we looked to see whether there was any tendency for the same four attributes to recur in combination. There proved to be one, but only one, such combination, viz., naturalistic – realistic – personal interaction low – not egocentric. This grouping occurred twenty-seven times among our sixty-four paracosm-cases. Of these twenty-two were the creation of boys, and only five the creation of girls.

THE PERSONALITIES OF THESE CHILDREN

What about the personality type of the child who creates one or more paracosms? Singer, discussing individual differences in fantasy-predisposition generally, links high-fantasy subjects with Broadbent's "long samplers," and even with obsessional personality [7, pp. 201-202]. We were working on a small and non-random sample of paracosmists, without a control group of persons who in childhood had never had a paracosm, and we were limited to a postal questionnaire; so we could only attempt a simple form of investigation. The data for this depended on question 23 of our thirty-nine-question form of enquiry. In that question, we had invited our respondents themselves to assess their personalities when their paracosms were active. We listed twenty-six adjectives, in alphabetical order, and asked each respondent to indicate those which he/she felt to have been particularly applicable to him/herself. Fifty-five paracosmists took part in this exercise in retrospective self-assessment (Table 3).

It is perhaps hardly surprising that "imaginative" should have been the adjective endorsed most frequently—by forty out of fifty-five paracosmists taking part; nor that the next most frequently endorsed should have been "bright"! "Dreamy" and "bad at games" came next with twenty-three each ("good at games" was only endorsed by nine). "Tender-minded" had eighteen endorsements ("tough-minded" only two). "Un-mechanically minded" was also endorsed by eighteen paracosmists ("mchanically-minded" by only five). These self-assessments, taken at their face value, suggest that paracosmic imagining can

Table 3. Frequency with which Each of Twenty-six Self-descriptive Adjectives was Endorsed

Imaginative		40
Bright		34
Dreamy; Bad at Games	(each)	23
Conscientious; Curious	(each)	22
Timid; Apprehensive	(each)	19
Tender-minded; Un-mechanically minded	(each)	18
Solitary		16
Reliable		15
Adventurous; Easy-going	(each)	12
Good at Games; Energetic; Single-minded	(each)	9
Gregarious; Mechanically-minded	(each)	5
Self-confident; Light-hearted	(each)	4
Scatter-brained; Lethargic; Outgoing	(each)	3
Tough-minded		2
Irresponsible		1

appeal to differing types of children, but that it especially appeals to the dreamier and more tender-minded individual who is less inclined than most to vigorous outdoor sports, and who is not mechanically-minded.

Singer, writing about fantasy play in general, said: "It seems reasonable to deduce that only children, first-born children, or children distantly spaced from other siblings, might show greatest day-dreaming tendencies" [7, p. 62]. To our surprise, we found, on reviewing the series of our first fifty-seven paracosmists, that very few of them were "only" children, though quite a number were separated in age from their nearest siblings by some years. As regards the quality of relationships with the family, one or two of our respondents felt themselves to be "ugly ducklings"; but for the most part they got on well with their families. Private worlds are not necessarily, and in our sample not usually, refuges from family hostility or misunderstanding.

USES OF A PARACOSM

Among imaginative activities, the creation of a private world constitutes, in several ways, a particular case. So what are the "biological" functions, or emphases of function, of paracosms? This is a question which is not easy to answer confidently at the present time, but we can derive certain pointers from the replies of our first fifty-seven respondents to our questionnaire. The questionnaire was sent to a self-selected sample of people who said that they had had paracosms as children, and who had volunteered to tell us about them. It seemed likely that each of these people had *enjoyed* his/her private world. But we did not know what *sort* of pleasure or enjoyment these children and young people had derived from their paracosms; so we used our questionnaire to try to find out. We worded question 21 thus:

> Can you now, looking back, identify the nature of the satisfactions you derived from your private world (even though, at the time, you would have found it difficult, if not impossible, to articulate them)?

Some of our respondents did not attempt to answer this question. The replies which were received do not lend themselves to neat tabular presentation, if only because many of them were multiple, but what matters is the nature of the areas to which they point. A number of the different kinds of satisfaction which respondents identified can be grouped together as all relating to the "scope" which private worlds, in different ways, provide. Perhaps it is that a paracosm, by providing fantasy with a focus, diminishes the likelihood that the imagination will be dissipated in desultory forays, and furthermore that, by acting as a framework within which imaginings can be built on one another, it gives these imaginings greater depth and solidity. There were repeated references to the delights of the life of the imagination in contrast to the "dullness" of reality. Many respondents emphasized the opening offered by private worlds for the expression of their personal interests.

Another cluster of replies referred to the satisfaction to be derived from the act of creation itself, and to the sense of achievement which creation can bring. Several respondents likened the satisfaction they derived from creating a paracosm to that which professional authorship now brings them. An artist likened the feeling to that which he now experiences when he is really satisfied with one of his pictures. Dan wrote of the satisfaction he derived from "the simple absorption of my whole personality." "Joy" was a word which several people used in this connection. A number of respondents cited as a satisfaction the feeling of being "in control" of a private world. "I enjoyed immense satisfaction," wrote Norman, "from the feeling that in all respects it was *my* world." Veronica said that her private world gave "a measure of control over the people who were making my schooldays a misery." Those whose paracosms took the form of imaginary national states were especially likely to refer to a satisfying sense of power.

It was to be expected that the word "escape" would figure sometimes in the answers to this question. A paracosm is evidently a convenient and comforting place to escape *to*. The escape can be *from* any of a variety of situations. Quite commonly, the escape was said to be from "the boredom of everyday life." Finally, there were those who, though they remembered the thoroughly enjoyable relaxation derived from their paracosms, were unable to identify specific satisfactions. They just remembered that their private worlds were "great fun."

CIRCUMSTANCES WHICH ENCOURAGE FANTASY

Sections III and IV of our questionnaire included a variety of questions about the circumstances of the childhood of the respondent. The answers we received yielded a wealth of lively comments. This information greatly illuminated each individual case, but for the series as a whole, it proved difficult to classify. It seems that one essential for the creation of a private world is plenty of leisure. Early in our search for cases a successful and cultivated American businessman remarked to one of us (R.S.) that he himself could never have created a paracosm in his own childhood because every moment of his "leisure" was spent on a newspaper route or some other way of earning dollars to keep the home going during the Great Depression. When we reviewed the childhood circumstances reported to us, we failed to elicit clear evidence of any factors *specific to paracosms*. On the other hand, again and again in the reports we found evidence of the factors described in the literature as being conducive to *fantasy generally*.

Different cultures, and different times, appear to vary widely in their tolerance of, and general attitudes to, fantasy of all kinds. This also applies to particular families. The imaginative life of a boy or girl will have the chance to flower in a situation where, as Singer says, "the family does not significantly impede the child's spontaneous make-believe play, or shame or mock the child in the course of it" [7, p. 199]. Singer also lists various circumstances which are positively conducive to imaginative activities generally. He writes [7, pp. 190-199]:

> These circumstances include: 1) An opportunity for privacy and for practice in a relatively protected setting where the external environment is reasonably redundant so that greater attention can be focused on internal activities. . . . 2) Availability of a variety of materials in the form of stories told, books and playthings. . . . 3) Freedom from interference by peers or adults who make demands for immediate motor or perceptual reactions. . . . 4) The availability of adult models or older peers who encourage make-believe activity and provide examples of how this is done.

As regards the younger children, the Australian, Ruth Griffiths, towards the end of her classic book, wrote [8]:

> The whole of this study goes to show how important in early childhood are such factors in the environment as space in which to develop, time in which to dream and think, and opportunities to play alone, as well as at times in the company of other children. Too much company is as great a hindrance to development as too little; to be continually stimulated by social impressions without time to absorb them is as bad as to be left too long alone.

EVIDENCE FROM LITERARY SOURCES

Our understanding of paracosms has been deepened by the use of an additional and different angle of approach, viz. the collection of evidence from literary sources. From published autobiographies and biographies we have amassed a wealth of material about spontaneous imaginative activities in general, in childhood and youth. (We have not concerned ourselves at all with purely *fictional* accounts of childhood.) In particular, we have already, with the help of various friends, collected from such resources fifteen cases of imaginary private worlds in childhood and youth (apart from the classical example of the Brontë children). These have enriched our understanding of the nature and origins of paracosms.

There is, moreover, an additional yield from this further group of paracosmists. Almost all of them later became famous, or at least well-known. The ordinary reader already knows something about their later lives, and has easy access to further information about them. Their life-histories, therefore, complement in a very helpful way the findings of our study of our first fifty-seven privately collected cases. Our questionnaire occasionally elicited scraps of information about the paracosmist's later life, but it did not specifically enquire into that topic. In any case, we had promised anonymity to our respondents. Most of our additional group of fifteen "autobiographical and biographical" paracosmists later became writers of prose or poetry. Of course, this could be because writers easily write autobiographies! Other explanations, however, seem more likely. For the sake of researchers who wish to pursue the subject, we list the fifteen names below. We ourselves hope to describe elsewhere some of the fascinating details of these cases. Here we shall confine ourselves, in each case, to just a few points. The cases are grouped, as before, in the three main age-periods, according to the age of the child at the inception of the (first) paracosm.

Published Paracosms Starting Between Three and Six

Charles Hamilton Sorley (1895-1915). (English poet, killed in the Battle of Loos.) His paracosm, shared with siblings, began when he was well under five. His biography describes it as "an imaginary kingdom 'up the line,' connected by a vast railway system" [9].

Alan Watts (born 1915). (English writer.) His paracosm lasted from four to eight. In his autobiography it is described as "an island kingdom in the middle of the Pacific, most incongruously named Bath Bian Street." The book reproduces his drawings of the islanders [10].

Thomas William Malkin (1795-1802). (A happy little English boy, who died in his seventh year.) His imaginary private world, which began when he was four or five, was Utopian and precociously sophisticated. It was called Allestone. His father, Benjamin Heath Malkin, describes it in detail in his biography of his son [11].

Kenneth Grahame (1859-1932). (English author of *The Golden Age, Dream Days*, and *The Wind in the Willows*.) His paracosm, when he was five or six, is reported in the biography of Peter Green, which also describes the emotional deprivation of his childhood [12].

Wystan Hugh Auden (1907-1973). (English-American poet.) His imaginary private world lasted from six to twelve. In adult life, he described it as "a private sacred world, the principal elements of which were two: a limestone landscape based on the Pennine Moors in the North of England, and an industry, leadmining." Later on in the same passage, he said of his paracosm, "I felt instinctively, without knowing why, that I was bound to obey certain rules"; and he discussed this compulsion at some length [13].

Published Paracosms Starting Between
Seven and Twelve

Robert Louis Stevenson (1850-1894). (Scottish writer.) His paracosm began when he was six. He shared it with his cousin and close companion,
Bob (Robert Alan Mowbray Stevenson). The classic biography of the writer
reports: "One of their chief delights was in the rival kingdoms of their inven-
tion—Nosingtonia and Encyclopaedia, of which they were perpetually drawing
maps." Louis' kingdom was Encyclopaedia [14].
    Clive Staples Lewis (1898-1963). (English scholar and writer.) He
was the younger, by three years, of two sons. His relationship with his father was
awkward and strained. Of his mother he saw less and less as time passed, for her
health was deteriorating. (She died when he was nine.) When he was six years
old, his family moved into a rather isolated house on the outskirts of Belfast. He
began to occupy himself by writing adventure stories; and soon these stories
were set in a mediaeval Animal-land. His paracosm extended over the whole of
his middle childhood and into the first part of his adolescence, developing and
changing all the time. During the school-holidays, he and his brother linked
together their respective private worlds, creating the single state of Boxen. By
the time that he reached the age of twelve, Boxen had been greatly modified, in
a direction symbolic of adolescent rebelliousness. In adult life, C. S. Lewis
earned high repute as a university teacher at Oxford, and eventually became
Professor of English Mediaeval and Renaissance literature at Cambridge. He
wrote successful books in many different fields. Of these, the most relevant to
our present topic is his autobiographical sketch [15]. In that book he describes
in detail the origin and nature of his paracosm. He stresses how different it was
from ordinary day-dreaming. He also emphasizes that it had no close connection
with his "Narnia" stories for children.
    Friedrich Wilhelm Nietzsche (1844-1900). (German philosopher.)
His "fairy tale world" seems to have begun early in middle childhood. Based at
first on toy soldiers and certain porcelain figures, it was increasingly elaborated,
and enriched with miniature paintings and the reciting of original poems. His
sister Elizabeth, in her biography of her brother, gives a detailed description of
their paracosm and other imaginative activities [16].
    Austin Tappan Wright (1883-1931). (American academic lawyer and
novelist.) At the age of seven, he created an imaginary country in the southern
hemisphere, called Islandia. He maintained and elaborated this up to the age of
seventeen, when he lost active interest in it. However, at about twenty-five, and
most exceptionally, he re-activated his interest in Islandia, and wrote its history;
his writings eventually developed into a long novel. He died, at the age of
forty-eight in 1931. It was not until eleven years later that his novel was published, but it was immediately successful [17].
    Thomas de Quincey (1785-1859). (English writer.) He started his
paracosm in concert with his brother William, who was five or six years older.

Thomas was perhaps eight at the time. He created a tropical island, called Gombroon, which, alas, was constantly dominated by William's imaginary country, Tigrosylvania. The continual struggle is described amusingly in Thomas' Autobiographic Sketches [18].

Claes Thure Oldenbourg (born 1929). (Swedish-American painter.) The elder son of a Swedish diplomat, he arrived at the age of seven, with his family in Chicago. At that time he spoke no English, and it was then that he started his imaginary private world. This took the form of Neubern, an island between Africa and South America, whose language was half Swedish, half English. From that time there still survive numerous scrap-books, filled with maps, Neubern documents and hundreds of colored scale drawings. In her book, Barbara Rose quotes Oldenbourg's facetious(?) assertion in 1966: "Everything I do is completely original—I made it up when I was a little kid" [19].

Peter Alexander Ustinov (born 1921). (British actor and dramatist.) In his autobiography, Ustinov describes how, at the age of eight or nine, he invented his Utopian private world after witnessing an incident of cruelty [20]. In a much modified form, this paracosm has persisted into adult life. Ustinov claims that it lends him valuable "detachment" and independence in his work for international agencies.

Jacques Borel (born 1925). (French academic and writer.) He also admits that his imaginary private world still, in some degree, persists [21]. His first paracosm began at the age of ten. It was, in large part, a response to big changes in his life, and to the social insecurity felt by himself and his mother. Its successive stages are described at some length in his prize-winning autobiographical novel *L'Adoration* [22], translated into English under the title *The Bond* [23]. He himself feels that his childhood paracosms truly helped him to live.

Published Paracosms Starting Between Thirteen and Eighteen

Anthony Trollope (1815-1882). (English novelist and public servant.) His imaginary private world started at the age of about thirteen, apparently in response to a poor relationship with his father and to his total academic and social failure at school. Even after entering the General Post Office as a clerk at the age of nineteen, he remained despondent and ineffectual for a number of years, and this is probably why his paracosm continued until he was twenty-five or twenty-six. In his autobiography he describes it in detail [24]. As in the case of W. H. Auden, "Nothing impossible was ever introduced." Eventually he became successful and popular—socially, in his work and as a novelist. He himself wrote of his private world as a "habit . . . which, I suppose, must have tended to make me what I have been"; and he came to see the paracosmic imagining of his youth as the precursor of his later novel-writing.

Published Paracosms Starting After Eighteen

Christopher Isherwood (1904-1986). (English-American writer.) At the age of about nineteen, as an undergraduate at Cambridge University, Isherwood made friends with Edward Upward. Together, they created a private world. This went through various stages of development and ended up as the imaginary village of Mortmere. The story is told in Isherwood's novel, *Lions and Shadows* [25]. Although, in the preface, he insists that the book, as a whole, is not autobiographical, it is probable that the paracosm parts are. "Chalmers" is Upward, more or less. The world of Mortmere represents a spontaneous and lively rebellious response to various dislikes shared by the two friends, but these dislikes are more sociopolitical than personal. Christopher and "Chalmers" are self-conscious about their village, and sometimes almost facetious. They hanker to make use of it in pursuit of their literary ambitions. Their paracosm, in fact, is an elderly and rather "decadent" one—very different from the imaginary private worlds of most younger paracosmists.

Further "privately reported" paracosms have trickled in to us, ever since we closed the dossier of our first sixty-four cases in order to analyze them. In a similar way, we expect to hear from time to time of an additional example of an imaginary private world found in a published autobiography or biography. Among the instances of the latter sort already found and listed above, the descriptions of the origin and nature of their respective paracosms, by Trollope, Borel, C. S. Lewis, and Ustinov are specially illuminating.

SUMMARY AND CONCLUSION

"Imaginative behavior," as Sybil Gottlieb has wisely said, "is not a mere intermission from life or a discharge of energy, it is a continuation of life and an expression of development on a sign level" [26]. We ourselves wish to emphasize that the imagination is not a mere handmaid of cognition. It has its own rules, and its own age-linked stages of development. Hence its importance, and the need to study it. The trouble is that it is not an easy field for investigation. It seems that it may be best to focus on a specialized part of the field. We have concentrated on the study of paracosms because they are remarkably well remembered in adult life. Our study, moreover, has been greatly enriched by the careful and detailed descriptions of certain autobiographers, as mentioned above.

We have defined a paracosm as a spontaneously created, but maintained and elaborated, imaginary private world. A true paracosm seems to derive from the personal developmental and emotional needs of a particular child or young person. This is why we have accepted Darius' paracosm—even though it did not start until he was twenty-one—whereas we are grudging in our acceptance of the private world of Christopher Isherwood and his student friend. It also helps us to understand why the fifty-four adults of our "privately reported" series were so pleased and excited by our questionnaire and by our general interest in the subject.

Among fantasies, there is a wide variety of types, which may be conceived as arranging themselves along a broad "spectrum." On such a spectrum, paracosms would, we think, lie fairly near to one end, close to "problem-solving" fantasies, with ordinary daydreams lying at the other end. In their basic motivation, paracosms seem to us to constitute one special development of the play of young children. In that connection, Jerome S. Bruner once wrote: "Play has the effect of providing practice not so much of survival-relevant instinctive behaviour but, rather, of making possible the playful practice of sub-routines of behaviour later to be combined in more useful problem-solving" [27]. Paracosms certainly seem to explore the child's expectations of life. It seems clear that the motivations of paracosmists are *not* merely escapist or compensatory. They vary widely, as is shown both by the published autobiographical cases and by the "privately reported" series. Many ex-paracosmists of that series refer to their desire, in childhood, for independence or control or power. The creation of an imaginary private world, like other imaginative activities, seems to be encouraged by such factors as cultural and familial tolerance of fantasy generally, the existence of leisure, and stimulation by the hearing of stories, the reading of books and the availability of suitable material on radio and television. High degrees of correlation with the general intelligence and "creativity" of the individual child have been plausibly suggested, but we have not demonstrated these.

We have admitted earlier the arbitrary nature of our sample of paracosmists. Nonetheless, some of the more definite findings of this preliminary study are of considerable interest. We have demonstrated that paracosms can start at any age between four and sixteen, but very rarely do so after the age of seventeen. We have shown that, in our series, 74 percent began during the seven to twelve age-period, and that the peak frequency of commencements occurred between eight and nine. We have demonstrated some interesting differences, in our series, between the paracosms of boys and those of girls. For instance, paracosms in which the degree of "Personal Interaction" was high accounted for only one of the boys', whereas they accounted for two-thirds of the girls'. With regard to individual temperament, we have shown that the creation, in childhood or youth, of an imaginary private world appeals specially to the dreamier and more tender-minded individual who is less inclined than most to vigorous outdoor sports, and who is not mechanically-minded.

REFERENCES

1. J. Keats, Letter to John Hamilton Richards, dated February 19, 1818.
2. J. L. Singer, *The Inner World of Daydreaming*, Harper and Row, New York, p. 16, 1975.

3. J. L. Singer, The Experience Type: Some Behavioral Correlates and Theoretical Implications, in *Rorschach Psychology*, M. R. Rickers-Ovsienkina (ed.), Wiley, New York, 1960.

4. S. Millar, *The Psychology of Play*, Penguin Books, England, pp. 152-153, 1968.

5. T. L. Smith, Psychology of Daydreams, *American Journal of Psychology*, *15*, pp. 465-488, 1904.

6. V. Bukovsky, *To Build a Castle: My Life as a Dissenter*, Andre Deutsch, London, pp. 22-24, 1978.

7. J. L. Singer (ed.), *The Child's World of Make-believe: Experimental Studies of Imaginative Play*, Academic Press, New York, 1973.

8. R. Griffiths, *A Study of Imagination in Early Childhood, and Its Function in Mental Development*, Routledge and Kegan Paul, London, p. 357, 1935.

9. J. M. Wilson, *Charles Hamilton Sorley: A Biography*, Cecil Woolf, London, p. 22, 1985.

10. A. Watts, *In My Own Way: An Autobiography 1915-1965*, Jonathan Cape, London, pp. 42-45, 1973.

11. B. H. Malkin, *A Father's Memoir of His Child*, Longman, Hurst, Rees and Orme, of Paternoster Row, London, 1806.

12. P. Green, *Kenneth Grahame: A Biography*, John Murray, London, p. 19, 1959.

13. W. H. Auden, The Place of Value in the World of Facts, in *Nobel Symposium 14*, A. Tiselius and S. Nilsson (eds.), Almquist and Wiksell, Stockholm, 1970.

14. G. Balfour, *The Life of Robert Louis Stevenson*, Methuen, London, p. 49, 1902.

15. C. S. Lewis, *Surprised By Joy*, Collins (Fontana Books), London, pp. 15-18, 1976.

16. E. von Forster-Nietzsche, *Das Leben Friedrich Nietzsches*, Druck und Verlag von C. G. Nauman, Leipzig, 1895, Vol. 1, Chapter 4, pp. 36-39, 1895.

17. A. T. Wright, *An Introduction to Islandia: Its History, Customs, Laws, Language and Geography*, New York, 1942. Reprinted by Arno (Utopian Literature Series), 1971.

18. T. de Quincey, *Autobiographic Sketches 1790-1803*, Adam and Charles Black, Edinburgh, pp. 72-77, 1862.

19. B. Rose, *Claes Oldenbourg*, New York Museum of Modern Art, New York, pp. 19-20, 1979.

20. P. Ustinov, *Dear Me*, Penguin Books, England, p. 258, 1976.

21. J. Borel, personal communication, 1981.

22. ____, *L'Adoration*, Gallimard (Collection La Chemin), Paris, pp. 65-75, 1965.

23. ____, *The Bond*, (N. Denny trans.), Collins, London, pp. 57-68, 1968.

24. A. Trollope, *An Autobiography*, Williams and Norgate, London, pp. 54-56, 1946.

25. C. Isherwood, *Lions and Shadows*, Methuen, London, 1953.

26. S. Gottlieb, Modeling Effects on Fantasy, in *The Child's World of Make-Believe*, J. L. Singer (ed.), Academic Press, New York, p. 157, 1973.
27. J. S. Bruner, Introduction, in *Play: Its Role in Development and Evolution*, J. S. Bruner, A. Jolly and K. Sylva (eds.), Penguin Books, England, p. 15, 1976.

CHAPTER 10

The Realities of Play

BRIAN VANDENBERG

Even the most casual observer of children knows that they spend a great deal of time playing. The reasons why children play, however, are much more obscure and difficult to discern. This chapter will sketch some of the current and past efforts to understand play, and how these efforts are reflective of the way we think about reality. A concluding section will playfully suggest an alternative reality of play based upon an existential framework.

PLAY: PRESENT AND PAST

Current Research

One area that has received considerable research attention is if and how play contributes to the development of insightful tool-using strategies. The impetus for this line of research can be traced to the insightful problem solving of Kohler's famous chimpanzee, Sultan [1]. Subsequent to Kohler's report, several studies were conducted to identify how chimpanzees arrived at insightful solutions to problems. This research concluded that, contrary to Kohler's Gestalt hypothesis, prior experience played an important role in insightful problem solving in chimpanzees. What was unclear was the way in which experience led to insight, although there was some evidence to suggest that the chimpanzee's free play might be an important factor [2].

This small pocket of studies lay dormant for about twenty-five years, until the issue was reintroduced by Bruner, who hypothesized that play provided the behavioral flexibility necessary for insightful problem solving [3]. Bruner and his colleagues examined this hypothesis in children, and used a stick-lure task that was similar to those used in the chimpanzee research [4]. The results of this study confirmed Bruner's hypothesis, and sparked a series of investigations that have provided additional evidence that play can enhance children's insightful problem-solving skills [5]. Despite important limitations in the research on this topic, including the fact that these studies have only examined preschoolers, research attention has begun to shift to identifying how play contributes to insight. Early evidence suggests that play might develop a generalized schema of action toward a set of materials that may later be used in the specific way required to solve the problem, and that the use of fantasy in play may enhance subsequent problem solving [6, 7].

These results converge with a second line of research on children's play aimed at assessing the cognitive and social benefits of fantasy play. This area of research, which began about the same time as the play and insight research, grew from a different impetus. Several theorists, most notably Vygotsky have suggested that the ability to engage in fantasy play is a watershed event in a child's development [8]. Fantasy allows the child to escape the confines of the literal; a stick is a stick, but it can also become a horse. The severence of an object from its usual meaning is an important step in gaining mastery of representational systems, and requires a sophisticated set of cognitive abilities. It has been hypothesized that if children could be encouraged to engage in fantasy play, it might result in the growth of important cognitive skills [9].

Piaget has also had his effect. According to Piaget, preoperational children are plagued by egocentric thinking which prevents them from decentering and taking another point of view [10]. This egocentrism is manifest in both cognitive and social areas. Dramatic play offers the opportunity, through pretense, to take another's perspective, and has come to be seen as a potential antidote for egocentrism [11].

The beginnings of dramatic play and the presence of preoperational thinking are characteristic features of preschool and kindergarten children. For this reason, the research on the effects of sociodramatic play has been conducted almost exclusively with children of this age. The usual methodology has been to provide one group of children with a fantasy play experience that is directed by an adult. These children are compared on a range of cognitive and social tasks to children who had not been given a fantasy play training experience. Researchers have utilized several different types of fantasy training experiences, have trained the children for various lengths of time, and have used a wide variety of social and cognitive outcome measures. In almost all the studies, a positive effect of some type has been found for the play training experience [9]. On the strength of these findings, recommendations have been advanced for including fantasy play as a regular part of children's school curriculum [12].

Despite a relatively large body of research that has documented the effects of fantasy play, doubts remain. It has been argued that in many of the studies, fantasy play has been confounded with adult tuition; that is, it is unclear whether the results are because of the fantasy play, or because of the active involvement of the adult tutors in the children's play [13]. Also, the effects of fantasy play have not been consistent from one study to another. One study might find that fantasy play enhances social but not cognitive skills, while a second study might find the reverse. This rather haphazard pattern of results that cannot be explained theoretically, coupled with some methodological complications, have led some to suggest that there is less here than meets the eye [12].

A third line of research has investigated the relationship between play and creativity. Intuitively, play and creativity seem to be close cousins; to "play" with something means to consider it from various alternative perspectives, and to thereby recast the familiar in a novel way. Wallach and Kogan, in their analysis of creativity, have suggested that the creative act involves just such a playful, permissive attitude or set [14]. An alternative perspective has been offered by Sutton-Smith, who has suggested that play is characterized by an "as if" posture that produces novel associations to the play objects [15]. These theoretical formulations have served as the springboard for empirical investigations of the play-creativity relationship.

Primarily as a result of Wallach and Kogan's thoughtful work, the research on play and creativity has operationalized creativity as performance on divergent tasks [14]. Divergent tasks are open-ended, and require the production of diverse and numerous solutions, while convergent tasks require the focusing of thought toward a single solution. As was the case with play and insight (which utilized convergent tasks), most of the evidence supports the hypothesis that play with materials can stimulate more creative responses about the materials. Furthermore, the evidence suggests that play enhances creativity through a generalized playful set, and not through the accumulation of specific associations about the materials. Thus, when children who play with one set of materials are asked to give creative responses to a second set of materials that they did not play with, they are still more creative than children who were not given a play experience [16]. Although not entirely clear, it appears that the playful set that enhances creativity may be ephemeral and easily broken [5].

The link between playfulness and creativity raises the question of whether children who are more playful are also likely to be more creative. Surprisingly, the research on this question is not very extensive. While no definite, or even tentative answers are apparent, what has emerged is a greater appreciation for the complexities. There is some evidence that playfulness in preschoolers may constitute a unitary dimension of personality, but these studies consist only of teacher ratings, and mental age sometimes has been found to be a covariate of playfulness [7]. For older children, playfulness is much more differentiated, often involving contradictory traits (e.g., happiness and sarcasm [17]). The difficulty in isolating a consistent and valid playfulness factor makes it difficult to investigate whether playful individuals are more creative.

The research on insight, fantasy play training and creativity began at about the same time, and are primarily concerned with examining the link between play and various cogntive abilities. This is true even for the fantasy play training studies that examined the social impact of play, since most studies measured social cognition using Piagetian based perspective-taking tasks. During the late

1960s and through the 1970s, Piaget's work influenced almost all areas of research on child development, and the cognitive focus of the play research probably indirectly reflects his presence. Freud, the other grand theorist of child development, also spawned considerable thinking and research about children's play, and for historical and conceptual completeness, it is important that we review his influence.

FREUD

In contrast to Piaget's cognitive emphasis, Freud focused on emotional and personality dimensions of development, and this emphasis is reflected in his treatment of play. Freud's conceptualization of play changed as his theory changed. In his early work, when Freud was focusing on the features of the id, he suggested that play provides a safe opportunity for children to vent forbidden impulses [18]. Later, as Freud began to focus on ego functioning, he averred that play allowed the child to master prior traumatic events [19]. Freud's theories of play were pushed into the realm of practice by psychoanalytic therapists who attempted to tailor psychoanalysis to children. Klein reasoned that therapy with children could be conducted in the same manner as psychoanalysis with adults, except that free play, rather than free associations, would be the source of dynamic material for therapy [20]. Thus, play came to be seen as: 1) a source of catharsis; 2) a source of mastery; 3) a therapeutic technique; and 4) a window into the psychodynamics of a child's personality.

These four emphases have resulted in distinct approaches to play. Play as catharsis has led to a raft of studies on the hypothesized benefits of the expression of repressed impulses that have continued to this day. The results generally have not supported the cartharsis hypothesis [21]. The mastery aspect of play has been pursued by ego psychologists, most notably Erikson [22]. Erikson has attempted to identify a link between children's play constructions and their ego concerns [23]. While Erikson's findings have been replicated, the interpretation of his results is highly controversial [5]. Unfortunately, there have been few other attempts to empirically substantiate the mastery aspect of play.

The use of play as a therapeutic technique has gained widespread acceptance in the treatment of troubled children. Unfortunately, this area also suffers from a lack of systematic research. This is particularly disappointing, since research might lead to a better understanding of how we can best help children with problems. Basic questions, like if and how a therapist should intervene in the child's play, beg for answers.

In contrast, play as a window into hidden personality dynamics has been a source of rich and extensive research. The reason for this is probably because of the development of the doll play technique, which has proven to be a simple, yet powerful tool for evoking the thoughts and feelings of children. The doll play technique has been used to investigate a host of issues, such as the effects of parental separation on children, children's attitudes toward people of other races, and the types of situation that are likely to engender aggressive feelings in children [24].

PLAY AND CULTURAL VALUES

Work and Play

The research on play has been conducted within a cultural context that views play as a frivolous diversion from the more important activities related to goal-directed behavior and work. We live in a culture where efficiency and productivity are essential to our material well-being. This focus has resulted in the linking of time and money. Workers "punch a clock," which documents their exchange of time (and productive labor) for money, and salaried employees, who do not fill out a "time sheet," are expected to spend even more than the standard amount of time on the job in exchange for this privilege. Fluctuations in the prime interest rate, which is the institutionalized, hypothetical estimate of the financial value of time, creates massive gyrations in the national and global economy.

Clearly, time, productive work and financial gain are intimately meshed. Since play is something done during one's "free time," it stands in opposition to those work related activities for which one receives financial remuneration. Not surprisingly, Western thinking about play has been influenced by this work-play dichotomy. The usual definitions of play, for instance, emphasize that play is voluntary (in contrast to work, which is involuntary) is not goal directed (whereas work is productive), and is intrinsically motivated (while work is extrinsically motivated) [2]. Since play is a nonproductive activity, it has been, until recently, overlooked as a topic of scientific investigation. In psychology, for example, undoubtedly the most heavily researched areas over the past eighty years are those addressing problem solving and IQ related issues. Essentially, this research is concerned with charting the parameters that are related to goal-directed, productive activity, and with identifying those individuals who are most facile at these activities.

The assumptions about the relative value of work and play are also evident in the current research on play and play training reviewed above. In all of this research, play is a treatment that is administered to enhance problem solving, creativity, or other cognitive skills. Play is important only as it bears on these other, more culturally valued skills. Much of the research inspired by Freud has a similar bias. The doll play studies are not really studies about play *per se*; rather, play is used as a window onto other issues considered to be of greater importance [25]. A similar criticism could also be made of the play and catharsis research. Frequently, children's aggressive activity in their play is used as an *outcome* measure of the effects of other, presumed cathartic experiences [26]. This research misses the point that it is the effects of the play that are hypothesized to be cathartic, and that it should be treated as an independent, not a dependent variable. This error suggests that the researchers were more interested in the issue of catharsis than play *per se*.

The juxtaposition of work and play also has led to some related theoretical conundrums. If work is associated with productivity and reality, and play is aligned with frivolity and fantasy, then why do children spend so much time playing; biologically, what are the adaptive benefits of this activity that seems to have no goal-directed consumatory value? This question is what has prompted much of the recent research. The assumption has been that since play has no overt connection to productive behaviors (e.g., cognitive, problem-solving skills), then the connection must be indirect, and hence the use of play as a treatment variable. While there is nothing inherently wrong with this approach, our cultural assumptions about play may have blinded us to other potentially fruitful ways of considering play. Before offering an alternative approach, it is necessary to first review a second theme that pervades the research on children's play.

Play and Reason

With few exceptions, the research on play reviewed above has been conducted with young children. The contempoarary research on problem solving, fantasy play training, and creativity has been conducted exclusively with preschoolers and kindergarten children; the doll play studies have targeted primarily this age group; and the research on catharsis has focused on children under ten years of age. This is also true of play therapy, as most discussions of play therapy presume a young child as the client [27].

The reason for this narrow focus is more than just an oversight. Both Freud and Piaget have argued that developmentally, the growth in reason results in the disappearance of play as an important factor in thought [28, 29]. In Piaget's terms, the play of young children reflects the distorting influence of the domination of assimilation over accommodation. With development, assimilation and accommodation became more differentiated and integrated, creating a more stable cognitive structure. Under these conditions, assimilatively dominated activity is less distorted, and play is more adapted to realistic goals and activities. Or, as Freud indicates, "play is brought to an end by the strengthening of a factor that deserves to be described as the critical faculty or reasonableness" [28]. These theories are compatible with the way that adults usually view children's play. Children outgrow their tendency to engage in playing house, school and other fantasy themes, and their beliefs in fairy tales and myths, such as Santa Claus, erodes as the children came to see their logical short comings (e.g., "How can Santa fly around the whole world in one night?" etc.).

This view rests on the epistemological assumption that adults are able to apprehend reality through the use of logic and reason. Childhood fantasy play and children's myths are developmentally idiosyncratic phenomenoa that disappear once the individual begins to develop these critical facilities. Not only is this perspective congruent with our everyday notions of reality, but it also reflects the implicit assumptions of science; it is because of the pervasive influence of science on Western thinking that this assumption seems intuitively obvious. This assumption, along with the work-play dichotomy, has limited our ability to clearly see the importance of play and fantasy for our understanding of reality.

PLAY RECONSIDERED: AN EXISTENTIAL APPROACH

Martin Heidegger, the existential philosopher, has turned much of Western thought on its head [30]. Where others have focused on epistemological questions that have led them to assert the importance of logic and reason, Heidegger has argued for the primary of ontology, leading him to stress the centrality of freedom, anxiety, death and authenticity in human life. Although the most complete statement of his theory, *Time and Being*, was first published in 1927, it was not translated into English until 1961. Even in its translated form the text is daunting, as Heidegger has invented a lexicon to express his unique ideas. The result is that his theory has, until quite recently, remained obscure. His work is now beginning to have an impact on psychology and the social sciences, through the work of Gadamer (a former student of his) and other hermeneutic philosophers who have elaborated certain aspects of his theory [31]. Attempts to explicate his theory have also recently appeared in important psychological journals [32], and more direct use of his ideas are certain to follow. Because of his very different focus, his theory offers a potentially rich source of new insights on play. While it is impossible to provide a detailed account of his complex work here, a brief sketch will be given of those aspects of his theory that are useful for providing a more enriched understanding of play.

According to Heidegger we are "thrown" into this strange and uncanny universe, and attempt to make ourselves at home in a place that is not of our own choosing and beyond understanding [30]. We are quite successful at taming the universe, of domesticating it, by dwelling within social, public norms and meanings that protect us from the awareness of the groundlessness of our existence. Although we create a home or a clearing for ourselves, the awareness of the uncanny lurks at the fringes of our consciousness. Anxiety, which according to Heidegger is a fear of "no-thing," carries the potential to make us aware of the uncanny, and of our uniqueness, our aloneness and our responsibility for our own lives. Rather than hide within the shelter of public meanings which create an inauthentic existence, anxiety points to the possibility of authentic, self-chosen meanings. Anxiety, then, is the uncanny awareness of the self as free to be authentic or inauthentic [33].

While we are thrown into the actual and factual conditions of our lives, we are not prisoners of these facts. Rather, the essence of being human is that we project possibilities into the future. While we are constrained by the givens of our lives, we express our freedom toward these facts through the projection of our future possibilities. Possibility is more fundamental than actuality, although the nature of the projected possibilities is tied to the actualities of our lives. This relation is reflected in Heidegger's notion of temporality. One of the unique features of being human is that we exist, which means, literally, to stand-out. Temporally, we stand-out of time; we straddle past-present-future and incorporate all three within ourselves. Past, present, and future are not separate self-contained aspects of time that exist independently. Rather, they are intimately linked into an organic temporality that is expressed by the way we project our possibilities. We orient our relationship to our past and present according to the ways we anticipate the future. Thus, we are not prisoners of the facts of our past, but are hopeful beings whose orientation to the future influence the way we consider our past and present.

Truth, for Heidegger, is a revealing or uncovering; in the process of uncovering from darkness, the world presents itself to us in a new and immediate way. The process of discovering truth is related to the process of "lighting-up" the uncanny, of bringing to light, and making safe a certain aspect of life that previously belonged to darkness. To do so means we must stray from the accepted forms of public meanings, venturing behind and around them to discover the truths that are hidden by them. It is potentially risky, since it overturns the safety of public meanings, and requires imagination.

Play takes on new meanings within this framework. Most contemporary perspectives of play consider it as a means for the acquisition of information, the exercise of cognitive functions, or an area for the elaboration of social skills. The passionate aspects of play are seen as epiphenomenon, or accompaniments to these purportedly more fundamental aspects of play. This attitude no doubt reflects the long tradition in Western thought to see emotions as subsidiary to reason. However, the centrality of passion, excitement, and tension in play may reveal other important features of play.

For example, a four-year-old friend of mine frequently pretends that she is a cheerleader. She dances, jumps, and twirls in youthful imitation of her older heroines. Certainly the situation can be considered as an opportunity to learn and practice social roles and physical skills, and creates new information that may be used in later situations. However none of these reasons explain why she has chosen this particular role to practice, or why she plays it with so much gusto. A clue to a more complete explanation is that her mother was a cheerleader, and has talked to her daughter about it. Thus, her daughter is attempting to construct a possible future for herself as she plays with the meanings of maturity and adulthood that has been presented to her by her mother. In its meaning, its immediacy and its emotional richness, her play is closer to wish and hope than learning and rehearsal.

Play is an instance of projecting one's future, and the thrill is derived from exploring possibilities. This view of play is contrary to the Freudian notion of play as mastery of past traumatic events. This is not to argue that children don't play-out and play-over events that have occurred in the past. However, the salience of these past events, the reason why they emerge in the present, is because of the way they influence, constrain and control the children's future. Whereas Freud argues that we are our past, and the play of children reflect this, this view based on Heidegger suggests that we are our future, and that we are concerned about our past because of the influence it has on our projection of future possibilities.

This perspective on hope and wishing has been addressed by May [34] and Yalom [35]. According to these theorists, wish provides the impetus for willing and action; wish is forged into responsible action through will. In Yalom's words [33, p. 300]:

> Wish, which May defines as "the imaginative playing with the possibility of some act or state occurring," is the first step of the process of willing. Only after wishing occurs can the individual pull the "trigger of effort" and initiate the remainder of the act of willing, commitment and choice, which culminates in action.

While May and Yalom have discussed the importance of wish in adult action, their analysis provides a framework for understanding children's play. Play can be considered as a childhood form of wishing that serves similar functions as adult wishing. The difference between adult wishing and childhood play is that the former is covert and private, while the latter is overt and public. The reason for this difference is developmental. As Piaget [10] and Vygotsky [8] have demonstrated, children "think out loud"; that is, the developmental basis of adult thought is childhood action, and the process of development is characterized by the internalization of overt action into covert thought. Thus, with development, play is internalized as wish.

Yalom has identified several ways that dysfunctions in wishing leads to more general psychological dysfunctions. According to Yalom, the inability to wish is a common therapeutic problem that can lead to a failure to feel, and ultimately, to conduct one's life with an energized, personally crafted meaning. At the other end of the spectrum, individuals who act impulsively on the most immediate wish have no organized future, since they cannot cope with the anxiety associated with delaying a wish.

It is likely that these dysfunctions of wishing in adults described by Yalom are also found in children. If play is the developmental precursor to wishing, then play therapy could be seen as a process of developing healthy wishing. What is critical is the children's capacity to wish, and its relationship to willing and action. For some children, indulgence in play (regardless of the content) may be required to liberate the child's capacity to wish, while for others, restriction and evaluation of play impulses may be required.

The passion and excitement of play also comes from other sources. Dramatic play, such as playing house, is a common form of play among pre-schoolers. In such play children enact common meanings associated with family membership, and there is undoubtedly a component of hopeful projection of future possibilities involved. However, the children frequently play with the script. New twists and alternatives are introduced and the script is bent to the desires of the children; perhaps more favorable child-oriented behaviors are assumed by the mommy and daddy players, or the children in the family are more angry, demanding, and powerful. The children are uncovering the limits and power of public meanings and at the same time, exercising their sense of freedom. This is, in a sense, an excursion into the uncanny, and something is being revealed. Thus, it is thrilling not only to consider one's future, but to journey into forbidden areas of darkness behind the public masks of conventionality and to become aware of one's freedom in the process. What children do in their play, adults do in their imagination; each penetrates behind the staid world of public meanings and respectable behavior, and there is a sense of exhilaration at the unmasking, and the freedom from the tyranny of the mask.

Play as unmasking is part of more general relation between play and anxiety. Safety is a prerequisite for play [5], and it is the safe confines of play that allow for the exploration of potentially threatening realities. For example, adults frequently play with infants by tossing them in the air while making ghoulish faces and strange sounds. If such activities were to be performed by a stranger, the infant would become extremely frightened. A trusted caregiver, however, provides the safety that enables the infant to travel to the edge of terror, and play with it.

Play derives its thrill from anxiety. But anxiety is buried and concealed in play, and because it is hidden, play carries a high potential for inauthentic modes of being. This issue becomes more focused with development, when issues of authenticity become more important, and when the modes of play become more varied and complex. Since anxiety is hidden, play provides the opportunity for an indirect flirting with anxiety without having to confront the profound challenges posed by it. And herein lies play's allure; that one can play with unmasking and venturing into the uncanny without carrying the weight of responsibility and isolation that a direct confrontation demands. The more common forms of adult play allow for "losing oneself" in passionate activity that recasts reality in a new and exciting (as well as controlled and artificial) way. In extreme forms, play can become a narcotic, and the passions of drug addictions, compulsive gambling, etc., are forms of inauthentic play that has become blind. However, when anxiety is more directly viewed and incorporated, such as in the arts, the potential for authenticity is enhanced.

SUMMARY

In summary, the exclusive focus on the play of young children is the back side of the belief in the importance of reason for intuiting reality; and treating play as ancillary to more valued concerns, such as problem solving, reflects the effects of the work-play dichotomy. New ways of considering play emerge when attention is given to the thrill and excitement in play. From an existential framework, play is the embodiment of the human capacity to wish; a capacity that is necessary for willing and responsible action. It is also a form of indirect unmasking and uncovering that has the potential for both authentic and inauthentic modes of being.

REFERENCES

1. W. Kohler, *The Mentality of Apes*, Harcourt, Brace, New York, 1925.
2. B. Vandenberg, Play and Development from an Ethological Perspective, *American Psychologist*, *33*, pp. 724-738, 1978.
3. J. S. Bruner, Nature and Uses of Immaturity, *American Psychologist*, *27*, pp. 687-708, 1972.
4. K. Sylva, J. Bruner, and P. Genova, The Role of Play in the Problem Solving of Children Three to Five Years Old, in *Play: Its Role in Development and Evolution*, J. Bruner, A. Jolly, and K. Sylva (eds.), Basic Books, New York, 1976.
5. K. H. Rubin, G. G. Fein, and B. Vandenberg, Play, in *Handbook of Child Psychology: Social Development* (Vol. 4), Mussen (ed.), Wiley, New York, 1983.
6. J. A. Cheyne and K. H. Rubin, Playful Precursors of Problem Solving in Preschoolers, biennial meeting of the Society for Research in Child Development, Boston, 1981.
7. B. Vandenberg, Play, Problem-solving and Creativity, in *New Directions for Child Development: Children's Play*, K. H. Rubin (ed.), Jossey Bass, San Francisco, 1980.
8. L. Vygotsky, *Thought and Language*, MIT Press, Cambridge, Massachusetts, 1962.
9. E. Saltz and J. Brodie, Pretend-Play Training in Childhood: A Review and Critique, in *The Play of Children: Current Theory and Research*, D. J. Pepler and K. H. Rubin (eds.), S. Karger, Basel, Switzerland, 1982.
10. J. Piaget and B. Inhelder, *The Psychology of the Child*, Basic Books, New York, 1969.
11. C. J. Brainerd, Effects of Group and Individualized Dramatic Play Training on Cognitive Development, in *The Play of Children: Current Theory and Research*, D. J. Pepler and K. H. Rubin (eds.), S. Karger, Basel, Switzerland, 1982.
12. J. E. Johnson and J. Ershler, Curricular Effects on the Play of Preschoolers, in *The Play of Children: Current Theory and Research*, D. J. Pepler and K. H. Rubin (eds.), S. Karger, Basel, Switzerland, 1982.

13. P. K. Smith, Social and Fantasy Play in Young Children, in *Biology of Play*, B. Tizard and D. Harvey (eds.), Lippincott, Philadelphia, 1977.

14. M. A. Wallach and N. Kogan, *Modes of Thinking in Young Children: A Study of the Creativity Intelligence Distinction*, Holt, New York, 1965.

15. B. Sutton-Smith, Novel Responses to Toys, *Merrill-Palmer Quarterly*, *14*, pp. 151-158, 1968.

16. J. L. Dansky and I. W. Silverman, Play: A General Facilitator of Associative Fluency, *Developmental Psychology*, *11*, p. 104, 1975.

17. J. N. Lieberman, *Playfulness: Its Relationship to Imagination and Creativity*, Academic Press, New York, 1977.

18. S. Freud, Creative Writers and Daydreaming, in *The Standard Edition of the Complete Psychological Works of Sigmund Freud*, Vol. IX, J. Strackey (ed.), Hogarth, London, pp. 141-154, 1959.

19. ____, *Beyond the Pleasure Principle*, Norton, New York, 1961.

20. M. Klein, *The Psychoanalysis of Children*, Hogarth, London, 1932.

21. A. Bandura, *Principles of Behavior Modification*, Holt, Rinehart and Winston, New York, 1969.

22. E. H. Erikson, *Toys and Reasons*, W. W. Norton, New York, 1977.

23. ____, Sex Differences in the Play Configurations of American Pre-Adolescents, *American Journal of Orthopsychiatry*, *21*, pp. 667-692, 1951.

24. H. Levin and E. Wardwell, The Research Uses of Doll Play, *Psychological Bulletin*, *59*, pp. 27-56, 1962.

25. H. B. Schwartzman, *Transformations: The Anthropology of Children's Play*, Plenum Press, New York, 1978.

26. E. Biblow, Imaginative Play and the Control of Aggressive Behavior, in *The Child's World of Make Believe*, J. L. Singer (ed.), Academic Press, New York, 1973.

27. V. Axline, *Play Therapy*, Ballantine, New York, 1969.

28. S. Freud, Jokes and Their Relation to the Unconscious, in *The Standard Edition of the Complete Psychological Works of Sigmund Freud*, Vol. VIII, J. Strackey (ed.), Hogarth, London, 1960.

29. J. Piaget, *Play, Dreams and Imitation in Childhood*, Norton, New York, 1962.

30. M. Heidegger, *Being and Time*, Harper and Row, New York, 1962.

31. H. Gadamer, *Truth and Method*, Crossroads, New York, 1985.

32. J. Faulconer and R. Williams, Temporality in Human Action: An Alternative to Positivism and Historicism, *American Psychologist*, *40*, pp. 1179-1188, 1985.

33. M. Gelven, *A Commentary on Heidegger's Being and Time*, Harper and Row, New York, 1970.

34. R. May, *Love and Will*, Dell, New York, 1969.

35. I. Yalom, *Existential Psychotherapy*, Basic Books, New York, 1980.

CHAPTER 11

E. Nesbit's Forty-First Year: Her Life, Times, and Symbolizations of Personality Growth

RAVENNA HELSON

GENDER, LITERATURE "FOR CHILDREN," AND MIDLIFE INDIVIDUATION IN AUTHORS

If one analyzes themes and characters in the best imaginative literature for children, one finds that heroic and comic stories are written more frequently by men and "tender" stories by women [1]. But stories vary also with historical period, and so does the nature and amount of difference in books by men and women [2]. In all periods there has been overlap: some women have written about aggression and achievement, some men about relationship. Yet "tender" stories by men, such as *The Wind in the Willows* or *Charlotte's Web*, are not the same as those by women, such as *Heidi, The Secret Garden,* or *The Children of Green Knowe*. The almost equal participation of men and women in children's literature has contributed to a valuable diversity of stories. There are "fantasies" for every reader.

Imaginative literature for children is not only varied but also rich. Its richness is related, I believe, to the fact that the stories are so often produced out of the authors' frustrations, disappointments and yearnings. Many have been written after personal crises in middle-age. For example, Charles Kingsley wrote one of the first fantasies for children, *Water Babies*, at age forty-six, when he was in a particularly thorny phase of his career as clergyman and academic [3]. Lousia Molesworth, late Victorian, wrote her best-known fantasies immediately before and after dissolving her marriage at age forty. Frank Baum began writing for children at age forty-one, after a serious heart condition forced him to give up his work as a salesman. *The Wonderful Wizard of Oz* appeared two years later. These and other stories illustrate very clearly what Jung described as the individuation process, in which the ego establishes a relationship to childish, shadowy, and contrasexual parts of the psyche, and to the psychic totality referred to as the *self* [4]. If the process goes well, there is a sense of new potential and growth, a "rejuvenation" of personality, and the stories are symbolized in ways that make them appropriate for children. To the extent that what has been repressed or underdeveloped is not the same in men and women, their individuation stories may be expected to show different patterns. The differences are instructive, but so are the similarities, and the individuality of each story is the most important of all.

This article examines portions of the life and work of an Edwardian author, E. Nesbit. Although she was a professional writer and journalist from the age of twenty-one, she produced nothing very good until she was forty. Between the ages of forty and fifty she wrote half a dozen books that make her one of the outstanding contributors to children's literature. Her most original works are not characteristically feminine, but I will try to show that some of her problems and sources of imagery were directly related to sex and gender. Her life, work, and the reception of her work were influenced by her culture in many ways, including its attitudes toward gender roles. And yet, her life story and the appeal of her work transcend gender, and I shall try to convey that also.

There is an excellent biography of E. Nesbit by Doris Langley Moore, all the more useful because it is written without psychological theory in mind [5]. There are also Nesbit's own recollections of her childhood [6]. She was an extrovert with an interesting life and a prolific output. Here I will focus on material that lends perspective to an understanding of her middle-age and to the series of three outstanding fantasies written at this time.

YOUNG ADULTHOOD

Anybody who attended meetings of the Fabian Society in London in the 1880s or 1890s would have known Edith Nesbit Bland and Hubert Bland. Edith was an attractive woman with quick, birdlike movements of the head and a direct, sympathetic manner. She was bohemian, aesthetic, boyishly feminine. Her husband Hubert had a charming and impressive manner. Edith much admired his physical strength, his intellectuality, and skill in debating. The Blands were Socialists. In the area of sexual mores Hubert held strong conservative views for people in general; he himself was an inveterate philanderer. For example, the youngest of the Blands' four children had actually been born to Alice Hoatson, nicknamed "Mouse," a friend of Edith's who lived in the family and served as a housekeeper. It wasn't all Hubert's fault that the Blands' marriage was tempestuous. Edith had emotional outbursts and eccentricities that were hard on the family.

Both Edith and Hubert enjoyed the company of fellow intellectuals and artists, and they entertained a lot. George Bernard Shaw, H. G. Wells, and many other Edwardians whose names one knows were among their close friends. Edith had a flair as a hostess, even when the Blands were quite poor, which they were for a long time. Soon after they married, (Edith seven months pregnant), Hubert contracted smallpox, and while he was critically ill, his business partner ran off with all his money. Soon after he recovered, he got a second case of smallpox. Edith was the sole provider for her husband and baby until Hubert began to take up journalism too. Adversity at this stage in Edith's life called out her courage and strengthened her endurance. But the habit of having to write a great many greeting cards, songs, horror stories, sentimental love stories, children's stories, and whatever would bring in money was probably one factor in the superficiality of most of her work.

She did not have disciplined work habits. She would delay writing until she had to shut herself off and work without stopping to meet a deadline. She could work this way because she was a very fluent writer, really too fluent for the best interests of her art.

Although Edith had serious aspirations as a novelist and especially as a poet, she did not believe in baring her soul before the public. In her view, this meant that she wrote "dramatic lyrics." Her sympathetic biographer, Doris Moore, describes her poetry as extravagantly artificial [5].

Edith craved attention, admiration, and affection. When a business meeting got too dull, she was the kind of woman who might interrupt the speaker to ask for a glass of water. She sent her books to eminent people and exchanged letters of mutual admiration. She was hurt if a friend, under her questioning, was reluctant to accord her a high rank as poet.

This narcissism and emotional dependence would seem to have had their origins in her childhood experience. She was the youngest of six children. Photographs show her to have been a darling child, and there is evidence that she often received attention and affection. But a brother died when she was in her infancy, and her father died of a lingering illness before she was four. After he died, his widow assumed financial control of the respected agricultural college of which he had been president. Then an older sister of Edith's developed tuberculosis and required considerable attention. So it is clear that in Edith's early years her mother had many preoccupations and was probably not a calm and consistently attentive "self-object" [7].

From earliest childhood, Edith suffered from fears. She describes a skit her brothers and sisters put on when she was about three. "I was the high-born orphan whom gypsies were to steal," she says, "and my part was to lie in a cradle, and at the proper time be carried away shrieking. I understood my part perfectly . . . and had rehearsed it more than once." Being carried away by her favorite sister was no reason for alarm. "Unfortunately," she continues, "there had been no dress rehearsal, and when on the night of the performance, the high-born orphan found itself close to a big black bonnet and a hideous mask, it did scream to some purpose, and presently screamed itself into some fit or swoon, was put to bed and stayed there for many days which passed dreamlike. But that old woman haunted my dreams, [and] haunts them still. . ." [6, p. 51] .

There were other incidents of this sort, phobias, and chronic night fears. From the age of seven she was sent off to one boarding school after another, first in England, later in France and Germany. She hated them all, longed to be with her mother, had frequent temper tantrums, could not do arithmetic, and continued to suffer from fears about skeletons, mummies, houses collapsing, and being buried alive. She was acutely sensitive to representations suggesting abandonment or of being overwhelmed by the unconscious.

Edith had written stories and poems from an early age. As she grew into adolescence and young adulthood, she adopted the attitude of taking conventional poses in what she wrote, rather than "baring her own soul." This must have been an effective means of controlling her emotions.

EARLY MIDLIFE

When Edith was thirty-six, her brother Alfred died, only four years older than she. His death may have influenced her, two years later, to write a series of recollections about her childhood. Most of her sketches treat the fears that I have mentioned and her unhappiness at school. The most pleasant of the recollections are about playing pirates and explorers with her brothers during several summer vacations in Brittany. In the course of writing these sketches, she found that memories began to flow in unexpected abundance and vividness—this was in 1898 when she was thirty-nine.

Soon after, she began what was to be her first great success. The Bastable stories were published first in adult magazines and later made into a book called *The Story of the Treasure Seekers*. These stories drew on her adventures with her brothers. The narrator is the eldest boy among six Bastable children, though there is an amusing pretense of disguising his identity.

Interlude: Peer Groups and Comic Style

In these real-life stories of imaginative children, E. Nesbit already showed two of the features for which she is well-known. One is the group of child characters. Victorian authors had used one child or a pair of children as central characters, and a relationship to admirable adults (usually female) figured prominently. In Edwardian fantasy, the child or animal peer group became pervasive, with adults cast in peripheral or villainous roles. Think of *The Jungle Book, Peter Pan, The Wind in the Willows*, and most of Beatrix Potter. This constellation was probably related to the loss of confidence in authority and the problems in sex roles that were painful in this era [2] . The group of child characters is so central in E. Nesbit's work that it is considered one of her contributions to children's literature. In her case, the exclusion of adults may have been, in part, a revenge for their abandonment of her. (This motivation could be attributed to several other Edwardian authors as well.) More importantly, it expresses the absence of adults as felt resources of personality. Instead there are internalized sibling figures and childhood ego states.

The second feature of these stories is that they are comic. In children's literature, the merely pleasant story may be written by men or women, but the highly comic story is usually written by men. The reason is that the usual plot is about pretending to be heroic and manly by exhibitionism and wish-fulfillment (as a little boy might do) rather than by actually being heroic through discipline, endurance, courage, and goal-direction. The comic story usually mocks both the heroic ideal and the unheroic aspirant to glory. Ambivalence about masculine identity is an important complex in men, but as women are not expected to be heroes, their failings in this respect do not arouse in them the intense, contradictory, and complex feelings that are expressed in the creative comic story. However, women may have urethral-phallic impulses that cannot be acknowledged. They may be critical of the discrepancy between male pretensions and performance, or resentful of male bullying. Fond as E. Nesbit was of her siblings, she had suffered from their teasing on numerous occasions. The boys loved to frighten her by running after her with a scary calf's head, and once they thought she looked so much like a flower in her new party dress that they planted her in the garden. An important source of humor in *The Story of the Treasure Seekers* was probably a little sister's pleasure at "creating" her siblings, mocking them a bit, taking on her big brother's preadolescent voice, and then pretending to disguise his identity as narrator at the same time she fused with it and asserted it. There is also in the story a father who can't support the family. The family home is saved not by the mock-heroic attempts of the children but by the dead mother's "Indian uncle." This suggests aggressive humor directed both at Hubert's failures in the masculine role of provider and also at the brothers, whose repeated borrowing for ventures that never worked out had been responsible for Mrs. Nesbit's eventual loss of her home [5]. The theme of seeking treasure to save the home will recur.

SUCCESS AND HARD TIMES

The Bastable stories elevated E. Nesbit's status as an author. Hubert was becoming better known also, and early in 1899 the Blands bought Well Hall, a manor house with an ancient moat, orchard, ghost, and authentic Tudor outbuilding. The move to Well Hall must have seemed a very happy milestone, a sign that Edith and Hubert had achieved a position in status-conscious Edwardian society. However, misfortunes began at once. And this was E. Nesbit's forty-first year.

First, the house was in worse shape than the Blands had realized. Much time, effort, and money were required to make it livable.

Then, Edith had a miscarriage or a stillborn child. Her last birth had been a stillborn, and she had been broken-hearted, refusing to give up the little body until forced to do so. This time she was especially grieved because she felt that she would never be pregnant again. Soon after this misfortune, Alice Hoatson gave birth to a child which for the second time turned out to have been fathered by Hubert. Edith again adopted the baby. The same month Edith's oldest sister, her "second mother," died.

After this, a physician who came to examine Edith told her that she must prepare for an immediate operation for cancer, and that her chances of recovery were remote. Three days later a specialist found the diagnosis to be entirely mistaken. The intervening week-end was carried off with the quiet drama of social entertaining as usual.

Finally, Edith's beloved son Fabian, very much like herself in personality, had a tonsillectomy just before his sixteenth birthday. The operation was performed at Well Hall. He was anesthetized, and never regained consciousness. After all else failed, Edith put hot water bottles and his sixteen candles around him but could not bring him back to life.

After Fabian's death, Edith was distracted, remorseful, bitter, and inacapable of work or social activity. In her grief she cried out her outrage at the injustices she had suffered, and the children overheard secrets that until then had been well kept. It is my central thesis that the pressure of these misfortunes at this point in her midlife brought about an introversion of libido, the effects of which may be seen in the fantasy that she now began to write.

FIVE CHILDREN AND IT

E. Nesbit's new stories appeared in Strand Magazine in 1901, and were later published as the book, *Five Children and It*. The stories are about four children and a baby whose parents have taken a house for the summer. The children are thrilled to be in the country, so our attention is displaced a bit from the "real-life" details of the setting. The house is painted white, but it is said to be quite mediocre. It may be taken as a self-image. It is located on the edge of a hill, between a sand-pit and a gravel quarry. At the bottom of a long incline there are lime kilns and a big, red brewery. If setting conveys mood, the mood here is depressed, even hellish. In comic style, E. Nesbit says that at sunset "the limekilns and oast-houses glimmered and glittered till they were like an enhanted city of the Arabian Nights." This suggests a place of wonders, but also where Scheherazade had to tell 1,001 serialized stories before she was reprieved from execution.

The children are digging a deep hole in the gravel-pit when they begin to find bits of shells. Their father has told them that long ago the gravel-pit was a seashore. Then they find in the hole a creature who identifies itself as a Psammead, or a sand fairy. It has "eyes" on retractible horns like a snail, ears like a bat, a tubby furry body like a spider, rat-like whiskers, and hands and feet like a monkey. Despite being this puzzling mixture of creatures usually thought ugly, the Psammead has an irritable dignity. He can grant wishes, although he has to swell his body up very large to do this and finds it tiring. He has one great fear, of getting wet. That would kill him. His wishes last only until sunset. After that things that have been wished for turn to stone. He grants the children one wish a day.

The book consists of a series of adventures in which the children get their wish but find that in various humorous ways it has led them into frustration or danger. Of course, getting her wish and then having everything turn out wrong is what happened to E. Nesbit at Well Hall. At one level, the theme is as depressed as the setting. But as one reads along, the stories are quite funny. They are also interesting, because the wishes explored and the consequences of their fulfillment evoke pleasure, excitement, and anxiety.

Five Children and It is dedicated to John Bland, the new baby born to Alice Hoatson, so a story about the baby is worth special attention. In this story one of the children becomes impatient with the baby, says nobody really wants it—otherwise the children wouldn't have to be taking care of it—and wishes (thoughtlessly) that everybody *did* want it. The Psammead has appeared unexpectedly, so this is the wish granted for the day. After staving off several people who want the baby, the children meet a band of gypsies who are determined to have it. The situation has become grim when the sun sets and all but one of the gypsies lose interest. The gypsy woman who remains is portrayed sympathetically. She still loves the baby but does not want to steal it, even though she has lost her own children.

The theme of the baby's not being wanted and then wanted so much that it was kidnapped by gypsies seems to refer to what Silvan Tomkins [8] would call a negative-affect "nuclear scene" created from E. Nesbit's early childhood experience and now amplified by recent traumata with analogs and "anti-analogs"—the latter being idealized scenes which capture the perfect negation of old dangers and disappointments and imply positive and active coping strategies [9]. The complex preconscious manipulations of the comic artist are apparent.

The Psammead

The Psammead is E. Nesbit's most original creation, and as he has a part to play in three of her books, it is important to try to understand what it is that has been discovered in this hole in the gravel-pit that was once a seashore. The Psammead controls admission to a world in which wishes are marvelously gratified and impossible dangers confronted. Thus he seems to be a gatekeeper to the unconscious. There are many characters in myth, dream, and fantasy that personify processes that go on at the threshold between everyday consciousness and altered states of consciousness. Some of them are toll-collectors, border guards, ferrymen, door-keepers—guardians of the threshold.

Frightening or austere aspects of the gatekeeper express the idea that the ego may be paralyzed or "turned to stone" if it enters the alien region without the right protection. Because of E. Nesbit's high anxiety, this protection was very important. The rules of the Psammead's magic—one wish a day, magic stops at sunset—served to control the exploration of wishes. Of course, gatekeepers are often portrayed as treacherous tricksters, sometimes because one is allowed through and then gets into trouble. The children were suspicious of the Psammead for this reason.

The ugliness of most gatekeepers, and certainly of the Psammead, may be understood in relation to Jung's statement that the shadow stands at the threshold of the unconscious. Jung said that the individuation process usually started with midlife depression and unpleasant awareness of oneself and of life that one would prefer not to think about. But of course this kind of knowledge is essential if one is to develop, and acquaintance with the shadow may bring wisdom and possibilities of growth.

This whole set of ideas is implicit in the Psammead. It is a mixture of snail, bat, rat, spider, and monkey—creatures with preponderantly unpleasant connotations, but in myth and folklore most of them have positive value too. In terms of Jungian type theory [10], the Psammead's seclusiveness, heavy rationality, and polymorphic animality express the inferior opposites of E. Nesbit's extroverted feeling and intuition. But the children *converse* with the Psammead, and in time they learn that he is philosophically sophisticated ("time is a figment of the imagination") and shrewdly down-to-earth. When the imaginative and well-read children ask him for wealth "beyond the dreams of avarice," he says, "I can't go beyond dreams, you know! How much do you want, and will you have it in gold or notes?" And after they choose gold, he tells them to hurry out of the sandpit or they will be buried in guineas when he starts to work. This earthiness in the treatment of magic, along with the rules of magic, are features much commented upon and admired in E. Nesbit's work. Their effectiveness seems to come from the liveliness of inferior functions brought into play.

Jung said that acquaintance with the shadow brings wisdom. The main wisdom in *Five Children and It* is increased awareness of shadowy thought processes and the illusory appeal of wish-fulfillment: getting what they want through the Psammead repeatedly involves the children in misery and complications. In a later book, the Psammead becomes a guide in further explorations.

The Psammead is not merely a guardian of the threshold; he himself, with considerable effort, brings about the wished for conditions. Thus he represents a creative process that operates *at the threshold*, and this means a comic process. The comic figure is trapped between greed and anxiety at the threshold where it cannot "grow up" or become differentiated, but does manifest great versatility and dexterity. This is the world of the preconscious with its hypnogogic illusions, distortions, and double meanings. Magicians and clowns play with these processes as on a tightrope, emotions superficial (must not get wet), rules used as a balancing stick.

The threshold region is often depicted with sexual symbolism. Comic fantasy by male authors often has a hero with phallic characteristics (Pinocchio, Dwarf Longnose, Peter Pan). Sexual experience is a dramatic and familiar gateway to altered states of consciousness, and of course the penis symbolizes change of state particularly well. A vivid example is Alice's fall down the rabbit hole and her extreme changes in size as she tries to enter the locked door at the bottom. If the unconscious is represented as a womb and the barrier is personified, the gatekeeper, in man's fantasy, is likely to be a symbol of maternal entrapment, such as the witch in Andersen's story, "The Tinder Box," or of paternal treachery, such as the false father in "Aladdin and His Wonderful Lamp." A relationship between central character and gatekeeper does not develop.

In E. Nesbit, the symbolism works out differently because she was female, and this is one reason for the novelty of the Psammead. The Psammead is located in a gravel pit. It has antennae that can extend or contract, and of course a snail's antennae are not really "eyes" but sensitive organs of touch. It has a tubby body that swells up in the process of gratifying the wishes of others. These and other details suggest that the Psammead is the underside of the female author as creator. Spiders, of course, spin "yarns."

Another woman author, well-known to E. Nesbit, had created fantasies in which children developed a relationship with a cuckoo (*The Cuckoo Clock*) and a lame raven (*The Tapestry Room*), who were first gate-keepers and then guides to inner worlds. This was Louisa Molesworth. Though it is reasonable to find that women's fantasies show a relation to their bodies and sexual experience, critics who have suggested a resemblance between the characters of Nesbit and Molesworth have not identified this as the source of similarity. Jung would describe their creatures as examples of a theriomorphic (earthy, primitive) animus. In his theory, the animus is a woman's guide to the unconscious.

In E. Nesbit's first famous fantasy, the children continue to represent her conscious personality with its absence of strong mature identifications. The Psammead is a representative of a variety of preconscious functions and processes, but he also has a perspective of centuries that makes him a primitive version of Philemon, the old man so important in Jung's experience of his psychic depths [11]. I think the conversations between the children and the Psammead represent what Jung called the transcendant function, a sustained communication between conscious and unconscious [12]. Once begun, the process continued, though new forces came into play.

THE PHOENIX AND THE CARPET

Five Children and It brought much public applause. The success was exhilarating, and the contact with the unconscious may have fired the author with new energies, because her next series of stories, later published as *The Phoenix and the Carpet*, were not depressive but manic.

It begins with the children setting off fireworks prematurely in their room. The damaged rug is replaced with a second-hand Persian carpet that, when unrolled, is found to have an egg-shaped stone in it. During an attempt on the part of the children to make magic with burnt offerings and sweet smells, the stone egg falls into the fire and hatches into the Phoenix. As the carpet proves to be of the flying variety, it takes the children and the charming, vain, self-congratulatory Phoenix on a number of adventures, including several visits to an ocean isle and subterranean locations. The Psammead, though he is called upon several times, never actually makes an appearance. The book has episodes more brillant than anything in *Five Children and It*, but it is looser, coarser, and some chapters are rather silly. (At this point, the carpet, symbol of the weavings of the imagination, is discovered to have worn thin.) Towards the end of the book there is renewed vigor and control, with undoing of massive destruction by fire and rich gifts for all.

The phoenix, immortal bird that arises out of its own ashes, would seem to be an appropriate symbol for E. Nesbit's renewal of creative spirit after her many misfortunes. Her story also reminds one of the Icarus myth because of the conjunction of fire, flying, and water. Phoenix symbolism and the story of Icarus have in common the theme of ascension and movement from high to low, or vice versa, through phases of fire, air, and earth or water. The book seems to celebrate the ability to dip down to indulge tabooed impulses or curiosities and to fly away not only unharmed but energized (inflated). But fear and anxiety play an important role in maintaining the cycle. One remembers Icarus' last anguished cry to his father for help as his wings failed and he fell to the sea: people with an "Icarus complex" have lofty ambitions but lack self-sustaining powers (mature adult identifications), and the fate they risk is succumbing to their unconscious destructive tendencies.[1]

E. Nesbit had a cycloid temperament, but there was probably something reactive about the mania in *The Phoenix and the Carpet* because her mother had recently died. In the last chapter of *Five Children and It*, an attempt to give jewels to the mother failed. In *The Phoenix and the Carpet*, the children are finally successful in salvaging a treasure and returning it to a mother figure in time to save the family home. They give their actual mother gifts, too. I regard

---

[1] It is unfortunately beyond the scope of this chapter to amplify the usefulness of the concept of the Icarus Complex in understanding E. Nesbit. See the review of the literature in Wiklund [13], especially the work of Fried, Murray, and Vaessen, and Wiklund's discussion of another woman author of comic fantasy for children, Astrid Lindgren.

these as attempts to restore value to the mother and to invest libido in a mother-identified personality. The manic energy may have accomplished something besides denial and defense, because the feminine self figures prominently in the last book of the series, *The Story of the Amulet*.

THE STORY OF THE AMULET

The third book of fantasy contrasts with the previous two in having a much more complicated and unified plot. Of all her books this is the one that E. Nesbit took the most trouble in writing. The plot and the order of emergence of different kinds of characters suggest that interrelated processes of confrontation and differentiation were going on in her psyche. Much of the material came from consultations with Wallis Budge, Keeper of the Egyptian and Assyrian Antiquities at the British Museum. They soon became friends, and then something more than friends. At one point Edith asked Budge to take her away from her marriage to Hubert. Budge was attracted to Edith and fond of her but he felt that his position at the British Museum precluded such an action. Extroverted feeling type that she was, Edith projected her thinking function on men, but now *The Story of the Amulet* involves, among other themes, the attempt to strengthen the thinking function in her own psyche.

At the beginning of the book, the four older children have been left with an old nurse. The father is away on duties as a war correspondent in Manchuria, and the mother is sick and has taken the baby with her to Madeira. The children find the Psammead in a pet shop. They buy him to remove him from this indignity. This is an important beginning, because in *The Phoenix and the Carpet* the Psammead was kept out of sight and used by the Phoenix to get the children out of jams in a cavalier, manipulative way. Now the Psammead regains his presence and austerity. Gratification of the children's own wishes is precluded, (though the Psammead still grants wishes of others when expressed in his presence, as his nature compels him to do). At once he puts them in touch with a higher form of magic than they have known before. They buy an amulet that he has observed in a curio shop. It is described as smooth, red, and softly shiny. In Wallis Budge's book on *Amulets and Superstitions* this exact one is described as a Tjet, the vulva of Isis [14]. (Scholars now call it the knot or girdle of Isis.) Isis, of course, was the Egyptian goddess much beloved for her resourcefulness and faithfulness as wife and mother. When Set tore her husband Osiris to pieces and scattered them, she found the pieces (all but one) and restored them. On another occasion she brought her son Horus back to life. Isis was a figure that would have appealed very much to E. Nesbit.

Back home, the children turn out to have only half of the amulet. The whole amulet, the Psammead tells them, would give generativity, integration, their heart's desire. But half an amulet is not without value: it will take them wherever they want to go to search for the other half. The "heart's desire" of the children is to bring back their parents and the baby. So now it is clear that this is a quest story, one that will describe E. Nesbit's search for the parts of herself that she does not know, with the hope of restoring the guiding factors in her personality and bringing a sense of renewed growth potential.

The amulet has strange marks on it that the Psammead says are important to be able to read. So the children take the amulet to a "poor learned gentleman" who lives upstairs. He is a scholar and says that the marks are pronounced "Ur Hekau Secheh" and that this is a Name of Power. (The term "Ur Hekau" was applied to an instrument used in the ancient mystic ceremony of "opening the mouth of the mummy," which served to establish communication between living and dead and to provide a dwelling place for the "double of the deceased." Wallis Budge had written about this. The symbolism is quite relevant to the story, if one regards the scholar as somewhat mummified.)

Under the instruction of the Psammead, the children sit down in a circle, put the half-amulet in the middle, and call out the Name of Power. The room becomes very quiet and very dark, and then a light comes and a serious sweet voice begins to speak. It tells them that they will have to go back in the past to find the other half of the amulet.

At this point there are already two important new characters. One is the poor learned gentleman, too gentle and dreamy to remember to eat his pork chops. He represents E. Nesbit's undernourished thinking function. The second is the voice of the amulet, which I take to be that of the Self, the whole feminine psyche.

The children's first venture (through an arch that appears when they hold up the amulet) takes them to a primitive village in very ancient Egypt. They manage to get inside a hut with a little maze inside that contains the amulet, but attackers appear, and they make a quick retreat to London.

Then they go to Babylon and ask to see the King, but he is away until evening fetching home his fourteenth wife. (The King and Hubert appear to have characteristics in common.) That evening three of the children commit sacrilege by asking the King directly for the other half of the amulet, and he condemns them to "the deepest dungeon." They have been separated from the youngest child, who has both the amulet and the Psammead, so the dungeon is deep indeed. However, the children call out their name of power and also a name they have heard the King use. A terrible fellow with a human-appearing body and an eagle's head appears. He is Nisroch, Servant of the Great Ones. I think he represents male power of the kind they have challenged or offended, and that this power can be terribly destructive to women if they turn its energy against themselves, as guilt or fear. But the children have called out "Ur Hekau Secheh" and are engaged in the mission of communicating with the past (or unconscious), so Nisroch serves this mission. The eagle's head suggests the power of vision. Nisroch obliterates a wall and brings into view the chamber of E. Nesbit's shadow, the imperious irrational, narcissistic (but still rather likeable) Queen of Babylon.

222 / ORGANIZING EARLY EXPERIENCE

The missing youngest child, the Psammead, and the half-amulet are with the Queen. This shows the great importance of the Queen for the quest. In the next adventure the Queen erupts from the past into London (because she had wished to do so "on her husband's next hunting trip" in the presence of the Psammead) and she causes a lot of very funny trouble in trying to retrieve her jewelry from the British Museum before another wish causes her visit never to have happened.

The children, the Psammead, and the poor learned gentleman go together to Atlantis, where they see the temples of Poseidon and observe the priests, kings, and bulls. Great waves break upon the land, a volcano begins to erupt, and they escape at the last nick of time. The primitive force of the masculine remains very dangerous and still impossible to assimilate.

On a trip to ancient Egypt the children encounter a somewhat sinister priest of Amen who becomes interested in them when he discovers that they can control fire (with a cigarette-lighter). Thus a power-oriented animus figure has emerged in human form to take part in the main plot. After several other adventures, the priest erupts into their life in London, and a struggle ensues. He has the half-amulet like theirs, but the apparent twain merge into one still incomplete half (children and priest are both desirous). As the priest has a somewhat unscrupulous passion for knowledge, his joining forces with the children adds intensity to the quest. However, the Psammead keeps him from taking over. Because of common interests, priest and poor learned gentleman are drawn to each other. At the scholar's suggestion, priest and children together find the amulet by going back to a very ancient past when it was "whole and unguarded." They do not tarry, because there is strong magic at this claustral place at the dawn of life, and death is all about.

The denouement is swift. The children receive a telegram that their father and mother are returning home with the baby. The priest and scholar, with the help of the amulet—again impressively described—become one person. The children give the amulet to the scholar-priest. The scholar-priest politely wishes that the Psammead could obtain his own wish to go back forever to the sands of the past, so the Psammead does. Everyone seems to have obtained their "heart's desire," but there is an unsatisfactory lack of relationship between the reunited family and the now impassioned animus "upstairs" with the amulet. One realizes that the reinstatement of "the three"—mother, father, and child—may be a regressive dream of the narcissist, and not a strong position at all. We shall return to the consequences for E. Nesbit presently.

The Story of the Amulet is E. Nesbit's most differentiated treatment of the individuation quest. Unlike most Edwardian fantasy, it has important characters who are human and adult, even if frail. It differs from *Five Children and It* in being much less defended by ambivalences and negations; it has more daring and a farther reach. It differs from *The Phoenix and the Carpet* in its lack of exhibitionism and manic defense, and in its sustained direction. Note that the characteristics of the style are related tothe psychological content of the story: it is concerned with increasing awareness of imperious and eccentric emotional states not well integrated into the personality (the author's shadow), an attempt to strengthen the thinking and planning functions (animus), and a vision – though flawed – of the possibilities of integration and renewal of personality through the Self.

E. Nesbit was now forty-seven. In the next two years she published several more books that show that she still had intermittent connection with the unconscious. Parts of these books are fascinating. But she seemed to have become ambivalent about the importance of the imaginative world and more concerned with love and responsibility (*The Enchanted Castle, The House of Arden, Harding's Luck*). Though these attitudes were probably a sign of personality growth, they may have led to changes in style and new characters that were not entirely successful. She never again wrote with the tautness that was the black-edged gift of the Psammead.

Did her quest make a difference in her life? Doris Moore describes E. Nesbit, approaching fifty, as still having the caprices and petulances of a child. On a trip to France, for example, shortly after the wedding of her daughter, she surprised custodians by taking a swim in the fountains at Versailles. Her bad moods were known to her household as "the Blights." But Moore quotes a letter Nesbit wrote to a young friend to show that she engaged in much self-examination about her temper and was working persistently to reduce its harmful effects.

The Queen of Babylon is so vividly and emphatically realized in *The Story of the Amulet* that one feels her creation may have changed the relationship between E. Nesbit and this shadow queen. But the passive, dreamy scholar and the dark priest were less life-like. In outer life, E. Nesbit had withdrawn some of her dependence on Hubert and Wallis Budge. Her conscious personality, however, was not able to take over the animus energies that now carried the power for personality change. This is the meaning, I believe, of the scholar-priest's being left "upstairs" with the amulet.

What happened was a cruel and unusual animus possession. Within a year after publication of the *Amulet* in 1907, E. Nesbit, who had never been able to do arithmetic, was engrossed in trying to learn mathematics so as to prove by cipher and Napierian logarithms that Bacon wrote the works of Shakespeare. She bought expensive rare books, studied Latin, and was undaunted by the antipathetic reactions of friends who thought the time, energy, and money that she poured into this pursuit was injurious to her creative productivity, responsible for considerable and long-lasting financial difficulties, and incomprehensible in one with a sensitive appreciation of Shakespeare and no capacity whatsoever for mathematics. Like a curse in a fairy tale, this passion lasted for ten years.

When Hubert died in 1914, Edith was devastated. She had no life-partner, no money, no work, no health, no children near, and World War I was grimly depressing. But three years later, a wonderful thing happened. At age fifty-nine she made a second marriage that was happy and peaceful. According to descriptions of her in her early sixties, a few years before her death, she was still charming, interested in almost everything, and deeply sympathetic to those with distressing problems. She retained her rapport with children, but was now less a child herself than a fairy godmother. She had become calmer, kinder, and more reserved. Moore quotes a friend from this time who felt that despite her social exterior she was "unworldly." She was often visited by an exceedingly amiable priest, the friend said, and "I gathered that she was often privately immersed in spiritual considerations, though she never at any time discussed them."

CONCLUSIONS

E. Nesbit grew up with strong fears of abandonment, poor impulse control, and, one may infer, ambivalence towards parental figures. However, there was also considerable achievement among her forebears and imagination among her siblings. Edith used what means her world offered to obtain the security and self-esteem that she needed so badly. She developed defensive patterns that would have kept her a "pseudo-writer"—one who writes to please an audience [15], had psychological processes of midlife not led her to closer contact with the unconscious.

Part of what Edwardian society offered her was a status as "modern woman." E. Nesbit was far from traditionally feminine in her literary ambition, use of her talent to support the family, friendships with men, love of sports and outings, and in her daring and adventurous spirit. On the other hand, home was precious to her. She was an erratic mother, but she shared the deep griefs of women over many ages after the death of a child. Her emotional dependence on Hubert and his compulsive philandering was a central aspect of her life and a painful exaggeration of traditional gender roles.

In some ways her work is "feminine." She could put babies into books as few other writers have known how to do, and her humorous domestic comments and attention to gender differences among siblings are those of a woman. In her experience of the unconscious, the Psammead served an important function, and I have argued that he was very much the creation of a woman. *The Story of the Amulet*, once analyzed, is clearly a woman's revelation of forces latent or ruling in her Psyche. But the basic characters in her three enduring fantasies are the immature children and the androgynous Psammead and Phoenix. No wonder that her work is not typically feminine. E. Nesbit had "both" family and career, but the inability to identify as an adult because of her dependence, emotional ambivalence, and boyishness is probably the basic dilemma underlying her comic style.

Works of creative fantasy usually emerge out of pain and limitation. This is particularly evident in Edwardian authors of fantasy for children, who all, male and female, had miserable childhoods, were severely handicapped in opportunities for mature identifications, and invented worlds of charm and delight without, or in opposition to, adult gender roles. E. Nesbit was one of those whose weakness and courage, limitation and imagination, made the Edwardian period a "golden age" in children's literature. Her fantasy is instructive today in another time of confusion and conflict in gender roles.

REFERENCES

1. R. Helson, The Creative Spectrum of Authors of Fantasy, *Journal of Personality*, *45*, pp. 310-326, 1977.
2. _____, Through the Pages of Children's Books and What a Psychologist Found There, *Psychology Today*, 7:6, pp. 107-112, 1973.
3. _____, The Psychological Origins of Fantasy for Children in Mid-Victorian England, *Children's Literature III*, *3*, pp. 65-76, 1974.
4. C. G. Jung, The Relations between the Ego and the Unconscious, *Two Essays on Analytical Psychology (Collected Works 7)*, Princeton University Press, Princeton, New Jersey, 1966.
5. D. L. Moore, *E. Nesbit: A Biography*, Chilton, Philadelphia, 1966.
6. E. Nesbit, *Long Ago When I Was Young*, Watts, New York, 1966.
7. H. Kohut, *The Restoration of the Self*, International Universities Press, New York, 1977.
8. S. Tomkins, Script Theory: Differential Magnification of Affects, in *Nebraska Symposium on Motivation*, H. E. Howe, Jr. and R. A. Dienstbier (eds.), University of Nebraska Press, Lincoln, Nebraska, 1979.
9. R. Carlson, Studies in Script Theory: I. Adult Analogs of a Childhood Nuclear Scene, *Journal of Personality and Social Psychology*, *40*, pp. 501-510, 1981.
10. C. G. Jung, *Psychological Types (Collected Works 6)*, Princeton University Press, Princeton, New Jersey, 1971.
11. _____, *Memories, Dreams, Reflections*, Random House, New York, 1961.
12. _____, *The Transcendent Function (Collected Works 8)*, Princeton University Press, Princeton, New Jersey, pp. 67-91, 1960.
13. N. Wiklund, *The Icarus Complex*, Department of Psychology, Lund, 1978.
14. E. A. W. Budge, *Amulets and Superstitions*, Oxford University Press, London, 1930.
15. H. Sachs, *The Creative Unconscious*, Sci-Art Publishers, Cambridge, Massachusetts, 1951.

CHAPTER 12

The Development of Romantic Ideation and J.M. Barrie's Image of the Lost Boy

DELMONT MORRISON AND
SHIRLEY LINDEN MORRISON

Romantic ideation has properties that differentiate it from other forms of thought. The characteristics of romantic ideation are perhaps best observed in the adult who is romantically in love. Although this romantic state is generally observed in adulthood, it is the position in this chapter that romantic ideation develops during the period of preoperational thought in childhood and is expressed in the negative image children have of self and the correspondingly idealized image they have of the person they love. These representations of self and the loved person develop because of the loss of the child's first love. These images provide the motivation for future romantic love and are also a source of creative imagination. J. M. Barrie, the creator of *Peter Pan*, developed a romanticized representation of a lost boy and a little girl-mother that had its roots in his early childhood. Because of his difficulties in understanding a rejected part of self, Barrie continued throughout his life to be preoccupied with these idealized romantic images. He searched for them in his life and developed them in his art. In what follows, the development of romantic ideation and the loss of first love will be examined as they relate to a persistent theme in the literary works of J. M. Barrie.

PREOPERATIONAL THOUGHT AND ROMANTIC IDEATION

Romantic ideation develops during the period between two and eight years when the child uses representational thought while in the egocentric cognitive state [1]. In this cognitive state children are greatly influenced by their perceptions and a system of preoperational representation that is not subject to reflective thought. As an organism that perceives and thinks, children are unique at this time. Their perceptions and conclusions regarding the world occur without the moderating affect of an adequate awareness of self and only a vague awareness of the cognitive state of others. Consequently, they can only know the world from their perceptions but are unaware of that influence on their conclusions. Lacking the cognitive capacity for consistent self-observation, the child's self-concept, both in terms of esteem and understanding, is unstable [2, 3].

Preoperational thought also tends to be unstable because everything is new and the child has no stable schemas for organizing old representations or constantly occurring new experience. New data are processed by two major cognitive systems. The first is assimilation, in which new experience is organized to be understood in terms of previously formed images. Some of the new images may be understood this way but the information that cannot be assimilated is dealt with by accommodation. In accommodation, pre-existing representations are modified to meet the requirements of the new information. As a result, new images emerge. A stable system of images, providing adequate information regarding the world, would result in adaptation. In this sense, preoperational thought is not adaptive thought because the systems of representation are unstable.

What are the characteristics of these first representations? To begin with, the child's image of events is greatly influenced by action and perceptual functions [4]. The fact that objects are not subject to the limits of space, time, and causality as adults know them, is important in terms of understanding how a child can perceive an ideally loved person. The child's sense of self and his concept of objects are both unstable and precisely because they are unstable, the image of the object is subject to the child's motivations rather than later developing systems of causality. Because the object is not known or defined by operational thought, it can have the multiple definitions available in the affective and motivational systems that determine preoperational thought. Importantly, first knowledge of the world is susceptible to perpetual confusion between objective and subjective, and the entire content of consciousness is inextricably mixed with ostensible reality and motivations of which the child is unaware. Objectification of experience begins when the child is cognitively capable of integrating at least two simultaneous sources of information available during an event. Initially these sources are not differentiated because of the child's tendency to be influenced by the dominant perceptual feature noticed or dominant affect experienced during the event. In the studies on the conservation of volume Piaget observed that by centering attention on changes in width or height the preoperational child is unable to conclude that the volume of water is conserved during transitions and end states [5]. Preoperational thought is dominated by immediate experience and does not coordinate or synthesize successive perceptions and images. Another related limitation is the fact that preoperational thought is irreversible in that the child has a limited capacity to perceive transitions during events or carry out transformations in thought. These cognitive limitations interact with affective states to influence the child's early interpersonal experience. For example, during an interpersonal event dominated by affect such as anger, the child cannot modulate that experience with other feelings toward the object of the anger, such as those associated with attachment. Although unstable, this thought is organized around systems such as analogy, metaphor, and simile. Such systems contribute to romantic ideation, but the major roots of romantic ideation are found in the realism, animism, and artificialism that dominate the child's first way of knowing the world [4].

REALISM, ANIMISM AND ARTIFICIALISM

Having an inarticulate conception of their own thought, children regard their own perspective as immediately objective and absolute. In realism, the child can attribute to the word the characteristics of the object it signifies. The six-year-old classifies the word "elephant" as strong because an elephant can carry people. For the individual in love, the loved one's name carries some of the affective power associated with the loved one's person. Partially because children have no stable concepts of causality, they consistently use a system of causation that would be considered as an inferior system of causality, or magical thinking, in later developing thought. Children believe that their own action, such as counting to a certain number, or holding their breath, can influence the outcome of an event they desire or fear, such as winning a game or losing a parent's love. In the child's experience this becomes a means of organizing and influencing the future: a magical cause. The nature of this participation in outcome is profound. In terms of cause and effect there is no relation of substance. There is, however, participation in outcome based on the child's compensatory wish. In the child's experience, the participation is between the child's will and the universal will. As socialized thought is acquired and operational thought applied to experience, this sense of participation is gradually modified and finally, for most persons, lost. For J. M. Barrie these motivational and cognitive states were part of an idealized romantic fantasy to be maintained, rather than modified, by experience. For Barrie, the first knowledge of the world organized by realism provided a sense of participation between the world as fantasy, and self. He had a sense of belonging to things and originating in things. Peter Pan and his shadow are one; both are lost without the other.

Lacking a stable system of reflective thought and a consistent system of judgment and reasoning, children attribute to nature the states that exist in them without their awareness. As Barrie expressed in his novels and plays, the child regards as living and conscious, a large number of objects that adults view as inert. Initially, in animism everything is alive and conscious. During the final stage of this animism only the moon, sun, and animals have this capacity. This intimate psychological oneness with nature is also encouraged by the child's use of artificialism, the conception that objects in nature are part of human creation. The imaginative use of artificialism, as well as realism and animism, is found throughout Barrie's account of Peter Pan's journey through Kensington Gardens and Neverland.

Realism, animism, and artificialism provide the child with cognitive systems for making events that are novel and unknown, and sometimes frightening, knowable in human terms. Assimilative functions are dominant and in that sense adaptation is poor. However, preoperational thought can also be used by children, when motivated, to make the world conform to their own needs. In this use, another form of adaptation is realized. To study operational thought and the development of concepts providing adaptive balance between assimilation and accommodation, one studies how a child, over a period of time, solves problems of volume, space, time, and object constancy [5]. To study preoperational thought, organized by children and adaptive to their own needs, one studies a child's play [6].

COMPENSATORY FUNCTIONS OF PLAY

Within the parameters of assimilation and accommodation, play extends the boundaries of assimilation in the context of protecting the child's developing awareness and evaluation of self. As new knowledge develops, the child finds in play a medium for an understanding that assimilates new information by a process that maintains the integrity of the self. In operational thought, representations are limited by interrelated conceptual systems. In play, representations are manipulated by the child to meet the needs of an evolving and poorly understood self-concept. It is important to note that the first representations of self will be organized by the preoperational system and only later will the child have the capacity to use operational representations. The result of this is a period of time approximately between early childhood and early adolescence in which the concept of self is a function of two different systems of thought. This conflict is initially explored in play. Although the possibilities of self are explored, the end result is the protection of self. Social play provides a medium for alternative views and conclusions, but social play is still dominated by wish and preoperational thought. Once operational thought is dominant, the representations in play become similar to more adult-like concerns and conclusions regarding current and future events. Play between ages three and eight provides an emotional distance from experience, where preoperational mechanisms can be used to explore the preferred images of self to arrive at compensatory conclusions. These conclusions, as in the case of Barrie, may not result in a stable sense of self, but rather in images of self that are "Betwixt-and-Between."

FAMILY ROMANCE

Reflective thought, influenced by preoperational systems or by the more stable conceptual systems of operational thought, contributes to the development of observations and evaluations of self. Self can be explored in play but it is in the context of the family that the child is forced into an awareness and a definition of self in the framework of having love and losing love. This event, as it is perceived and understood by the son within the system of preoperational thought, is a major factor for the male in the development of romantic ideation [7]. Whoever is identified by the child as the major source of gratification becomes the object of a wish to possess. Gratification is mostly a function of another person and the child's erogenous bodily functions at this time. The erogenous zones contribute to the first representations the child has of an emerging sense of self, as well as the corresponding growth in the recognition of others [8]. At an affective level the child's egocentric tendency to center on dominant perceptual features results in a categorization of the parent into separate emotional states. During the emotional event in which the parent is encountered, the parent is known by the affective qualities of that event. For example, the mother is seen as the "bad" or "good" mother of that event. This cognitive limitation results in the child having an unstable representation of the mother and self and a consequent failure to perceive and know the interrelated affective qualities of object and self which exist beyond each event [9, 10]. The lack of reversible thought also contributes to an instability in the child's concept of both self and parent. The dominance of affect in the egocentric cognitive state limits the child's awareness of other information and the feelings experienced are not understood as a psychological state of a differentiated self. Thus, the early conceptualization of other people, particularly parents, is greatly influenced by affect, and preoperational thought with its limited capacity to decenter or synthesize. If another person is viewed by the child as powerful, in terms of the ability to attract the love of the person the child loves and wishes to possess, a competitive relationship evolves. It is the unevenness of the Oedipal struggle, both in the child's fantasy and in reality, that forces the child into one of his most enduring compensatory conclusions.

In the classic Oedipal conflict, operational thought will provide the four- to six-year-old with the relative comparison of bigger or lesser than, yet his egocentrism will cause him to confuse his own competitive wishes with those of the rival. The images involved are multiple and greatly dependent on the child's perception of the rival and the loved person. Importantly, the images involve an evaluation of self. There are now aggressive and sexual components of self that previously had not been a major focus of awareness. These emerging representations become sources of anxiety as their possible future implications are vaguely explored in fantasy. In the context of first love and competition for this love, images of self are incorporated into a system of negative evaluations and anxiety. The conclusion is the equation of love with an unexplored and essentially frightening aspect of self. Because of anxiety, images that were becoming the objects of consciousness, or operational thought, are now beyond the conclusions of that system. These representations form the newly developing affective unconscious. The child resolves the Oedipal conflict through anxiety-reducing systems of preoperational thought, such as identification, obsessive-compulsive ritual, reaction formation, repression, and denial.

LOSS OF FIRST LOVE

As a result of these operations, thoughts remain egocentric with an inarticulate image of self that becomes equated with love, a sense of mystery, and the unexpected. It is the child's beginning awareness of a part of self as imperfect and undesirable that motivates the search for the idealized romantic object who is self sufficient, all powerful, and highly desirable: all the attributes the child feels he does not possess. However, by being worthy of the love of the idealized person, the child begins to regain a sense of self as complete and perfect [7]. Romantic ideation develops soon after first love is lost and under the influence of that system this vaguely known side of self must be explored and finally expressed in the possession of a love that replaces the original. Like play, this possession will be compensatory. In the wished for state, the beloved will reciprocate in feeling, ideas, and sexuality, not in terms of the common prosaic systems of operational thought, but rather by the system in which the narcissistic love was first discovered and then rejected: preoperational thought. The variable affective qualities of self result in the preoperational child, or the adult using preoperational systems, having difficulty in maintaining the identification of self and object in different emotional contexts [10]. The object and self are not differentiated from the affective event. For stable operational concepts to develop, the individual must discriminate between how s/he feels about the loved person and how the loved person actually exists beyond that personal event. If the object of love is known over time and the systems of socialized and/or operational thought are applied, the love becomes one more of companionate love rather than romantic love [11].

When shared with another person, romantic ideation, like play, is both compensatory and exploratory. It is compensatory in that a relationship can be a modality to examine an unfulfilled self in a system of thought and love that is not constrained by operational thought. It is exploratory in that a final definition of self and love can be examined within that old system, and with time, definitions of self and love can be made in the framework of a system of thought in which assimilation and accommodation are in relative balance. It is precisely that lack of balance which we see in J. M. Barrie where his conclusive self-image remains in the static state of "Betwixt-and-Between." It becomes a theme which will permeate Barrie's life and his art: the romantic ideation of the eternal and lost boy.

ROMANTIC IDEATION: THE LOST BOY

It began with the accidental death of Barrie's brother, David, whose skull was fractured in a skating accident on the eve of his fourteenth birthday. Barrie was six years old and had lived in the shadow of David who was tall, handsome, athletic, and scholastically promising; he was also the favorite child of the mother, Margaret Ogilvy. In contrast, James was small, the runt of the family; he lacked the physical appearance and academic promise of his brother. Years later, in *Margaret Ogilvy*, a tribute to his dead mother, James Barrie records this negative image of himself as a very small and ordinary boy while David was so special for him [12]. Barrie never knew his brother, David, because he had lived in boarding school all of James' life; his knowledge of this romanticized brother came from Margaret Ogilvy.

Overwhelmed with grief at David's death, Margaret Ogilvy went into a deep and prolonged depression. In her darkened room she lay in bed with the family christening robe beside her, crying constantly, and oblivious to her family's needs. Barrie recalls how the young James would peek into the darkened room many times and then retreat to the stairs and sob. Finally, an older sister sent him to Margaret Ogilvy to tell their mother that she had another son. When he entered the dark room, Margaret Ogilvy called out, "Is that you?" The boy was hurt by the tone and responded, "No, it's no him, it's just me" [12, p. 232]. Even his mother was touched by the pathetic little figure and reached out to embrace him. Thus began Barrie's search for lost love and the identification of self with the ideal, romanticized image of the dead brother, David.

Aspects of Barrie's use of preoperational thought are seen at this period. The name "David" becomes powerful and magical for him; the fusion of object and word demonstrate the contribution of realism to the process of romantic ideation. For the rest of Barrie's life the name David will surface in his art, the symbol of the ideal boy. It is a part of Barrie's identification. He will try to become and remain the idealized David and he will search for that romantic figure. This early preoccupation will limit his capacity to accommodate to new experience. As he listens to his mother's memories and vision of the dead David, the young Barrie accommodates to and finally identifies with this image [6]. Later, Barrie writes that he had an intense desire "to become so like him [David] that even my mother should not see the difference" [12, p. 234]. He wore David's clothes; learned how to emulate his whistle. He is no longer in touch with the "old self" as he competes with the idealized brother, the product of his mother's fantasy. The compensatory wish results in an identification transforming the dead David into the living James. While this resolution will lead Barrie to enormous creativity, it will also prevent him from consciously knowing the "old self" through operational thought. A part of self vaguely understood by preoperational systems becomes lost and a new self based on a wish for love evolves. Because of anxiety neither self could be adequately explored, and, consequently, in many ways Barrie was the lost boy.

For David, and subsequently a part of Barrie, will remain a boy forever, and thus the eternal state of boyhood becomes powerful and magical as well. Barrie could identify and compete with the dead David while he still remained a boy, but he found the situation to be impossible as he himself moved into manhood.

Growing up was very painful for Barrie; it forced him into an awareness of himself as a sexual and aggressive male that he rejected. It was also complicated by the fact that physically Barrie never attained the stature of five feet; he was tiny, more boy-like than man. While he was strongly attracted to females, he was also sexually repelled by them. His diaries record repeated nightmares of waking up and shrieking because he found he was married [13, p. 12]. Yet he did marry a beautiful young actress, Mary Ansell, and never sexually consummated the union, a fact brought out fifteen years later when they divorced. The idealization of eternal boyhood is contingent on Barrie's identification with his dead brother, David, but it is also coupled with another important fantasy: Margaret Ogilvy as a child, the "little girl-mother."

ROMANTIC IDEATION: THE "LITTLE GIRL-MOTHER"

It was Barrie who brought his mother out of her depression. For hours he would sit on her bed and listen to her stories about the dead David. At first Barrie was jealous but then as he "became" David for his mother, and subsequently for himself, the lost love for David became a strong tie between them. Then Margaret Ogilvy shifted her stories to herself and her childhood. When she was eight years old, her mother had died and she became the "little mother" of the house, caring for a five-year-old brother and becoming her father's housekeeper. There were innumerable stories about life in Kirriemuir, but always at the center was the image of a "little girl-mother" who wore a magenta frock with a white pinafore and carried her father's supper in a flagon to the distant places in Scotland where he worked as a stonecutter. Months after David's death Margaret Ogilvy recovered from her depression, but the stories continued.

What Barrie had experienced at age six would forever be the center to which he would return: this part of himself that he did not understand as a child, nor as an adult. He would try to replicate the "family romance" with his dead brother and his mother, more precisely with those ideal-images that she had shared with him: her own romantic ideations which formed a part of his identity. It was the great bond between them.

Their intimacy continued after Margaret Ogilvy could leave her bed. She shared her childhood memories with her son by telling him innumerable stories. They read many books together, again sharing the things of the imagination, and then Barrie, still a child, began to write his own stories—even he is not sure how it began: "On a day I conceived a glorious idea, or was it put into my head by my mother. . . . The notion was nothing short of this, why should I not write the tales myself?" [12, p. 254]. He did write them, up in the garret of their house, and he ran down the stairs to read each short chapter as it was quickly completed to the waiting Margaret Ogilvy. Not only was she a part of the creative process of writing, she would later provide the content and substance of characterization for Barrie. It was her stories that would become his stories.

These stories about life in Kirriemuir, *Auld Licht Idylls* (1888), are not only told from Margaret Ogilvy's perspective, but from her experience as a child sixty years ago. Barrie was twenty-eight years old when he wrote and published these tales, and the center of his creative vision is the little girl-mother whom he idealizes and adores. Barrie, aged thirty-six, wrote: "I soon grew tired of writing tales, unless I see a little girl, of whom my mother has told me, wandering confidently through the pages. Such a grasp as her memory of her girlhood had upon me since I was a boy of six" [12, pp. 239-240]. Time nor age will alter the vivid image of the "child-mother" who lived in the richness of Barrie's imagination. Even Margaret Ogilvy's laughter remains in her son's memory as that of a "merry child," eternally ageless; she is his ideal who was sent by God "to open the minds of all who looked to beautiful thoughts" [12, p. 227]. While Margaret Ogilvy never read these words which her son had written in tribute to her, she knew her power over him, and she delighted in being the focal point for his writing. Barrie records a conversation between his mother and sister as Margaret Ogilvy tells Jane Ann, "He tries to keep me out [of his writing] but he canna; it's more than he can do!" [12, p. 328]. When mother and son discuss the need of a writer to know both man and woman, she chides the young Barrie ". . . I'm the only woman you know well." He replies, "Then I must make you my heroine" [12, p. 261]. And so he does.

Because the romantic ideation between mother and son was reciprocal, it became more powerful and credulous for both of them. In contrast, Barrie's relationship with his father appears to have provided him with little emotional sustenance. A large, strong, quiet man, David Barrie never shared an intimacy with his son; nor is he mentioned in Barrie's autobiographical writings beyond a cursory "a man I am very proud to be able to call my father" [12, p. 244]. Barrie's intimacy was exclusively with Margaret Ogilvy. As an adult, Barrie corresponded daily with his mother. She carefully preserved the hundreds of letters from him, always sleeping with the latest one beneath her sheet; they found Barrie's last letter there when she died.

Thus, it is not surprising that Barrie was reluctant to give up this intimacy of his childhood. Besides the stories he wrote, he created little theatricals and performed them in Margaret Ogilvy's washhouse, a prototype for the house he would later create for Wendy. This creative, fruitful period lasted until Barrie reached age twelve. Then he entered Dumfries Academy, where sports were more important than stories about a little girl carrying her father's supper in a flagon. Still, writing remained the primary compensation for Barrie, as he wrote plays for the school's drama club; so it would always be.

During his adolescence and young manhood, Barrie was miserable. His short stature and lack of success with women were painful for him. At his mother's insistence, he reluctantly entered the University of Edinburgh. Desolate, he became taciturn and diffident; it was one of the loneliest times in his life. At age twenty-one he was already looking back at what he felt he had lost, what he could never regain. For Barrie there is a supreme value in remaining a child, yet there is also great pain for a boy who remains "Betwixt-and-Between" in an adult body, in an adult world.

"BETWIXT-AND-BETWEEN:" CONFUSED IDENTITY

Barrie's confusion with his identification also permeates his art. While he recorded volumes of personal notes regarding his "Betwixt-and-Between" status, he artistically tried to work through these complexities in a novel, *Tommy and Grizel* [14]. It was written shortly after his marriage to Mary Ansell, who is transparently converted to Grizel while Barrie becomes Tommy. Like Barrie, Tommy agonizes over his marriage to Grizel. Friends from childhood, they genuinely love each other, but Tommy cannot fulfill Grizel's sexual passion: she has matured while he is still a boy. Barrie describes their plight [13, pp. 341-342]:

> He told her all that love meant to him and it meant everything that he thought Grizel would like it to mean. They had a honeymoon by the sea . . . Tommy, trying to become a lover by taking thought, and Grizel not letting on that it could not be done in that way. . . . He was a boy only . . . and boys cannot love. Oh, is it not cruel to ask a boy to love. . . . He was a boy who could not grow up. He gave her all his affection but his passion, like an outlaw, had ever to hunt alone.

That the Barries' marriage had never been sexually consummated was revealed by Mary Barrie later during their divorce proceedings; it was a humiliation that tortured him just as it had confused Tommy. Barrie's empathy for Tommy's plight is evident. For Barrie the lost love appears to have occurred when he began to be conscious of his mother as a mature female and himself as a maturing young man. He goes on to say that had Tommy lived in a "younger world, where there were only boys and girls, he might have been a gallant figure!" [14, p. 43]. Indeed, Barrie defines genius as "the power to be a boy again at will" [14, p. 183]. But Barrie has placed Tommy in the context of a real world, and though it is the context, not Tommy, that is at fault, Tommy experiences a violent, tragic end. Ironically, it is the death of the young adult Tommy that will give birth to Peter Pan for Barrie will take this same problem and approach it from a child's perspective.

Barrie's obsession with eternal boyhood is demonstrated in his statement, "Nothing that happens after we are twelve matters very much" [12, p. 250]. Much of Barrie's wished-for self was known by preoperational understanding and it is this modality that defines his art and his genius. Peter Pan does not have a mature male body nor does he function in an adult world; indeed, he refuses to grow up. Peter first appears in *The Little White Bird* where he has escaped the fate of adulthood when he was seven days old: he flew out of the nursery window and back to Kensington Gardens [15]. Yet mortality has stamped him, and once there he had temporarily lost his power to fly. He was neither a boy nor a bird. Old Solomon Caw, the Birds' Potentate, christened him: "You will be a Betwixt-and-Between" [15, p. 166]. And so he is, for Barrie has given his old problem a new metaphor. The tension of the two worlds and the pain of Barrie's sexual vacillation between those two worlds still exists.

A SEARCH FOR THE LOST BOY: GEORGE LLEWELYN DAVIES

Yet Barrie's context and perspective of the child in this work is not solely his; the co-author of *The Little White Bird* was five-year-old George Llewelyn Davies. It was two years after Margaret Ogilvy's death that Barrie noticed this beautiful little boy who was wearing a bright red velvet Tam-O-Shanter and playing in Kensington Gardens. There were three Davies boys; George had two brothers: Jack was four and Peter was still in his pram, but it was George who captured Barrie's affection and soon started to dominate Barrie's life.

Barrie was captivated by the beautiful little boy. His note books are filled with the things George said, experiences they shared and George's reactions to them. From these notes Barrie reveals that George is thinly disguised as a fictional character named David in *The Little White Bird*. For George is Barrie's idealized dead brother, the lost boy whom his mother loved, and the boy for whom he has been searching: the most conscious image and definition of himself.

Thus when George responds to Barrie's stories Barrie incorporates these perceptions into his own; he describes the creative process: "[This] is our way with a story: First I tell it to him [George], and then he tells it to me, the understanding being that it is quite a different story; and then I retell it with his additions, and so we go on until no one could say whether it is more his story or mine. . . . The interesting bits about the ways and customs of babies in the bird-stage are mostly reminiscences of [his], recalled by pressing his hands to his temples and thinking hard" [15, p. 159].

Another example of George's contribution to the work and Barrie's capacity to create literary images with a child's preoperational thought, includes the following description of the Serpentine Lake in Kensington Gardens: "It is a lovely lake and there is a drowned forest at the bottom of it. If you peer over the edge you can see the trees all growing upside down, and they say that at night there are also drowned stars in it" [15, p. 154].

Or as Barrie and George stroll together in the Broadwalk (Kensington Gardens), the fictional little boy, David, wonders "if it began little, and grew and grew, until it was quite grown up, and whether the other [smaller] walks are its babies. . . ." [15, p. 144]. It is a child's perception of the world, and for Barrie it was not simply charming, it possessed a viability and richness beyond rational thought. More importantly, it held a clue to his own confused identity.

THE "LITTLE GIRL-MOTHER:" SYLVIA DAVIES

Just as the images of the dead brother, David, were coupled with the love of Margaret Ogilvy, so in Barrie's mind was little George connected with his beautiful mother, Sylvia. Like her son, Sylvia, too, is thinly disguised in *The Little White Bird* as David's mother. She is as physically gorgeous as her sons to whom she is devoted. Just as her boys, especially George, embody the ideal tenets of boyhood, Sylvia becomes Barrie's romantic ideation of motherhood.

To make Sylvia his own "mother," Barrie rechristened her. Because everyone else called her Sylvia, he chose to call her by her middle name, Jocelyn. Barrie was financially successful with his plays and he was generous with his money. He sent her presents, theatre tickets; offered her excursions, dinners, diversions of all kinds. He flirted with her outrageously, safe in the knowledge that she adored her barrister-husband, Arthur, who was as handsome as his wife. Barrie was confident that he would never be sexually tested. The lovely Sylvia without her boys could not have charmed Barrie; it was this combination of mother and sons that drew and captivated him. In *Peter Pan in Kensington Gardens* Peter rapturously says to his little girl friend: "Oh, Maimie . . . do you know why I love you? It is because you are like a beautiful nest" [15, p. 242]. The metaphor is appropriate for Sylvia. Surely, she was his mother, too, as he "played" with her sons.

And he did indeed play with them. For Barrie, this play afforded an opportunity to explore the self yet the end result was to protect the self; it was compensatory based on preoperational thought. This grown man's play with children invoked magic rather than linear causality; thus it was a creative process analogous to art. For Barrie, play and the creative process merged in the summer of 1901. He and his wife, Mary, stayed at Black Lake Cottage, a five-minute walk from Tilford Cottage where the Davies Family were vacationing. For the entire month of August, Barrie played with George and his brothers; it was another search for the lost boy.

NEVERLAND

The basis for their day-long adventures was Barrie's favorite boyhood book, *The Coral Island*. Thus the lake became a South Seas Lagoon; the boys were pirates; even Porthos, Barrie's St. Bernard dog, wore the papier-mâché mask of a lion. Spontaneously, Barrie invented the script, pausing to photograph the boys or jot down ideas. He became Captain Swarthy, a dark, sinister figure who frequently forced the boys to walk the plank into the shallow waters of Black Lake. That Sylvia and Arthur had to interfere when the use of real arrows and long-bladed knives was interjected says something about Barrie's own absorption in the play with his young companions, now aged eight, seven, and four [13].

To commemorate that summer, Barrie took thirty-five photographs of the boys and used them as illustrations for a book, *The Boy Castaways of Black Lake Island* [13, p. 88]. He published it himself. How rich and personal the experience was is indicated by Barrie's wish not to make this project a commercial venture; he printed two copies of this book—one of which he gave to Arthur Davies, who promptly lost it on a railway carriage. That this summer was the creative genesis of *Peter Pan and Wendy* is clearly documented in Barrie's notebooks [16]. In his magical approach to experience, Barrie used the perspective of the child to resolve the tension of the two worlds: his old problem of identity. Using the beautiful young boys as links to his own first images of the world, Barrie creates what is essentially a tragic character arrested in time.

THE ETERNAL BOY: PETER PAN

The recurrent themes which permeate Barrie's life and art pervade his creation of Peter Pan: the desire to remain a boy forever in the Neverland of childhood and the possession of the little girl-mother. Compelled to explore these themes, Barrie used his art to explore himself. Unlike Tommy, Peter is saved by the context of Neverland where the male's tension is resolved by the fact that he will never grow up. Peter explains this to Wendy's mother: "I don't want ever to be a man . . . I want always to be a little boy and have fun." With passion he elaborates, "O Wendy's mother, if I was to wake up and feel there was a beard!" [16, p. 206]. Even in play, Peter gets anxious when Wendy pretends that he is the father of the lost boys, as she is their mother. Seeking her reassurance, he asks, "It is only make-believe, isn't it, that I am their father?" Sensing her annoyance, he apologizes, "You see . . . it would make me seem so old to be their real father." And when Wendy, in exasperation, asks what Peter's feelings for her are, he replies: "Those of a devoted son, Wendy" [16, p. 133]. The sexual titillation and nuances are there, but the tragedy of Tommy and Grizel takes on a light comic tone with Peter and Wendy, for as a boy Peter has responded appropriately and it is inconceivable that, sexually, anymore might be expected from him. Surely, Wendy, as a child, does not possess Grizel's need for sexual passion, yet Wendy, too, is fated to mature.

Peter chooses Wendy to be the "mother of us all"; she is a child, the little girl-mother whom one can visualize with a magenta frock and a white pinafore. Wendy knows, in the first paragraph of *Peter Pan and Wendy* that "[age] Two is the beginning of the end" [16, p. 13]; she must grow up. Unlike Peter, she has no choice—unless she remains in Neverland. Her ultimate rejection of Neverland is her betrayal of Peter: she grows to be a mature woman with a daughter of her own. Ironically, it is the reversal of the betrayal between Tommy and Grizel, but the focal point is the male who can't or won't mature while the female can't or won't stop growing. Even in Neverland the tension exists of the character caught up in two worlds. Barrie says of Wendy's maturity: "You need not be sorry for her. She was one of the kind that likes to grow up" [16, p. 211]. Yet when Peter later visits Wendy, she is embarrassed that she is an adult and feels "something inside of her crying Woman, woman let go of me" [16, p. 214]. The pull of the two worlds splits Peter and Wendy, just as it did Tommy and Grizel.

For just as Wendy laments her loss of childhood and Neverland, Peter misses the "little mother" and what she represents. Her primary function is to tell him stories and while she bullies, bosses, and cajoles him, she exudes warmth, security, and love. When Peter sees Wendy as an adult, he is horrified that she has broken her promise to remain the little girl-mother. They are separated by their choices: Peter Pan will never grow up and always remain in Neverland, while Wendy, now a woman with a young daughter, must face her mortality in the context of a real world.

Peter sobs at Wendy's betrayal, at the loss of the mother whom he had come to take to Neverland, and Wendy can no longer comfort him for "She was only a woman now" [16, p. 218]. As Wendy leaves the room, Peter's crying wakes her daughter, Jane. It is a re-enactment of the first meeting between Wendy and Peter. When Wendy returns, Peter looks at Jane and tells Wendy that "She [Jane] is my mother" [16, p. 219]. Wendy sighs as Jane and Peter fly off to Neverland. Someday as Wendy's hair turns white, it will be Jane's daughter, Margaret, who will fly to Neverland with Peter. It is the compromise between Peter and Wendy: each generation of Wendy's daughters shall be Peter's "mother" in turn, and "thus it will go on," says Barrie, "so long as children are gay and innocent and heartless" [16, p. 220].

Peter Pan will remain the eternal boy; it is someone else who fathers the daughters, who in turn become Peter's little girl-mothers. It is a perfect solution for Peter possesses the desired female object and does not have to confront "growing up" which means male maturity and sexual function.

No one knows how conscious Barrie was of Peter Pan when he first created him, but his notes indicate an increased awareness of Peter's relevance to himself. Eleven years later, Barrie wrote: "It is as if long after writing Peter Pan its true meaning came to me—Desperate attempt to grow up but can't" [13, p. 297]. Six years after this entry, Barrie added to the stage directions when Peter says he wants always to be a little boy: "So perhaps he thinks, but it is only his greatest pretend" [13, p. 298].

CONCLUSION

Beginning in that darkened bedroom with a child's perception and wish for love and a depressed mother's wish for a lost boy, and a lost girlhood, Barrie excluded from consciousness the first images he had of himself. In the process he lost the representation of himself or females as mature adult lovers and he identified with an idealized childhood of a mother and son. While he was reworking this fantasy with Sylvia Davies and her sons, his relationship with his wife was deteriorating beyond repair. He was confused and repelled by mature sexuality in himself òr in females and throughout life he was subject to serious bouts of depression. He loved boys in the widest sense of that word and was most alive when he could use them as androgenous muses who helped him to create the romantic images in his books and plays. Really, he loved the boy David that he saw in the various young boys he pursued and the idealized image of himself as that David. He never seemed to have resolved these conflicts. Written when he was seventy-seven, his last, and unsuccessful, play was named *The Boy David*.

Beyond the conflict was the creative imagination. There had never been a play before like *Peter Pan* with a magic place in time where children can fly. Neverland is a metaphor for one resolution of the family romance as well as a creative expression of preoperational thought. Barrie knew he was taking a chance when he had Peter turn to the opening night audience and ask them if they believed in fairies. They answered "yes" with conviction that night in 1904. They have been saying "yes" ever since.

REFERENCES

1. J. Piaget, *The Origins of Intelligence in Children*, International Universities Press, New York, 1952.
2. S. Coopersmith, *The Antecedents of Self Esteem*, W. H. Freeman, San Francisco, 1967.
3. W. Damar and D. Hart, The Development of Self-understanding from Infancy Through Adolescence, *Child Development*, *53*:4, pp. 841-864, 1982.
4. J. Piaget, *The Child's Conception of the World*, Littlefield, Adams and Company, Totowa, New Jersey, 1979.
5. J. H. Flavell, *The Developmental Psychology of Jean Piaget*, Van Nostrand Company, Princeton, New Jersey, 1963.
6. J. Piaget, *Play Dreams and Imitation in Childhood*, W. W. Norton and Company, New York, 1962.
7. S. Friedlander and D. Morrison, Childhood, in *On Love and Loving*, K. S. Pope (ed.), Jossey-Bass, San Francisco, 1980.
8. A. Balint, *The Early Years of Life*, Basic Books, New York, 1948.
9. M. Mahler, F. Pine, and A. Bergman, *The Psychological Birth of the Human Infant: Symbiosis and Individuation*, Basic Books, New York, 1975.
10. R. Melito, Cognitive Aspects of Splitting and Libidinal Object Constancy, *Bulletin of the American Psychoanalytic Association*, *39*:1, pp. 515-534, 1982.
11. E. Walster and G. W. Walster, *New Look at Love*, Addison-Wesley, Reading, Massachusetts, 1978.

12. J. M. Barrie, *The Novels, Tales and Sketches of J. M. Barrie*, Vol. III, *Margaret Ogilvy*, Charles Scribner's Sons, New York, 1901.

13. A. Birkin, *J. M. Barrie and The Lost Boys*, Clarkson N. Potter, Inc., New York, 1979.

14. J. Barrie, *Tommy and Grizel*, The Press of the Readers Club, New York, 1943.

15. ____, *The Little White Bird or Adventures in Kensington Gardens*, Charles Scribner's Sons, New York, 1902.

16. ____, *Peter Pan*, Penguin Books, Great Britain, 1967.